THE FREUDIAN CALLING

THE FREUDIAN CALLING

EARLY VIENNESE PSYCHOANALYSIS AND THE PURSUIT OF CULTURAL SCIENCE

LOUIS ROSE

WAYNE STATE UNIVERSITY PRESS   DETROIT

02 01 00 99 98   5 4 3 2 1

Library of Congress Cataloging-in-Publication Data

Rose, Louis.
    The Freudian calling : early Viennese psychoanalysis and the
pursuit of cultural science / Louis Rose.
        p.   cm. — (Kritik)
    Includes bibliographical references and index.
    ISBN 0-8143-2622-6 (pbk. : alk. paper)
    1. Psychology—Austria—Vienna—History—20th century.
2. Psychoanalysis—Austria—Vienna—History—20th century.
3. Vienna (Austria)—Intellectual life.   4. Freud, Sigmund,
1856-1939.   I. Title.   II. Series: Kritik (Detroit, Mich.)
BF108.A92R67   1998
150'.9436'13—dc21   97-37080

An earlier version of chapter 2 first appeared in *Psychoanalytic
Quarterly* 61, no. 4 (October 1992) and was later reprinted in
Rediscovering History: Culture, Politics, and the Psyche,
edited by Michael S. Roth. It is reprinted here with the permission of
the publishers, Stanford University Press. © 1994 by the
Board of Trustees of the Leland Stanford Junior University.

Kritik: German Literary Theory and Cultural Studies Series
Liliane Weissberg, Editor
*A complete listing of the books in this series can be found
at the back of this volume.*

For

Carl E. Schorske

CONTENTS

ACKNOWLEDGMENTS

The author wishes first to express appreciation to the Fulbright Commission, whose grant supported an extended period of research in Vienna. A sabbatical leave from Otterbein College, and a contribution from the college's Ursula Holtermann Fund assisted final preparation of the manuscript.

In Vienna, my research into early psychoanalysis benefited greatly from the advice of Dr. Ernst Federn, Dr. Harald Leupold-Löwenthal, and Dr. Hans Lobner. My thanks go to Markus Freund, Elisabeth Menasse-Wiesbauer, and Johannes Reichmayr for our discussions of Vienna's past and present.

I am grateful for the comments on earlier versions of the manuscript provided by Anthony Grafton, Thomas Knock, Arno Mayer, Anson Rabinbach, Michael Roth, and Jerrold Seigel. Much of the second chapter of the book appeared in the *Psychoanalytic Quarterly*, where I received the editorial assistance of Josephine Shapiro. I wish to express appreciation to Peter Taylor for his suggestions on the final manuscript.

At Otterbein, Mary Ellen Armentrout and Patricia White helped to track down sources with persistence and patience. Aaron Thompson cleared away technical difficulties in the printing of the manuscript. Andy Spencer provided invaluable advice on translation. Pat Lewis read the final manuscript, and I am grateful for his comments and encouragement. Here I warmly recall the counsel and memory of Ursula Holtermann, a refugee from Nazi Germany in 1933, and a professor of history for over thirty years.

Arthur B. Evans, director of Wayne State University Press, extended his time and assistance at each stage of publication, for which I express my thanks. My gratitude goes to Janet Witalec for her editorship. I wish to thank Sandra Williamson for copyediting the manuscript. I am greatly appreciative of the critical judgment and generous spirit of Liliane Weissberg, editor of *Kritik*.

In important measure, this book derives from a dialogue with Jim Amelang on psychology and the study of culture. I am grateful to him not only for his reading of the early and final versions of the manuscript, but also for his comments on the history of the cultural sciences.

From my wife, Cynthia Laurie Rose, I have begun to acquire knowledge in the fields of experimental psychology and perception. I am thankful for her tolerance.

Finally, I acknowledge my gratitude to the person to whom this book is dedicated, whose work and teaching have given full expression to history as both a craft and a commitment.

ONE

COMMITMENT
TO THE CAUSE

I

The first organization for the study of psychoanalysis and the diffusion of Sigmund Freud's ideas emerged from a small group of followers who in 1902 began to meet with Freud on Wednesday evenings at his home. In 1908, the group took the name Vienna Psychoanalytic Society. Like Freud, those disciples most deeply dedicated to psychoanalysis referred to it as "*die Sache*": the cause. Within the Freudian movement, they discovered a calling—an inward commitment and, in Max Weber's words, a "life-task."[1]

In the view of Freud and the Viennese, their calling belonged as much to culture as to psychology, and not only because that early circle included writers and critics, as well as medical practitioners. From the founding of the society at the turn of the century to its forced disintegration under the *Anschluss* in 1938, Freud and his followers defined the comprehensive exploration of culture as one of their fundamental pursuits. The publication of *The Interpretation of Dreams* marked the beginning of a collective odyssey, the appearance of *Civilization and Its Discontents* its point of culmination. Throughout that journey, Viennese Freudians remained conscious of themselves as the vanguard of a new cultural, as well as psychological, vocation.

This book will trace the evolution in Vienna of an early psychoanalytic science of culture, examining how the work of cultural interpretation became essential to the Freudian calling in the years before the First World War, and how that work was continued in the war's immediate aftermath. In doing so, it will explore Freud's own writings in light of the discussions and projects of his Viennese circle. As he constructed his theory of civilization, Freud answered and deepened the Viennese aspirations toward both inward vocation and new cultural understanding. Those aspirations embodied a notion of psychoanalysis which combined, in Aristotelian terms, *episteme*—the rational understanding of "the first principles and causes"[2] in mental life—and *technē*—the exercise of a craft, or art, in psychological research and interpretation. Inspired by their sense of calling, Freud and other Viennese disciples sought to build a new cultural science—what they referred to as applied psychoanalysis—employing the theories and techniques of individual psychology.

As he gave expression to the aims and struggles of his Viennese followers, Freud expanded the boundaries of the project he shared with them. In 1907, he founded the *Papers on Applied Psychology (Schriften zur angewandten Seelenkunde)*, the first publication devoted to the psychoanalytic interpretation of art, mythology, and literature. He prevailed upon Hugo Heller, Viennese bookseller, publisher, and member of the Psychological Wednesday Society, to print the first volumes. His biographical study and aesthetic analysis of Leonardo da Vinci—the seventh volume in the series—Freud presented first to the members of his Viennese circle, as he did the essays which would comprise *Totem and Taboo*. In 1913, with Otto Rank and Hanns Sachs, Freud founded *Imago: Zeitschrift für Anwendung der Psychoanalyse auf die Geisteswissenschaften*—Journal for the Application of Psychoanalysis to the Cultural Sciences—again published by Heller. With the publication of *Totem and Taboo* in the pages of *Imago*, Freud directed the application of psychoanalysis toward the domain of communal organization and behavior, and finally, toward history.

As Freudian cultural exploration in Vienna and other cities expanded, the question of its incorporation into Freudian theory and its role in professional training became increasingly insistent, sparking new debates within and beyond the international psychoanalytic movement. In 1926, when Viennese authorities refused to license Theodor Reik, one of Vienna's first lay analysts, as a therapist, Freud responded with the pamphlet, *The Question of Lay Analysis*, in which he called on the reader to envision the creation of a college of psychoanalysis. Within its precincts, he wrote, "analytic instruction would include branches of knowledge which are remote from medicine and which the doctor does not come across in his practice: the history of civilization, mythology, the psychology of religion and the science of literature."[3] Ultimately, in 1929, with the writing of *Civilization and Its Discontents*, Freud rooted psychoanalytic theory in the dynamic interaction between psyche and culture.

For Freud and his Viennese circle, the cause included both a vision of culture and a sense of calling: as the cultural vision widened, so the idea of vocation also underwent transformation. At the turn of the century, the vision expressed in their work derived closely from the German humanist concept of *Bildung*, with its emphasis on self-education and inward transformation. Character development and the sources of individual creativity drew intensive Freudian study. The figure of the artist, balancing tenuously the demand for self-discipline and the impulse to self-expression, embodied for the Viennese circle the ideal and burden of culture. Following from their concern for character and creative labor, their focus on artistic activity ranged from characterization on the stage to the creative process itself, and finally the relationship between the artist and his work, as in *Leonardo da Vinci and a Memory of His Childhood*. Thus did analysis of art and the artist open the field of applied psychoanalysis.

With the notion of culture, the Freudian sense of vocation received new meanings. Prior to joining Freud's circle, those who became psychoanalysts viewed character and creativity through a moral lens. Inspired by their own sense of mission, they called on the artist to safeguard moral responsibility from a world in crisis. Once within the Vienna Psychoanalytic Society, however, they moved from the moral interpretation of art to the psychology of creativity. Their focus as cultural critics shifted from ideals to experience, from *Bildung* to *Erlebnis*. Helping to generate that shift, Freud in his biography of Leonardo concentrated his analysis on the image in art, and on its relation to inward experience. Seeking to preserve their demand for responsibility, and to strengthen their original sense of calling, Freud at the same time aimed to transform his followers from moralists into psychologists.

On the eve of the First World War, Freud and the Viennese began to expand their focus from art to society. In *Totem and Taboo*, the vision of culture encompassed ritual behavior and communal customs, while the theme of inward rage and sublime recovery, also surfacing at that time in "The Moses of Michelangelo," published with *Totem and Taboo* in the pages of *Imago*, passed from individual psychology to collective psychology, from personal to societal history. Moving from the study of individual creativity and inward experience to the exploration of society and history, Freud incorporated within his cultural science the idea of a universal drama of community, within which the creative images of art could acquire a new meaning. With the outbreak of the First World War, however, that drama confronted destruction: community lost might not be regained, while recovery of the self and of society appeared to Freud a matter of deep uncertainty. Cracking the classical foundation of their cultural studies, the war forced upon Viennese Freudians the vocation of modern social science. In the wake of the conflict, with the shattering of European societies and the deepening of individual malaise, Freud and his followers, concerned with the problem of community lost and regained, turned their attention to the seemingly unorganized collectivity—the crowd—and continued with more intensity their studies of social organization and disintegration, carefully assessing the possibilities of reconstruction.

With the end of the first decade of the peace, Freud brought the psychoanalytic study of human drama, collective behavior, and the self within a comprehensive theory. Written in 1929, *Civilization and Its Discontents* explored the foundations of community and the fate of the individual as a social being, bound to civilization in the shared dualism of Eros and death. In Freud's final vision, communal life revealed itself as tragic destiny. The path from moralism to a psychology of culture ultimately brought that destiny into conscious view.

II

Who formed the psychoanalytic vanguard in Vienna? In the years before the First World War the Vienna Society had a fluid structure and a shifting base of membership. It drew on lay and medical professions, and incorporated diverse cultural and clinical interests. Furthermore, a greater number of members occupied the fringes of the organization than toiled at its center.[4] The society did not represent an official school with a consistent number of instructors and students until after the war; yet, a small number of active members emerged from the beginning as an intellectual and professional vanguard of Viennese psychoanalysis. Those members fulfilled essential functions as advocates of a new intellectual movement either by their attendance at meetings from the days of the informal gatherings at Freud's home, by the publication of psychoanalytic articles, or by applying Freudian theory and method in their own occupations as doctors or writers.

Sixteen members will come under chief consideration in this book. Freud and four physicians—Wilhelm Stekel, Alfred Adler, Max Kahane, and Rudolf Reitler—founded the Psychological Wednesday Society in 1902. Paul Federn, also a general practitioner, joined the group a year later. Music critic David Bach came to the society during the first three years of its existence. By the end of 1905, Eduard Hitschmann, a physician, and Max Graf, a music critic, had also become members. Graf became well known to later psychoanalysts as the father who compiled the case history of the animal phobia of his son, "little Hans." In 1906, Otto Rank, an aspiring writer, entered the circle and immediately took on the task of recording the minutes of its meetings. Two of the first practicing analysts, Maxim Steiner and Isador Sadger, began to attend the meetings in 1907. A few months after Sadger joined the society, he proposed for membership his nephew, the journalist, Fritz Wittels. In 1908, Victor Tausk, a former lawyer and writer, introduced himself to Freud, and in the following year entered his circle. In 1910, Hanns Sachs, a lawyer with literary ambitions, became a member. Finally, Alfred von Winterstein, president of the Vienna Society after the Second World War, joined the group in 1910, and Theodor Reik, a student of psychology and literature, entered in 1911. Not only were these members' occupations equally divided between the medical and nonmedical, but several among the physicians pursued second careers as writers and cultural critics.

At the time of the appearance of the Viennese Freudian movement—the years between the founding of the Wednesday circle in 1902 and the official creation of the Vienna Psychoanalytic Society in 1908—Freud's psychological theory rested on four pillars: the concept of repression, the idea of the unconscious, the libido theory, and the theory of the Oedipal complex of childhood. In *Studies on Hysteria*, published in 1895, Josef Breuer and Freud defined repression as the exclusion of an idea or affect from conscious memory under the influence of a traumatic experience. In *The Interpretation of Dreams*, Freud transformed that definition to refer to that mental agency which established a closed boundary between two distinct psychological spheres, unconscious and conscious, and which manifested itself in the ego's resistance to pursuing conscious recognition of the contents of the unconscious mind. Mental energy within the unconscious reflected the endurance of instinctual drives and wishes, and derived permanent, generative force from obedience to the pleasure principle—the ceaseless striving after the discharge of energy or the reduction of psychic tension, the fulfillment of which was experienced as the sensation of pleasure. The individual's oldest wishes for gratification—humanity's most ancient impulses—which the unconscious wove into fantasy, and to which adhered the greatest mental energy, experienced the harshest repression. The unconscious region of the mind, Freud concluded, provided the original mental formation of the individual. That region, the psychic laws which governed it, and the modes of expression peculiar to it became open to intellectual exploration and understanding through dreams, to the extent that such visions permitted a "return of the repressed." Psychoanalytic technique could elucidate the unconscious wishes and images behind dream formation after the dream itself became a part of memory—when, in other words, it became attached to conscious language.

In 1905, in *Three Essays on the Theory of Sexuality*, Freud explored the central role of childhood sexual instincts in unconscious mental life and in the psychological development of the individual. The book began with a definition of libido: "The fact of the existence of sexual needs in human beings and animals is expressed in biology by the assumption of a 'sexual instinct', on the analogy of the instinct of nutrition, that is of hunger. Everyday language possesses no counterpart to the word 'hunger', but science makes use of the word 'libido' for that purpose."[5] With the first moments of life there began the striving after libidinal gratification. Owing to the unconscious energy of the libido, and the malleability of libidinal aims, the earliest forms of bodily pleasure and the earliest sensations of desire, despite suffering repression, retained their uniquely powerful role in the development of the individual. Through the process of sublimation, the ego channeled early sexual strivings into nonsexual aims, and thus even the most exalted of such aims did not fail to express an original element of longing.

The original seeking after instinctual fulfillment, and the hostility to what interfered with that fulfillment, led to the Oedipal configuration of childhood, the psychical complex into which ultimately flowed the individual's earliest libidinal life. Freud first referred publicly to its significance in *The Interpretation of Dreams:*

> Being in love with the one parent and hating the other are among the essential constituents of the stock of psychical impulses which is formed at that time and which is of such importance in determining the symptoms of the later neurosis. It is not my belief, however, that psychoneurotics differ sharply in this respect from other human beings who remain normal—that they are able, that is, to create something absolutely new and peculiar to themselves. It is far more probable—and this is confirmed by occasional observations on normal children—that they are only distinguished by exhibiting on a magnified scale feelings of love and hatred to their parents which occur less obviously and less intensely in the minds of most children.[6]

The case of "little Hans," published in 1909, confirmed for Freud not only that hostile wishes toward the father arose from feelings of sexual rivalry over the mother, but also that such wishes generated within the son an unconscious fear of punishment.[7]

In *The Interpretation of Dreams*, Freud made his first published reference to the possible contribution of psychoanalytic discoveries to an understanding of art—in this case, an understanding of the relationship between the psychological content of the Oedipal complex, and the content of drama: "If *Oedipus Rex* moves a modern audience no less than it did the contemporary Greek one, the explanation can only be that its effect does not lie in the contrast between destiny and human will, but is to be looked for in the particular nature of the material on which that contrast is exemplified."[8] Commenting on the impact which the fate of Oedipus exerted upon the audience, ancient and modern, Freud continued,

> His destiny moves us only because it might have been ours—because the oracle laid the same curse upon us before our birth as upon him. It is the fate of all of us, perhaps, to direct our first sexual impulse towards our mother and our first hatred and our first murderous wish against our father. Our dreams convince us that that is so. King Oedipus, who slew his father Laïus and married his mother Jocasta, merely shows us the fulfilment of our own childhood wishes. But, more fortunate than he, we have meanwhile succeeded, in so far as we have not become psychoneurotics, in detaching our sexual impulses from our mothers and in forgetting our jealousy of our fathers. Here is one in whom these primaeval wishes of our childhood have been fulfilled, and we shrink back from him with the whole force of the repression by which those wishes have since that time been held down within us.[9]

Yet, resistance did not prevent the spectator from attaining, through the language of the tragic poet, a piece of self-recognition: "While the poet, as he unravels the past, brings to light the guilt of Oedipus, he is at the same time compelling us to recognize our own inner minds, in which those same impulses, though suppressed, are still to be found."[10]

In 1907, Freud offered the inaugural contribution to the *Papers on Applied Psychology: Delusions and Dreams in Jensen's "Gradiva,"* his study of a writer's reconstruction of the dream process within a creative story.[11] The dream mechanism as produced by the creative writer could, Freud found, be understood through psychoanalytic method, thus not only reaffirming the laws of unconscious mental processes, but revealing a new source of literary meaning. Within the story and the fictional dream, the survival of the image of Gradiva—an ancient bas-relief which the central figure encounters at the ruins of Pompeii, and which provides the focus of his emotion and memory—granted the opportunity for interpretation. Thus, through the study of the unique, creative image, as well as in the analysis of dramatic performance, one could begin to apply psychoanalytic understanding to cultural science.

III

This book will chart a mutual endeavor undertaken by Freud and his Viennese circle. It will not provide an institutional account of the movement in Vienna. Indeed, much has already been written on personalities, schisms, and professional reorganizations, and I have little to add to the literature on those subjects. Where conflicts within the movement and changes in its organization become significant for the theme of this study, they will be considered, but it is my hope nonetheless that the book, by retaining its focus on the Viennese Freudian approach to cultural science, will not seem overly narrow in scope to the reader seeking an institutional history or group biography. The method to be followed here will have each member's work and ideas offer a perspective on the work and ideas of his associates, and, in this way, provide an intellectual account of a shared, if not always harmonious, effort. In taking this route, the book will also provide a vantage point from which to observe Freud's work as part of the Viennese project, bringing into focus the ways in which he responded to that project and gave it direction. Thus, this study will remain centered on the effort which Freud and his Viennese followers pursued in cultural science before the First World War, and will conclude by considering to what extent the intellectual motives and aspirations of that effort continued into the postwar period.

The route traced here presents only one among several possible paths to an understanding of the subject. Of equal interest would be to chart the development of an interpretation of culture and society which emerged from psychoanalytic clinical practice and experience, or from the gradual expansion of Freudian metapsychological theory. This book will restrict itself to that work of Freud and the Viennese which they specifically defined as psychoanalysis applied to the cultural sciences. By keeping to the boundaries of this path, however, we can reach a new perspective on the relation of the movement to its intellectual surroundings.

The reader will note that what Freud and his followers referred to as *Geisteswissenschaft* is here translated as cultural science, although elsewhere in psychoanalytic writings the term has been commonly rendered as mental science.[12] Cultural science, however, seems to me to characterize more fully the fields reached by applied psychoanalysis, and to indicate more exactly the aspirations of

Freud and the Viennese in making such applications. Both the *Geisteswissenschaften*—the "sciences of the human spirit," or humanistic disciplines, including classical studies, literature, and art criticism—and the *Kulturwissenschaften*—the "sciences of culture," or social sciences, including anthropology, sociology, and religious and ethnographic studies—defined the fields into which Viennese Freudians brought psychoanalysis. Early in the nineteenth century, German-speaking scholars endeavored to unite those diverse disciplines through a history of the spirit, whether that history denoted the stages in which Spirit embodied itself in the world and shaped the awareness of humanity, as G. W. F. Hegel defined the historical process, or evoked the spirit of an age and civilization, as Jacob Burckhardt approached the investigation of the past. By the turn of the twentieth century, however, humanist scholars and social researchers sought grounding in the sciences of the mind. Psychologists themselves offered ways to join their work to the cultural disciplines, most notably the experimentalist Wilhelm Wundt, who in the ten volumes of his *Völkerpsychologie* sought to demonstrate that consciousness derived as much from cultural practices and ideals as from those physiological and perceptual processes which he explored in his Leipzig laboratory.[13] Interpreting the career of the art historian Aby Warburg, E. H. Gombrich traced one of Warburg's principal motives to "the hope of basing a scientific explanation of cultural progress on the well-proven results of psychological research."[14]

The figure of Aby Warburg recalls themes essential to Freud and his followers in the application of psychoanalysis to cultural studies. Like Warburg, the Viennese Freudians studied the artistic image as a psychological problem, a problem which they too believed came most vividly to view in the art of the Renaissance; they investigated works of art not only as expressions of inward, emotional experience, but as manifestations containing traces of the instinctive actions of humanity; and finally, they approached art as the inheritor and vehicle of, in Warburg's term, "pathos formulae" (*Pathosformeln*), images of suffering.[15] Here are markers which we will encounter again as we chart the evolution of Freudian cultural science from its focus on artistic images to its concern with drama. Along that path early Viennese psychoanalysis moved from the study of individual creativity to the examination of community. In combining the humanities and social sciences under the rubric of *Geisteswissenschaft*, *Imago* not only emphasized the role of individual psychology within cultural and social life, but, more specifically, interpreted with that psychology the images of suffering—the formulae of pathos—transmitted by art, drama, and history.

Examining the formation of a Freudian cultural science requires following the transition from a concern with art and individual creativity to a focus on drama and community. To help clarify that development, this study will ask the reader to bear in mind Aristotle's definition of tragedy and mimesis in the *Poetics*, a copy of which Freud kept in his library throughout his life: "Tragedy, then, is an imitation of an action that is serious, complete, and of a certain magnitude; in language embellished with each kind of artistic ornament, the several kinds being found in separate parts of the play; in the form of action, not of narrative; through pity and fear effecting the proper purgation [catharsis] of these emotions."[16] In his moving discussion of ancient and modern theater, Francis Fergusson demonstrated how the imitation of an action, single and complete, manifested itself in diverse forms within a tragedy, not only through its plot, but through its language, characterization, and rhythm of development.[17] The psychoanalyst and Viennese emigré, Hans W. Loewald, noting Fergusson's expansion of the Aristotelian notion of mimesis, found that such a widened conception also illuminated the phenomenon of transference in the analytic situation. "The transference neurosis," Loewald wrote, "is such an imitation of action in the form of action, or, more correctly, it develops from such imitation in action of an original action sequence and remains under the formative influence of that original action, although in its total development it is uniquely a creature of the psychoanalytic process."[18] The Aristotelian concept of imitation, he explained, could be translated into psychoanalytic language as "re-enactment and repetition."[19] The social psychologist Serge Moscovici emphasized the idea of mimetic activity as essential to Freud's theory of ego identification.[20] Exploring the concept in yet another direction, this book will trace the notion of dramatic mimesis in Freud's approach to the study of community and in his understanding of the historical process. For Freud, the catharsis theory in the cultural sciences helped to explain the release of affect in the work of art, and the communication between artists and their audiences. To interpret the transmission of affect and ideas across generations, and to account for the influence of history on the life of the community, he turned as well, it will be argued, to the theory of mimesis.

In her book, *Ancient Art and Ritual*, published in 1913—the year in which *Totem and Taboo* appeared—Jane Ellen Harrison, a leader of the Cambridge school of classical anthropologists and like Freud a strong admirer of the work of James Frazer, emphasized two distinct aspects of mimetic ritual: the imitation of an action, on the one hand, and the reexperiencing of emotions, on the other. In commemorative ritual, participants "*re*-present" an action, not merely for the purpose of "copying" a significant act, but for reliving its emotion. The "desire to re-live" expressed itself even more strongly in anticipatory, or preparatory, rituals, in which "the action is mimetic, not of what you see done by another; but of what you desire to do yourself. The habit of this *mimesis* of the thing desired, is set up, and ritual begins. Ritual, then, does imitate, but for an emotional, not an altogether practical, end."[21] "Art and ritual," Harrison argued, "are at the outset alike in this, that they do not seek to copy a fact, but to reproduce, to re-enact an emotion."[22] Such an interpretation, she concluded, received support in the very origin of the Greek word, *mimesis*, which did not refer to imitation in the strict sense, but to the activity of mimes, or actors in dramatic performances. The player sought "to emphasize, enlarge, enhance, his own personality; he masquerades, he does not mimic."[23] Similarly, E. H. Gombrich, in his biography of Aby Warburg, reminded his readers that in German-speaking scholarship the concept of mimesis referred not only to imitation, but "to the action of 'miming', in other words to all kinds of expressive movement, particularly to facial expression and bodily gestures."[24] As both Harrison and Gombrich indicated, the mime did not simply copy physical behavior, but, through ritual or dramatic action, reembodied emotional experience.

Tracing a theory of mimesis within the evolution of Freudian cultural science will require that we bear in mind both elements of the Greek notion: the reexperience of an emotion and the imitation of an event. In this way, we will recognize a path leading from analysis of expressive features in Renaissance painting to speculation on the historic action which initiated the process of civilization. Finally, if Aristotle's definition of tragedy helps us to see how the psychoanalytic investigation of art led to the study of community, his idea of history in the *Poetics* may also be worth noting: "poetry tends to express the universal, history the particular."[25] Indeed, Freud's approach to history first centered on that action, not only single and complete, but specific to one time and place, whose consequences extended across generations, and from which humanity sought continually to recover. That attempt at recovery placed the most severe demands on individual consciousness.

Throughout its development, the Freudian approach to cultural science retained its individualist perspective, stressing individual motives and actions in the artistic process, the communal drama, and the events of history. That perspective, we will argue, had an important moral source in the pre-analytic lives and work of Freud's followers. Within the Viennese psychoanalytic movement, that early moral impetus, what we may describe in Weberian language as an ethic of inward responsibility, became channeled into a commitment to the cause, a sense of calling. By exploring the origins of that commitment in the prepsychoanalytic period, by examining the relation of that calling to the project for a science of culture, and by charting the evolution of that project before and immediately after the war, this book will allow us to reconsider the position of Vienna as the city of origin of the Freudian movement. In this way, too, it will identify the survival of a moral impetus and classical aspiration within a modern, psychological approach to culture.

This study—an essay concerning the first Viennese psychoanalysts as moral critics and cultural scientists—follows a specific train of thought, or intellectual goal, within the Freudian movement in Vienna, from the formation of the earliest circle around Freud at the turn of the century to the reemergence of the movement in the immediate aftermath of war. In following that train of thought, we should of course remember that early ideas of culture and of the psychoanalytic calling never became completely lost in later formulations. As this book traces the evolution of the cause, it will examine the extent to which those previous notions of culture and mission continued to guide the Viennese circle. The journey of the original Viennese psychoanalysts began as a moral pilgrimage; we must consider how moralists first entered the domains of psychology.

TWO

MORAL JOURNEYS

I

In defining their role as a vanguard for the cause, Viennese psychoanalysts did not ignore intellectual predecessors. Frequently they looked back to thinkers who helped prepare their way. Of particular interest was Friedrich Nietzsche. Members of the Vienna Psychoanalytic Society found remarkable similarities between Nietzsche's psychological theories and those of Freud. On 1 April 1908, during the society's first meeting devoted to Nietzsche's life and thought, Paul Federn commented that "Nietzsche has come so close to our views that we can ask only, 'Where has he not come close?'" Federn pointed out that the philosopher had grasped "the significance of abreaction, of repression, of flight into illness, of the instincts—the normal sexual ones as well as the sadistic instincts."[1] At the second meeting on Nietzsche, however, Freud drew attention to a distinction between his own work and that of the philosopher.

> And thus he begins with great perspicacity—in endopsychic perception, as it were—to recognize the strata of his self. He makes a number of brilliant discoveries in himself. But now illness takes hold. Nietzsche is not satisfied with correctly fathoming these connections, but projects the insight gained about himself outward as a general imperative [*Lebensan-*

25

forderung]. To his psychological insight is added the teaching, the pastoral element that derives from his Christ ideal. . . . The degree of introspection achieved by Nietzsche had never been achieved by anyone, nor is it likely ever to be reached again. What disturbs us is that Nietzsche transformed "is" into "ought," which is alien to science. In this he has remained, after all, the moralist; he could not free himself of the theologian.[2]

To free oneself of the moralist—the step which Nietzsche could not achieve—Freud demanded of his own followers. He chose his words carefully. He knew that the core of his recruits had joined the movement out of a sense of moral outrage with the world. He expected, even counted on, this alienation, righteous anger, and earnest sense of calling. Freud set himself the task of molding his moralists into psychoanalysts. In accomplishing this task, he opened a new phase in the history of Viennese psychoanalysis. Moralists-turned-psychologists would play an indispensable role in organizing and defending Vienna's Freudian movement.

This chapter will identify the coordinates of the moral journeys completed by those disciples. Like their spiritual ally, the critic Karl Kraus, the moral *enragés* in Freud's early circle had perceived within Viennese society a crisis of responsibility, what the writer Hermann Broch would describe as a "value vacuum."[3] In response, they, like Kraus, sought to destroy intellectual illusions which masked the extent and depth of the crisis. Authentic heirs of the Enlightenment, they firmly believed that ethical responsibility must follow from intellectual clarity. That demand for clarity, however, also fostered the search for psychological truths—for principles and causes in mental life, and for the laws of their functioning. Thus, the origins of the Freudian movement in Vienna lay in the contribution of moral estrangement and anger to the demand for a scientific understanding.

The anger of future psychoanalysts can be traced to the impact on them of political and social changes in late nineteenth-century Austria. The Austrian Constitution of 1867 had offered support and protection to the middle class, especially its Jewish members, and had furthered the Liberal agenda for political and cultural reform. Constitutional guarantees of individual rights, together with steps toward greater secularization of education and the appointment of a Liberal ministry, promised conditions for complete freedom of conscience, an opportunity of unusual significance in clerical and aristocratic Austria. Forces of reaction, however, suppressed that promise, and in the aftermath members of the middle class quietly abandoned faith in it. Instead, they pursued cultural assimilation with the Catholic aristocracy.

Toward the turn of the century, there came into being a group of university students and young Viennese writers for whom the preservation of moral responsibility in a hostile world now seemed especially urgent. Victims not only of political reaction, but of moral betrayal, these righteous individuals found themselves not only under siege, but spiritually isolated. That sense of urgency and alienation led the young philosopher Otto Weininger inward to a stringent analysis of his own ethical consciousness and a consuming quest for personal redemption. Others pressed outward, along the path followed by Karl Kraus. In Kraus's journal, *Die Fackel* (*The Torch*), bourgeois *enragés* attacked corruption throughout society. Thus, moral pilgrimage followed two routes. For some, introspection held the promise of a redemptive vision. Those from whom society could not escape judgment sounded the prophet's call for contrition and reform.

The core of Freud's first recruits belonged to these intellectual cohorts. From the prepsychoanalytic writings of the Viennese Freudian vanguard, the worldview of the moral critics emerged strongly. It could be found in a physician, such as Eduard Hitschmann, or a layman, such as Theodor Reik; in a critic, such as Max Graf, or a publicist, such as Fritz Wittels. Most importantly, it could be seen in Otto Rank and Hanns Sachs, the founding editors of *Imago*. Moral outrage at the world provided them with a dissenting consciousness and a sense of mission. It did not, however, endow them with a critical method or a positive commitment. The psychoanalytic movement channeled their personal mission into a collective cause, and their moral rage into intellectual radicalism. At the furthest reaches of moral criticism, their explorations and questioning led to Freud's circle, and the science of psychoanalysis.

To understand the origins of the Viennese psychoanalytic movement, it will be necessary to begin with the social and intellectual context in which Freud's inner circle formed their notion of Viennese history. This chapter will explore the vanguard's moral reaction to the world of late nineteenth-century Vienna, concentrating on the attitudes of those members who worked in the area of applied psychoanalysis and who continued to defend the cause after the schism with Alfred Adler. (Adler's opposition to psychoanalysis began at least as early as 1909, although he did not withdraw from the Vienna Society until 1911.) Close attention will be paid to the decided affinity between the views of the Viennese psychoanalysts and those of Karl Kraus in the years before they joined the movement. Gradually, as we shall see, those who eventually became Freud's recruits turned from the examination of conscience to exploration of the psyche, and so finally to the meetings of the Vienna Psychoanalytic Society.

II

With the insurrection of 1848, Austrian Liberals launched a battle for political change within both the Habsburg monarchy and the city of Vienna. After nearly twenty years of political bargaining and disastrous Habsburg military adventures, the Constitution of 1867 finally created a Liberal ministry, expanded the powers of parliament, and formally recognized equality before the law and freedom of conscience. The Liberal Party, however, retained its share of power through a narrow franchise and debilitating concessions to the aristocracy and imperial officials. The year 1879 saw its permanent defeat in national politics and, with the conservative ministry of Count Taafe, a successful reaction against its reforms. In the city of Vienna, the party managed to hang on to the reins of power until 1897, when Karl Lueger, at the head of the populist and anti-Semitic Christian Social movement, ousted it from office.

Throughout this period, elites of the liberal middle classes and intelligentsia sought political and cultural partnership with the aristocracy. They hoped that humanist instruction and self-cultivation —*Bildung*—would create a unified educated class both to lead a reformed state and to nourish cultural life. As Carl Schorske has explained, with the defeat of political reform, the middle class fostered with ever greater energy the pursuit of cultural integration. Consequently, appropriation of the traditional aesthetic culture of the Catholic aristocracy became the most vital component of assimilation. To cement their alliance with the lower nobility and imperial administrators, Viennese industrialists, bankers, lawyers, and professors promoted that aesthetic culture through instruction and patronage in the fine arts, theater, and music. An "amoral

Gefühlskultur"[4] united those social strata within Vienna's "Second Society." As Schorske wrote, "Elsewhere in Europe, art for art's sake implied the withdrawal of its devotees from a social class; in Vienna alone it claimed the allegiance of virtually a whole class, of which the artists were a part."[5] Throughout the middle classes and intelligentsia the ideology of "art for art's sake" served as an ideology of assimilation.

In their background and education, the Viennese psychoanalysts received fully the liberal inheritance and its dilemmas. The occupations of their fathers offered a cross section of the economic and professional groups that provided the chief support of Austrian liberalism.[6] More than half of those occupations belonged to the liberal professions or the civil service. Friedrich von Winterstein fit the model of Vienna's "Second Society" in wealth and prestige. A privy councillor and vice-governor of the Austro-Hungarian Bank, he handed down the title *Freiherr* to his son Alfred. Hanns Sachs's father and uncles became successful lawyers, and they expected Sachs to continue in their vocation.[7] The physician Salomon Federn counted patients among the "Second Society," but found his friends and associates among reformist, middle-class supporters of Social Democracy. The elder Federn provided a link with the revolutionary tradition of 1848, having fought at the side of fellow medical students in the streets of Vienna.[8] Eduard Hitschmann's grandfather was a physician, his father a banker and accountant, one of his brothers a bank director, and another brother a lawyer.[9] Of the six fathers in business, we know the specific occupations not only of Mathias Hitschmann, but also of Rubin Wittels, a broker on the Vienna stock exchange, Leopold Adler, a produce merchant, and Eduard Bach, first a bookkeeper, later the owner of a hat business. After her husband's death, David Bach's mother became a laborer in a "textile business."[10]

The victory of the liberal Constitution of 1867 encouraged Marcellin Reitler, deputy director of the *Nordwestbahn*, to give practical meaning to new intellectual freedoms. In 1868, his name appeared as editor of the bulletin of the Society for Utilization of Intellectual Work, a short-lived association intent on organizing cultural activities and finding work for writers, artists, and linguists.[11] In his book on the administration of the rail system, Reitler demanded that the railroad bureaucracy be handed over to legal, medical, and technical specialists, with entrance and promotion based on *Recht*.[12] Hermann Tausk, a firm believer in the Habsburg monarchy as the guardian of a liberal empire, accepted a post in the government press office in Sarajevo after working both as a school-teacher and as editor of his own literary journal.[13] Otto Rank recorded the occupation of his father, Simon Rosenfeld, as civil servant.[14] Whereas Marcellin Reitler held a directorship in the *Nordwestbahn*, Max Reik, Theodor Reik's father, struggled to support a large household as a railway inspector.[15] Thus, the largest group of the psychoanalysts' fathers covered the spectrum of the liberal professions and state service.

With the exception of Rank's household, each family provided its son with the education of a classical *Gymnasium*. Wilhelm Stekel and Victor Tausk attended German *Gymnasien* in non-German possessions of the Habsburg empire, Stekel in Bukovina and Tausk in Croatia. Rebelling against her Orthodox Jewish upbringing, Stekel's mother enrolled her son in a Protestant, coeducational middle school. After graduating, Stekel moved on to the German *Gymnasium* in Czernowitz.[16] At his *Gymnasium*, Victor Tausk helped lead a student protest against the teaching of religion.[17] Four Viennese psychoanalysts graduated from the *Akademisches Gymnasium* located in the Ringstrasse district of the capital. During the Revolution of 1848, Viennese liberals had placed the *Akademisches Gymnasium* on their political agenda. In that year, reformers won the elimination of clerical control of the school, and four years later the government declared it a state *Gymnasium*. Throughout the late nineteenth century, "successful manufacturers and business people, noted physicians and lawyers or high administrative officials" sent their sons—including Rudolf Reitler, Paul Federn, Eduard Hitschmann, and Max Graf—to the *Akademisches Gymnasium*.[18] The liberal middle class turned the institution into a stronghold of secular education in conscious opposition to the aristocratic *Theresianum* and the religious *Schottengymnasium*.[19]

While the parents of the psychoanalysts ensured that their sons received educations in practical professions, they also provided them with opportunities to acquire the aesthetic culture so highly prized by the Austrian bourgeoisie. They expected that art would give way to law or science at the university, but their sons refused to relinquish their creative aspirations. During *Gymnasium*, Wilhelm Stekel spent as much time as possible reading and writing poetry, but decided that the study of medicine offered the best path out of Czernowitz to the University of Vienna. At the time he started his career in general practice, however, he also began work on a novel.[20] Max Graf devoted himself to music. Before entering the university, he recalled, "without benefit of a great deal of training I had been composing day and night—songs, violin pieces, chamber music—and like many young people I was obsessed with the one thought of giving utterance to my musical feeling."[21] When he graduated from the University of Vienna's school of law in 1895, Graf sought employment as a music critic.[22] Hanns Sachs dutifully enrolled in the university's school of jurisprudence, "a young man who was supposedly studying law but not living up to the supposition."[23] His interests were "centered in literature, almost to the exclusion of everything else."[24] Sachs did not take his final examination for a doctorate in law until July 1907, four years after completing his course work.[25] In 1905, Victor Tausk abandoned his legal career, and his wife and children, to try a career as a writer, publishing his first efforts in his father's journal. After months of poverty in Berlin, he gave up the literary vocation.[26] Having passed his graduation examination for the school of law in 1909, Alfred von Winterstein turned immediately to publishing his poetry.[27] These psychoanalysts knew well the world of literary ambition and devotion gripping the younger generation of Viennese liberals.

All but two of the psychoanalysts under discussion were Jewish.[28] In nineteenth-century Vienna, the German-speaking, Western Jews of the Habsburg lands trusted that constitutional reform would secure equality before the law, careers open to talent, and freedom of conscience and education. The political program of the Liberal Party conformed to their intellectual and social aims: in Hanns Sachs's words, "full assimilation without apostasy."[29] Some of the psychoanalysts' families could point to significant successes. During the first round of liberalization following suppression of the rebellion of 1848, Salomon Federn became one of the first Jewish general practitioners in Vienna.[30] In the final decades before the First World War, however, the triumphs of Lueger and the Christian Social Party exerted ever greater pressure on middle-class Jews to seek cultural assimilation or religious conversion. The Jewish bourgeoisie experienced viscerally the historical conflict in Viennese liberalism between the ideology of gradual progress through political and educational reform, and the drive toward cultural and religious integration with the aristocracy.

Although apostates against tradition, these future psychoanalysts stood against full religious assimilation. Nor did they share in much of the striving after cultural integration with the upper orders.[31] Their families had preserved a commitment to liberalism's reformist program and a faith in Jewish upward mobility through education and professional advancement. As the turn of the century approached, however, the sons nurtured few hopes for the realization of those agendas. Amidst middle-class desertion and defeat, personal moral commitment seemed to them essential as a last defense against the assimilationist options. Without an institutional mooring for the liberal cause and faced with the expanding tendency among the Viennese bourgeoisie toward assimilation, they hammered out a highly individualistic and moralistic response. The disappointment of a young, liberal intelligentsia grew finally into a profound sense of moral alienation.

III

In their social position, professional education, and religious training, Freud's future disciples sustained the legacy of Austrian liberalism. Radical moral dissent, however, drove a wedge between them and that tradition. That break with the past initiated the journey which would bring them to the psychoanalytic movement. The moral discontent of their youth not only expressed itself in their writing at the time, but left its imprint in their later memoirs. In both types of writing, psychoanalysts concerned themselves chiefly with the shaken values of the Viennese bourgeoisie in a time of reaction, sharply emphasizing that the drive to integrate with the aristocracy corrupted their social class.

The origins of the striving toward assimilation, Max Graf wrote, could be traced to the rise of a "new society of finance nobility, industrial and business *arrivés*, and their allies, the old Viennese aristocracy: a society with riches, cosmopolitan attitude, love of pleasure, and like every upwardly mobile caste, energy for making newly gained ground its property."[32] It masked its humble origins in the "monstrosity of the Roman, Greek, Gothic and Renaissance building decoration" which embellished the Ringstrasse, the bourgeois "wreath" crowning the imperial and aristocratic Inner City.[33] Bourgeois elites adopted the behavior of the aristocracy and aspired to its privileges and honors: "The new industrial and Stock Exchange men, streaming with wealth, crowded themselves into the court society to receive orders and titles from the Emperor. When they gave parties in their new houses, they invited aristocrats as window dressing. The young sons of Viennese manufacturers dressed themselves like aristocrats and aped their accent and manner."[34] To solidify their inward identification with the aristocracy, "new plutocrats" joined with the old nobility in building and patronizing the Viennese palaces of art.[35]

In his memoirs, Hanns Sachs recalled with bitterness how the nobility, like a silent, corrosive force, emptied parliamentary process and the rule of law of meaning:

> Austria was a constitutional monarchy with all the usual trappings: a charter of liberties, two houses of parliament, responsible ministers, independent law courts, the usual machinery of government. Yet, it was an open secret that none of all these institutions possessed a scrap of real power, not even the bureaucracy. This power was in the hand of the Austrian "eighty families." . . . Closely knit together as they were, yet without any trace of organization or leadership, their amorphous, anonymous, irresponsible power could only work in one way: to inhibit any innovation, to exclude all new forces from coöperation.[36]

Those in power, and those who wanted power, kept constitutional forms and the ideal of law as covers for favoritism, patronage, and political extortion:

> Political parties and elections, heated parliamentary debates, the voting of laws and the creation of public offices to execute them, all this went on just as in a grade A democracy. But all this was a false front made for outsiders and those afflicted with congenital blindness. To get anywhere it was necessary to have backing from "above" either directly or, if that was not possible, through one of the henchmen to whom the ruling class had delegated the execution of its power. Without that no move, however strictly within the bounds of the constitution, could prosper; with it any law could be infringed or somehow circumvented.[37]

In the process of carrying out its strategy of assimilation, the middle class sacrificed its cultural identity and ethical responsibility:

> The style of life of the privileged class became, as a matter of course, the pattern after which the middle class tried to model its conduct, imitating it down to the slightest mannerisms. (The rich Jews, after they had surmounted the religious barrier, were easily in the forefront.) The result oscillated between simple and downright snobbism and high, exalted aestheticism; one variant of this attitude, called *fin de siècle*, boasted that it

preferred "beauty"—but a beauty in inverted commas—to morals, and proudly called itself "decadent."[38]

No psychoanalyst felt a greater sense of rage against that moral defeatism than Fritz Wittels. In 1904, the year of his graduation from Vienna's school of medicine, Wittels published his first polemic, *The Baptized Jew*. For the young pamphleteer, religious conversion embodied the crisis consuming liberalism. Virtually every baptism, Wittels wrote, had at bottom the overriding motive of "social ambition [*Strebertum*]."[39] The docent desired to become a professor, the lawyer set his sights on a judgeship or ministerial post, and the parvenu ached to attend the hunts and feasts of the high nobility. The Constitution of 1867, Wittels reminded the reader, guaranteed equality before the law, established freedom of religion, and declared public offices open to every citizen. Yet Jews had been excluded from positions in the ministry, the bureaucracy, the judiciary, the officer corps, and the university, had regularly found their promotions blocked in those institutions, and faced continuing exclusion from local administrations and private enterprises. Too many Jews made peace with the new politics and society. In parliament, in local councils, and in the press, they relinquished the "battle for *Recht*."[40]

In Wittels's worldview, the most severe consequence of the drive toward assimilation consisted in the crime against oneself. Official baptism marked the last victory over conscience among "those Jews who have allowed it all to take place, and so sacrificed their personality."[41] To the young Wittels, the most disturbing aspect of assimilation within the Jewish middle class lay in the act of self-betrayal. That breach of faith governed Wittels's view of society. Social life depended on a moral covenant: "Each individual citizen has the right to demand that his trust, his belief in honesty, not be injured, at least not through a falsely *solemn* assertion, and therefore the perjury through which an individual man is deceived is as culpable as the one through which generations are overthrown."[42] Disappointment, mistrust, and "disharmony with society"[43] now dominated the consciousness of Western Jewish youth. Within their spiritual life, absolute negation continuously undermined the impulse toward moral affirmation:

> It [Western Jewish consciousness] is, on one side, the method of analytical reason, the spirit of relentless criticism, undermining everything, a Mephistophelian orgy of the destruction of all that which has become obsolete, worn out, traditional: "for all things, from the Void called forth, deserve to be destroyed." On the other side, it throws itself with blind passion on everything new, seizes it, works it through, spreads it over the globe, for since he [the young Western Jew] has destroyed the old, he must seek happiness and satisfaction in what is still unexplored, what is hardly understood, until such time that, furiously disappointed, with his harlequin's sword he plays catch with the stars that a short while ago he himself fastened onto the heavens.[44]

In Wittels, blank rage and the longing for virtue combined to produce a sense of estrangement, even despair. Feeling betrayed by his class and his coreligionists, he committed his judgments to print as a warning to individual conscience and a public indictment for the day of reckoning.

Wittels expressed most ardently and darkly the disillusionment and embitterment shared by the moral *enragés* among Freud's eventual recruits. Their trust betrayed, these future disciples viewed Viennese society and politics as an elaborate game of mirrors. Glittering words and polished moral surfaces endlessly reflected and distorted each other. Disoriented and perplexed, they searched for a core of integrity and authenticity in the world around them. Although aware of the social purposes and political strategies of the ruling class and their assimilationist, middle-class allies, they initially identified individual ethical obligation as the antidote to the system of corruption. Their moral disappointment and anger marked the first important turn from the path laid down for them by the liberal tradition.

IV

Psychoanalysts were not alone in their puritanical intensity. In equal measure and for similar reasons, the writers Otto Weininger and Karl Kraus burned with righteous indignation. Yet, despite their common anger at the political destruction of their moral hopes and their fury at the turpitude of the middle class, moral *enragés* did not steer in the same direction. Weininger turned inward for solace and reflection, while Kraus and allies on his journal, *Die Fackel*, pushed outward to the commotion and confrontation of the public arena. The reactions of future psychoanalysts also divided between inwardness and engagement. Freudians, however, later differentiated themselves from both Weininger and Kraus by leaving the moral forum for the fields of science.

Throughout his university education, the philosopher Otto Weininger lived in intellectual self-exile. Emerging at the age of twenty-one from extremes of withdrawal and estrangement, he declared he had found the key to the ego's salvation from moral corruption. At the same time, Weininger also claimed to have discovered the path from moral philosophy to scientific psychology; he thus became for future psychoanalysts a figure with whom to reckon.

Within Viennese intellectual circles, Weininger incarnated the penitent who, in isolation from society and its corrupting influences, hoped to guarantee his own salvation. In the young philosopher's Manichaean vision, the forces of morality and antimorality warred continually for mastery of the soul. His book, *Sex and Character*, published in 1903, defined those contending forces in sexual terms. Men embodied the principles of character, self-knowledge, and moral independence. The principle of sexuality governed women, rendering them incapable of intellectual consciousness and moral pride. Weininger arrived at this conclusion after having established his "psychology of individual differences,"[45] founded on an analysis of the balance between male and female psychic forces within the individual. In a chapter entitled "Talent and Memory," he explained that this new science of characterology, or "theoretical biography," would "deal with the investigation of the permanent laws that rule the mental development of an individual. . . . The new knowledge will seek general points of view and the establishment of types."[46]

The central concern of characterology, however, became neither the "psychology of individual differences" nor the discovery of developmental laws, which Weininger thought solved in any case, but the study of character as "the ruling force of the Ego."[47] The ego, Weininger wrote in "Talent and Memory," had to be understood as the "will to value [*Wille zum Wert*]."[48] To express that will, the artist or philosopher chose to live apart from the world, lay aside anger, and "acquiesce in his loneliness."[49] The chapter "Talent and Genius" explained that the genius could endure such isolation because his personality contained the complete range of human psychological types.

Weininger's thought showed no such complexity, but degenerated into Manichaeanism and misogyny. His moral independence became a denial of life, and his intellectual iconoclasm yielded to pious introspection. In woman, who, dominated by the principle of sexuality, lived without moral consciousness, he found a destructive force against which to do battle. According to Weininger, the Jews, his former coreligionists, also lacked moral enlightenment, with the exception that they retained the possibility of self-renunciation and a return to the ascetic ideal. "The birth of the Kantian ethics, the noblest event in the history of the world," he exalted, "was the moment when for the first time the dazzling awful conception came to him, 'I am responsible only to myself; I must follow none other; I must not forget myself even in my work; I am alone; I am free; I am lord of myself.' "[50] Weininger held in contempt those for whom "the earth can only mean the turmoil and press of those on it."[51] The torment barely concealed in his ideal ended in suicide.

On 24 February 1904, two years before joining Freud's Wednesday meetings, Otto Rank wrote in his diary,

> I am now reading Otto Weininger, *Sex and Character.* What happened to me while reading the sections, "Talent and Genius" and "Talent and Memory" stands forth uniquely as an event in my reading of literature. Everything which is expressed as special in these two chapters, I myself had already experienced earlier in me, and at many points I thought Weininger could have added there still one thing or another that belongs within the domain of this complex of thoughts. And hardly had I thought that and formulated the supplement, when indeed I came upon it also in the book; it stood there almost in my own words.[52]

What most appealed to Rank in Weininger's philosophy was the modern conception of an invisible moral elect and the possibility of confirming one's membership in that new moral vanguard through introspection.

Rank grew up within a struggling, lower-middle-class Jewish family in Leopoldstadt. His father, suffering from alcoholism, frequently became violent toward his wife and two sons. Rank's older brother attended *Gymnasium* and eventually studied law. When Rank finished his early schooling, however, his father started him on a program of vocational training, which concluded with three years in the machine section of an advanced technical school.[53]

Rank's journals, kept after 1903 while he worked as an apprentice and finally a clerk in a machine factory, expressed despondency and confusion. He began several literary endeavors in 1903 and 1904: a notebook of poems, one act of a play, and a short story. Echoing Weininger, Rank described the artist as the embodiment of the ideal of intellectual and moral self-reliance: "Highly gifted spirits are always fine observers of mankind, deep psychologists, because they concentrate in themselves the whole concept of humanity; they have the tendencies of all possibilities of mankind in themselves and can develop them in ideas."[54] In the realm of philosophy, Weininger's "will to value" had succeeded Schopenhauer's "will to life" and Nietzsche's "will to power."[55] It provided a sense of consolation, as well as independence. "Kant's ethic: There are only duties toward oneself. I have only to answer for me to myself. I stand *alone*, am *free*, am my own *master*. Weininger."[56] Like Weininger, Rank welcomed isolation from society as the condition of moral freedom.

Gradually, Rank drifted from Weininger's program. Under the influence of Freud's work, he slowly relinquished his goal of spiritual transcendence, endeavoring instead to fathom the inner world of psychic conflict. In the summer of 1904, his family physician, Alfred Adler, introduced him to *The Interpretation of Dreams*.[57] Strongly impressed by the book, Rank began to abandon his moral investigation of genius. His journals turned into drafts of a book on the libidinal sources of creativity, published finally as *The Artist* in 1907. According to Rank, the psychological conflict between unsatisfied libido and forces of suppression raged most intensely within artists, who, in the creative process, never ceased renewing their efforts to allay in themselves the feeling of want.

Wilhelm Stekel employed a similar conception of psychic struggle to explain Otto Weininger's life and work. Weininger's inner battles, however, led not to temporary repose, but frenzied disequilibrium. His rage against sexuality and women, Stekel wrote, finally resulted in a "pathological illusion of grandeur."[58] Meanwhile, another physician, Eduard Hitschmann, sought to separate the psychological wheat from the moral chaff in Weininger's philosophy. In Hitschmann's view, Weininger's psychological method needed to be preserved from the philosopher's all-consuming redemptive mission. In his review of P. J. Möbius's pathography of Arthur Schopenhauer, Hitschmann stated that Otto Weininger's characterology, in contrast to psychopathography, signified "a genuine and practical psychology" which did justice both to the personality and the demands of science: "Psychology set out to become theoretical biography, whose task consisted in the research of constant laws of the mental development of the individual [*Individuum*], in the determination of types."[59] What caused the collapse of that scientific project? Schopenhauer's division of the world into will and idea provided the key: "Hypersexuality with idealistic struggle, powerful instinctual drive at war with asceticism, longing for mental peace, clarity, and intensive, undisturbed capacity for work, gradually led to the accumulation in him of hatred and contempt for—the essential female."[60] Schopenhauer's own life and work became dominated by the same striving after redemption and struggle to transform sensual urges into spiritual powers, the psychological phenomenon "characteristic in this 'Schopenhauer type.'"[61]

From spiritual exercises to psychological exploration: the way led to Freud. Viennese psychoanalysts differentiated their work from the endeavors of thinkers, past and present, who searched the psyche for an assurance of salvation. Psychologists, such as Weininger, who presumed to offer a route to personal redemption, opened dangerous moral paths. For Freud's disciples, to explore and illumine, not to transcend, inner conflict finally defined the true vocation of psychology.

V

Although notoriety came quickly and overwhelmingly to Weininger, he never purposefully sought access to the public stage. Led by Karl Kraus, however, others from the camp of moral critics sought assiduously to expose to scrutiny the veins of corruption running throughout society. If psychoanalysts came to define themselves in opposition to seekers after redemption, such as Weininger, several of them saw in Kraus a potential brother-in-arms. Among Freud's most loyal adherents were those who had taken their moral criticism and intensity into a campaign against the corruption of culture. Like Kraus, they extended their offensive to an attack on the false moralism of the prevailing sexual ethic, and its social and psychological consequences. They concluded with Kraus—and against Weininger—that the liberation of sexuality established the necessary condition for the liberation of morality. In this fight, one of their number, Fritz Wittels, formally joined forces with *Die Fackel*. Not only Wittels, but Sachs, Reik, and Graf started on the road to psychoanalysis, to use Wittels's description of his mentor Kraus, as "anticorruptionists."[62] Although they soon parted ways with Kraus, they traveled furthest with him in the years before they joined the movement.

As a satirist and polemicist, Karl Kraus concentrated and channeled the moral fury of Viennese youth, giving it direction and identifying its targets. His satire did not rely on exaggeration or invention to expose its objects. Rather, he used his opponents' own words against them. In the cold light of Kraus's essays, the true intentions behind distended and contorted expressions of venal writers, politicians, and propagandists stood revealed. Throughout his lifetime Kraus tirelessly purged Viennese prose so as to restore words to their authentic meanings. As on the printed page, so too in drama and the arts. Kraus became the leader of those who have been called the "last puritans," those critics "who rejected the use of art as a cultural cosmetic to screen the nature of reality."[63] A zealous muckraker and austere guardian of the word, Kraus sought above all else to preserve the sanctity and immediacy of language.

Like the anger of the psychoanalysts, Kraus's ire, especially his fury against Viennese liberals, fed on a sense of betrayal. His outrage and disenchantment toward both the careless journalism and political compromises of the liberal *Neue Freie Presse* produced some of the most deeply searing polemics of his early career. Kraus's bitterness, however, reflected disappointment and estrangement far less than it expressed complete absorption in the fight. Walter Benjamin summarized in a few words the origins of Kraus's method:

> Here we find confirmation that all the martial energies of this man are innate civic virtues; only in the *mêlée* did they take on their combative aspect. But already no one recognizes them any more; no one can grasp the necessity that compelled this great bourgeois character to become a comedian, this guardian of Goethean linguistic values a polemicist, or why this irreproachably honorable man went berserk. This, however, was bound to happen, since he thought fit to begin changing the world with his own class, in his own home, in Vienna. And when, recognizing the fu-

tility of his enterprise, he abruptly broke it off, he placed the matter back in the hands of nature—this time destructive, not creative nature.[64]

Kraus began his own moral odyssey with a condemnation of the withdrawal and introversion of the new bourgeois aesthetic culture. His first pamphlet, *The Demolished Literature*, attacked the Viennese literary representatives of "art for art's sake"— Hugo von Hofmannsthal, the young Arthur Schnitzler, and the artists, critics, and hangers-on of *Jung Wien*—for their moral detachment and psychological resignation. Their work, Kraus maintained, exalted the virtue of personality without understanding its significance. Nor did it comprehend the individual's confrontation with the world. Naturalism had no influence among them: "'Secret nerves' the phrase now went; one set about observing 'mental states,' and wanted to flee the ordinary clarity of things."[65] Kraus's wrath focused on the "shallow impressionism" of their spokesman, the writer Hermann Bahr, whose critical judgments contained "vague potshots" without "purposeful aggression."[66]

With an aim not unlike Kraus's, Hanns Sachs in 1910 published a translation of Rudyard Kipling's *Barrack-Room Ballads* to make available poetry which "refused to bow to the principle of 'art for art's sake.' "[67] From Kipling's work one learned that the foundation of the British Empire came from criminals, youths dissatisfied with "cramped bourgeois life,"[68] and the poor, all outcasts who served the government, but were in turn abused by it. In *The Barrack-Room Ballads*, according to Sachs, "artistic form is only the expression of a striving for the factual."[69]

Similarly, in 1911, Theodor Reik's first publication, a study of his Viennese contemporary, the writer Richard Beer-Hofmann, warned against the introversion and amorality of Vienna's "culture of aesthetes."[70] In subject matter, Beer-Hofmann's first stories centered on reflections and memories of the "favorite of the salon," "men of the world" without commitments or attachments.[71] Like Arthur Schnitzler's Anatol, Beer-Hofmann's hero remained the "cool observer of his own ego" and "refined dissector of his own moods."[72] In that early stage of his literary career, Beer-Hofmann "ran the risk that his fertile, but chaste inwardness would evaporate into the elegant, tasteful, 'merely beautiful'; that he would see art as a refuge for persons unsuited for the confusing rush of life, as a place of asylum for psychological drifters."[73]

Despite their shared starting point, the paths of Kraus and the psychoanalysts soon diverged sharply. Theodor Reik concluded that Beer-Hofmann had rescued himself and his art by turning to psychology. Works such as *Miriams Schlaflied* depicted the survival through the generations of Jewish spiritual identity. In this way, Beer-Hofmann's introspection finally led to recognition of the silent bonds between individuals and generations. His inwardness thus produced "insight into the lawfulness [*Gesetzlichkeit*] of our life, the physical and spiritual."[74]

Hanns Sachs's own "striving for the factual," his endeavor to see the psyche as one would, in Kraus's words, see the "ordinary clarity of things," ultimately led him away from the work of moral criticism. Literature guided Sachs in an unforeseen direction, ending at Freud's evening lectures at the University of Vienna. "The connecting link," wrote Sachs, "was formed by my boundless admiration for Dostoevski. I wanted to find, led by the hand of science, the secrets of the soul which he had almost succeeded revealing in their nakedness; I hoped to tread in broad daylight the obscure and labyrinthine paths of passion which he had traced."[75]

To strip reality of all artifice, Karl Kraus delved even further into the corruption of society. Although fighting his own battles, Kraus again found common ground with psychoanalysts. In his eyes, society revealed the depth of its corruption and the insatiability of its appetite by simultaneously attacking moral freedom and natural drives. Thus, the moralist preached sexual freedom, for in the domain of sexuality, intervention by the authorities "always produced the most wicked antimorality."[76]

Crimes perpetrated in the courtroom, the arena in which society sought to complete its victory over individual freedom, became special targets of Kraus's condemnation and despair. In 1906, the prosecution of the madam of a brothel, Regine Riehl, drew Kraus's fire, in part as an example of the diversion of moral scrutiny from issues of genuine public importance: "Society despises her [the prostitute] more deeply than the corrupt public functionary, than the most venal bureaucrat, and the journalist most easily bribed, rages against the prostitution of women as if it endangered the most important social interests, and considers the corruption of men a matter of individual ethics."[77] The Riehl case, however, demonstrated to Kraus more than the existence of the persistent confusion between civic concerns and matters of private morality. Interference by the state in sexual life opened sexual desire to criminal exploitation.

Although Riehl was accused and finally convicted of the economic exploitation and physical mistreatment of her employees, her establishment, Kraus pointed out, had existed for years under the protection and patronage of the authorities. Riehl's trial unmasked a system of social control. Wardens existed for exploited segments of the population, in this case, prostitutes: "The usurious landlady of the bordello is an assistant to the authorities, an executive organ of morality."[78] To keep watch, the state also appointed "guardians of morality"[79] and a "moral police":[80] judges, prosecutors, and magistrates. The procuress occupied the anomalous and dangerous position of go-between for members of society and the state. At any time, the state could choose to make an example of her. The abused and alienated had no recourse to justice. In reality, social mores were the rules with which society kept a banished population confined:

> The invaluable possession of humanity in graciousness and elementary naturalness is outlawed. Around it, a barbed wire fence; behind this begins the order of society. From the latter, when it becomes dark, hordes of scornful men scurry into the unholy district. For those, however, who live within, no path leads into the order of society. Often the blood of those who cannot feel pride in being ostracized sticks to the barbed wire. But always those from the order of society spring across; they have contempt for those expelled by day, because these must submit to their love at night. So those on the other side have for centuries preserved a heroic passivity toward the order of society, which daily devises new, malicious sport against them.[81]

Morality and sexuality fell prey to the same corrupt forces.

Die Fackel's cause won over young Viennese writers who shared —or, perhaps, aspired to—Kraus's fervor and indignation. Victor Tausk explained to his fellow psychoanalysts that Kraus's "greatest merit" lay in his struggle against the "vulgarization of thinking and feeling."[82] From 1907 to 1909, Fritz Wittels contributed to *Die Fackel* a series of articles arguing for the legalization of abortion, open treatment of venereal disease, enlightened sexual education, and unrestricted sexual freedom for married and unmarried alike. Through association with *Die Fackel* and his membership in the Vienna Psychoanalytic Society, Wittels intended to be the first to unite the work of Kraus and Freud. In the introduction to the publication of his essays in book form in 1909, Wittels explained that sexual misery created by the "artificial quieting of passion" constituted the invisible suffering of "bourgeois society."[83] Freud's teachings confirmed Kraus's indictment of society and had to be brought before the public: Freud "must put up with others carrying into life the truths he discovered. Men must live out their sexuality, otherwise they become cripples. One will surely not suppress this blessed truth out of the consideration that it is unpopular. Freud has pointed out new paths to psychology. Perhaps it belongs to the better part of virtue to travel early these newly opened paths."[84]

When writing his memoirs, Wittels recalled the educational zeal and transcendent urgency which Kraus's defiant piety inspired in him: "Kraus was the reformer and I his learned counsellor, as Melancthon to Luther, very much secularized."[85] Wittels would take up the sword with Kraus—"But how could one be Kraus's collaborator and not attack!"[86]—and devote himself to formulating the intellectual rationale for the polemicist's demands. To fulfill his self-conceived mission, he turned to Freud: "I considered him a scholar who forged the weapons with which Kraus and I would tear to bits a world of hypocrisy and hysteria."[87] The new psychology would release humanity's moral sensibility and sexual longing from an empty, omnivorous ethic.

Kraus's recent biographer, Edward Timms, has shown that Wittels departed from the views of both Kraus and Freud on how to apply psychology toward his goal.[88] For Kraus, the naturalness of sexuality stood in stark contrast to the public's—and Wittels's—unholy hunger for sensationalism. Kraus wrote, "Whoever places on the title page of a book this motto: 'Men must live out their sexuality, otherwise they become cripples' is an honest fellow who is serious about sexual enlightenment and for whom nothing is more important than sexuality, with the possible exception of success."[89] Similarly, as Wittels expected, Freud took exception to his follower's advocacy of unlimited sexual license. At a meeting of the Vienna Society devoted to Wittels's proposals, Freud explained that the book

> stems from two different sources—from, so to say, a paternal and a maternal source. The first one, represented by the *Fackel*, goes part of the way with us in its assertion that suppression of sexuality is the root of all

evil. But we go further, and say: we liberate sexuality through our treatment, but not in order that man may from now on be dominated by sexuality, but in order to make a suppression possible—a rejection of the instincts under the guidance of a higher agency. The *Fackel* stands for "living out" one's instinctual desires to the point of satiating them [*ausleben*]; we distinguish, however, between a pathological process of repression and one that is to be regarded as normal.[90]

Freud later informed Wittels and the society that his own "personal relation to Kraus was such that, even before Wittels became one of our collaborators, he had had the idea that the cause [of psychoanalysis] could obtain an effective helper in Kraus."[91] In October 1904, at the time when Freud actively began to seek recruits from outside the medical profession, he initiated communication with Kraus. After an occasional exchange of letters and information stretching over two years, Kraus sent Freud a copy of "The Riehl Trial." Freud took the opportunity to raise the possibility of the two joining forces. In a letter dated 11 November 1906, he wrote, "My heartfelt thanks for sending me the reprint. I had, naturally, already read the 'Riehl' case in the *Fackel*. Some of it is 'beautiful to the point of tears.' People will once again praise your style and admire your wit, but they will not feel ashamed, which is after all what you want to attain. For that, they are too many, and feel themselves too secure in their solidarity. We few should therefore also stick together."[92] The project for an alliance, however, came into the world of Viennese cultural life stillborn. Like Kraus, Freud emphasized that repression of sexuality not only distorted natural drives, but undermined moral ones. Thus, in the views of both, liberation of the moral impulse required liberation of the sexual. Freud, however, wanted neither a redemptive quest, nor a prophetic mission attached to the understanding and liberation of sexuality. A psychology which sought insight into the laws of the unconscious and its sensuous reality had to distance itself not only from strivings for personal deliverance, but also finally from the puritanism of rage. For Freud, such distance defined the condition of scientific understanding—and of the sublime in art. For Kraus, that distance created an opportunity for corruption. In ethics and science, unity between Freud and Kraus had only been temporarily forced upon them by their common antagonists.[93]

VI

The process of education within the Vienna Psychoanalytic Society can be interpreted in part as an endeavor to transform awareness gained from moral indignation into a new scientific consciousness. As Freud wrote to Carl Jung, with reference to prospective allies in Switzerland, he hoped to "be able to draw the moralists to ΨA rather than let the Ψ-analysts be turned into moralists."[94] Although the alliance between Freud and Kraus never transpired, Freud continued in those first years of the Vienna Society's existence to search for recruits among cultural critics. When Max Graf joined the society in 1905, Freud pressed him to bring to the cause his associates from the literary professions.[95] Graf himself embodied the critic-turned-psychologist that Freud valued so greatly among his followers. His personal odyssey epitomized the moral journey of the early disciples of Viennese psychoanalysis.

Psychology completed Graf's journey through the Wagnerian subculture of his Viennese youth. Renouncing the quest for prophetic powers or personal salvation so ardently pursued by Viennese Wagnerians, Graf turned to psychological investigation. Wagner no longer appeared to him as a visionary or private messiah, but rather as a historical and psychological problem. The historical problem consisted in the composer's attempt to assume the role of prophet and restore the supposedly lost connection between art and society. The psychological problem lay in the internal conflicts which produced Wagner's need for personal redemption.

In the 1870s, Wagner's aim to regenerate German cultural life with a new art found enthusiastic followers among university students in Vienna. Disappointed with the inadequacy of liberalism's political reforms and dissatisfied with its rationalist view of man, they looked forward to a society in which the populace would enjoy full political participation, economic equality, and social unity. Bonds of community would draw sustenance from the emotions, which art would bring to the center of social life. Their movement was short-lived. After leaving the university, those students genuinely committed to the rights of humanity helped found Austrian Social Democracy. Malcontents descended with Wagner into right-wing German nationalism and anti-Semitism.[96]

Graf described that first generation's "idealism" as the source of a distorted picture of the composer: "According to their own images, the fighters of German battles sketched the image of Wagner: the image of the German epic poet, the herald of heroic emotions, the master of every strong and triumphant art."[97] The culturally regenerative force within Wagner's art proved artificial: "[His] artwork did not, like Greek tragedy, stand at the beginning of an age, a civilization, a people, but at the end, as a grandiose *resumé*. . . . It rests on the fragments of an old culture and attempts to resolve its highest conscious forces once more into unconscious ones."[98]

The university generation of the 1890s, Graf's cohort, lost interest in the composer's vision of cultural transformation. Instead, they adopted the message of personal salvation proclaimed in *Parsifal*: "No music in the world spoke so to our passions, our longing, our torments. . . . Thus we saw in Wagner not, like that old generation, the bard of heroic emotions, but the great musical sorcerer of all wounds and mental suffering."[99] The new Romantics, like the first Wagnerians, clung to a belief in the power of art to transcend conflict, whether that conflict be societal or psychic.

According to Graf, psychology finally dissolved Wagnerian illusions. The science of the mind uncovered the meaning of art in the inner foundations of creativity. Subjected to psychological analysis, works of art revealed their creator's "psychic type."[100] In the case of Wagner, musical creation expressed longing for release from inner struggle. The source of his creativity from the conception of *The Flying Dutchman* to the completion of *Parsifal* came from his ceaseless effort to escape the psychological conflict between forces of sensuality, power, and health, and those of denial, disgust, and sickness. In *Parsifal*, Wagner finally embraced the Schopenhauerian prescription for inner freedom: extinguishing desire.

Behind Graf's analysis of Wagner, art, and psychology stood the figure of Friedrich Nietzsche. In *The Birth of Tragedy out of the Spirit of Music*, the young Nietzsche exalted Wagner's aim to regenerate society through art and to revive the force of instinct within music. Wagner's Viennese followers, however, observed the philosopher's estrangement from the composer and his renunciation of Wagnerian idealism. Graf, together with other Viennese of his generation, incorporated Nietzsche's new teachings: "A great guide, our instructor in the battles of spiritual life plunged with violent force into the chasm of eternal night. Honor to the memory of Friedrich Nietzsche!"[101]

Nietzsche, according to Graf, had suffered internal struggles similar to those of Wagner. *The Birth of Tragedy* presented Greek tragic drama as the constructive, yet uneasy interplay of forces furiously battling each other within the philosopher: "Dionysos is the moving principle—the struggle, the tumult of instincts, the swirl of passion; Apollo gives order and binds. . . . A passionate, Dionysian underworld, over which the eyes of Apollo look out with blessed clarity: so the image of the Greek world appeared to him, a grand likeness of his inner being."[102] Aeschylus, the "Dionysian dramatist,"[103] gave voice both to the wordless, instinctive compulsion of music, and to the philosopher's own suffering. To the young Nietzsche, Wagner seemed to be the Greek tragedian's modern incarnation. As his inner conflict became more severe, however, Nietzsche's view of the world, and of the composer, became more trenchant. Bayreuth did not sublimate unconscious desire, but served up stimulants and dangerous illusions. In the end, Nietzsche renounced completely the goal of cultural transformation: "He had seen the world as a Dionysian Romantic: now it appeared disenchanted to him, the fantastic cloud appeared to tear and with hard, clear vision he saw the forces which moved the world at work."[104]

"The degree of introspection achieved by Nietzsche had never been achieved by anyone, nor is it likely ever to be reached again. What disturbs us is that Nietzsche transformed 'is' into 'ought,' which is alien to science. In this he has remained, after all, the moralist." With that comment, Freud not only distinguished the ideas of Nietzsche from those of psychoanalysis. He also reminded his followers of their own journeys to the Vienna Society, and the inner vigilance required to protect the identity and autonomy of the movement. Their seeking after redemption or prophecy had finally to be renounced; the striving toward clarity remained to them. Those who stayed the course permanently left their earlier, sacred vocation for a secular one. Moral indignation and protest marked those psychoanalysts' initial break with their society and their past, while their commitment to the movement marked the second, decisive one.

The early Viennese recruits to psychoanalysis undertook journeys of a great distance, during which they discarded their moral absolutism for a framework within which to interpret scientifically the dualism of the psyche. Yet, awareness of the dynamics between repression and desire, and the duality of ego and id, never belonged to science alone. With the unique exception of Karl Kraus, Viennese moralists sought desperately to discount psychic dualism, either by exalting the dictates of conscience or by glorifying the demands of instinct. Nietzsche became for them a cipher in which they read either message as the spirit moved them. Within the psychoanalytic movement, therefore, Freud attempted to bring his recruits not only to psychological understanding, but to inward acceptance of the ineradicable dualism of the human soul. In the process, their moral perception and intellectual awareness became imbued ever more deeply with tragic consciousness. Thus, those psychoanalysts who continued their journeys followed a path leading not only to the discoveries of *The Interpretation of Dreams*, but to the final conceptualization, in *Civilization and Its Discontents*, of the eternal struggle between Eros and death.

It was, perhaps, ironic that conscience originally led these individuals to the movement. Yet, righteous anger certainly provided impetus and confidence to support Freud's intellectual revolution. Nor can one overlook the importance of their fervent sense of commitment. Even the schisms which consistently plagued the movement in Vienna reflected the uncompromising character of its members. More significantly, however, psychoanalysis in its turn utilized and affirmed their sense of mission, giving it new content and direction. Among the members of the Vienna Society, moral intensity preserved itself in the dedication of their lives to the movement. For the Viennese, psychoanalysis meant "the cause," an odyssey which became a life's work.

A Viennese journey: dissatisfied youths became moralists, moralists became psychoanalysts. Thus, the Freudian movement in Vienna came into being as a transformation of its opposite.

THREE

A CULTURAL VOCATION

I

The beginnings of the Viennese psychoanalytic movement can be traced to a single book, *The Interpretation of Dreams*. In its pages, the explanation of the unconscious origin of dreams, and the articulation of the laws which governed their formation, brought into a new light the causes and first principles of mental activity. The book also described a new intellectual craft, for in the interpretation of dream life lay a technique for conferring new meaning on psychic and cultural phenomena.

Freud's dream book resonated with the ancient striving toward clarity. To the ancients, the dream, the murkiest of mental creations, allowed the trained interpreter to illuminate the direction of a person's life. The vision granted to the seer revealed purpose. By contrast, to future Viennese psychoanalysts reading *The Interpretation of Dreams* soon after its publication, the book conveyed understanding of the origins, not the ends, of the visions contained in dreams. Yet, these modern individuals too searched for a purpose, and in the dream book they discovered a calling. For Freud's earliest disciples, such a book exerted enough influence to create a community of shared commitment and resolve. Thus, *The Interpretation of Dreams* brought to Freud a circle of followers, the recruits who carved footholds for psychoanalysis in Vienna before the First World War and helped ensure its survival after the deluge. In the Viennese psychoanalytic movement, that cadre not only confirmed its inward sense of commitment, but also created and sustained a new center of cultural activity.

The first meeting of the Wednesday evening discussion group took place at the suggestion of Wilhelm Stekel. Max Kahane, who had attended Freud's university course, had introduced Stekel to psychoanalysis.[1] In 1901, Kahane published a textbook, *Outline of Internal Medicine for Students and Practicing Physicians*, in which he explained the aim of analytic therapy: "This procedure (psychoanalysis) attempts to trace the symptoms of illness to unconscious impulses, whose expression they are, and trusts that an expansion of the power of the will necessarily coincides with the enlargement of consciousness."[2] In January 1902, Stekel reviewed *The Interpretation of Dreams* for the Viennese daily, *Neues Wiener Tagblatt*, announcing that Freud's work marked the beginning of a "new era in psychology."[3]

In the same year, Freud, responding to Stekel's suggestion, invited three practicing physicians, with Stekel, to join the Wednesday discussion circle—Kahane, Rudolf Reitler, and Alfred Adler, all of whom had attended Freud's lectures in the amphitheater of the university's Psychiatric Clinic.[4] In 1901, Reitler had opened the "Thermal Cure Institute for Dry Air and Heat Treatment."[5] Soon, however, he became the first practicing analyst from the Wednesday group. In 1899, Alfred Adler's investigations into the work of Jean-Martin Charcot and Pierre Janet on the treatment of neurosis had led him to Freud's lectures; during 1901, he reestablished contact with Freud.[6] As members of the society gradually drew friends and colleagues to their small circle, they retained the policy that all new members enter the group officially at Freud's invitation.

At the amphitheater in which they heard Freud speak, potential recruits received their first introduction to the cause. In the winter semester of 1907-08, a patient of Freud provided Alfred von Winterstein with an introduction to Freud's home at Berggasse 19. During their initial meeting in Freud's study, the Professor, as Freud's Viennese followers addressed him, invited the student to attend his lectures. "Years earlier," Winterstein wrote in his memoir, "I had read *The Interpretation of Dreams* for the first time, which affected me with such force that it indicated a lifelong direction to the weak compass needle of my inner self."[7] Upon completing his legal studies in the summer of 1908, Winterstein reenrolled at the university to pursue a program in psychology and art history, with the aim of training in psychoanalysis.[8]

In those early years before the First World War, Winterstein recalled, Freud altered the customary format of the university lecture course. The Professor adopted the unique procedure of requiring prospective students to meet with him in order to obtain permission to register for his course. Freud departed further from tradition by transforming his lecture on some evenings into a seminar, with each student speaking on a theme for discussion. "Attempting to remain unnoticed, therefore, did not work," according to Winterstein, "one would be called upon to take part."[9] Years later Winterstein summoned up the atmosphere in the lecture hall in the Psychiatric Clinic, where usually ten to fifteen listeners assembled on Saturday evenings to hear Freud: "Before the first row of seats were placed small chairs; on them and in the first rows of benches listeners took their places. The newcomers, out of shyness, attempted to situate themselves closer to the edge of the not all too large circle of light from the lamp which burned above the rostrum."[10]

The small illumination within the darkness of the amphitheater remained a vivid impression on Hanns Sachs, as he recalled his first attendance at the lectures, where "the only light came from a few bulbs suspended above the table and chair of the lecturer; the ascending rows of empty benches in the dusk gave the room a somewhat sepulchral aspect."[11] Reading *The Interpretation of Dreams*— "No other book made life seem so strange and no other book had explained its riddles and self-contradictions so fully"[12]—had inspired Sachs to attend Freud's lectures in the winter semester, 1905. Initiation into the mystery approached; Sachs remembered that "I had persuaded a cousin of mine, who was a medical student, to come with me; I hoped that his presence would give me support. In these unusual and gloomy surroundings I felt more panicky every moment and as a middle-aged gentleman, evidently the professor, entered, I started toward the door, whispering to my cousin a hurried explanation that we were at the wrong place."[13] Before they could make their way past him, Freud indicated the semicircle of chairs near the rostrum and "said in the politest way: 'Won't you come nearer and be seated, gentlemen?' "[14] Sachs remained in attendance at this lecture, and those that followed, drawn not only by "zealous interest aroused by what he had to say,"[15] but by the Professor's "faultless elocution and careful accentuation."[16] The lectures, Sachs explained, "became the pivot around which my private universe revolved."[17] Fritz Wittels, who attended Freud's lectures in the spring semester, 1906, wrote that Freud's "method of exposition was that of the German humanist, lightened by a conversational tone which he had probably acquired in Paris."[18] Recalling the scrupulous but relaxed nature of Freud's presentation, Wittels continued: "Amiably, almost enticingly, he dealt with the representatives of traditional psychology, reminding us of the way in which Hauff's Satan genially appeals to his victim Hasentreffer with the words: 'Come along over here; it doesn't hurt a bit!' "[19]

Those seeking an inward calling found in Freud's lectures an appeal to their sense of commitment. The circle of light within the amphitheater signified not only illumined vision, but participation in a new community. That fellowship, for Viennese Freudians, sustained both a new consciousness and a new inner purpose. In this way, the psychoanalytic community became for them a new vanguard of cultural activity.

David Bach, one of the first lay participants in the Psychological Wednesday Society, enunciated the need for such a vanguard community. In a series of articles written for the Social Democratic *Arbeiter Zeitung* and entitled "Austrian University Troubles," he described the disillusionment of young intellectuals with the university and the professions.[20] Bach himself graduated in 1897 from the University of Vienna's school of philosophy, writing in the curriculum vitae of his graduation forms that he intended to embark on the study of experimental psychology.[21] Instead, he pursued a career in journalism. In January 1904, he joined the staff of the *Arbeiter Zeitung* as a music critic, having already established his credentials at the paper with contributions on philosophy and the university system. In October of the same year, the young writer succeeded Josef Scheu as music editor. Bach remained with the *Arbeiter Zeitung* until forced to emigrate in 1934, the year of authoritarian reaction in Austria.[22]

Bach's series of articles on the university system appeared in December 1903. They decried the absence in Vienna of an "intellectual culture [*geistige Kultur*]"[23] that could function as both a center of learning and a bridge to society at large. The failure of the university to fulfill either goal stemmed first from "the culture-inhibiting power of Catholic reaction."[24] During the previous century, the virtual exclusion of Protestant philosophers from the university had limited the influence of both the German Enlightenment and its Romantic critics among Viennese intellectuals; among the Viennese masses, by the end of the century the anti-Semitic Christian Social movement—"leaders of the plebs, who are now spokesmen in Vienna and Lower Austria"[25]—had come to hold sway. Finally, the nationalist conflicts plaguing the Habsburg monarchy joined in preventing the university from becoming an open, flourishing center of critical learning and scholarship.

How did Bach conceptualize a new intellectual culture for the university? He drew his ideal from the past, the German and Austrian *Vormärz*, when, according to Bach, German cultural life did not recognize the intellectual and social boundaries currently imposed by the university. "Was there ever," he asked, "a society in Vienna like that which gathered together in the homes of Humboldt, Rahel [Varnhagen], and Henriette Herz, and many others?"[26] Closer to his own day, the circle which had surrounded the Berlin physicist Hermann Helmholz provided him with a model of pure intellectual endeavor and universalist aspiration. According to Bach, only once—in the aristocratic salons of the *Vormärz*—did Viennese cultural life approach those models. Yet, in such places, "exclusively art and nothing else was nurtured,"[27] leaving even Catholic scholars without footholds in society.

Without a critical, intellectual center, what academic and social role did the university in fact play at the turn of the century? From each school of the university came the type Bach labeled the "scholar-bureaucrat [*Wissenschaftsbeamte*]."[28] That figure answered the narrow and self-serving wishes of both state and student: the government wanted lawyers, judges, medical examiners, and teachers who would faithfully carry out its policies; students sought comfortable careers and secure posts. The university produced the intellectual expected of it: "The state needs judges; but we receive judicial bureaucrats. The state needs teachers; but we receive imperial and royal officials of instruction. The state needs doctors; of these we receive not a one. The state, however, is pleased to have bureaucrats of sanitation."[29] According to Bach, only physicians and educators could still achieve direct contact with the populace; the state, however, refused to provide them to those in greatest need of their services. Further, the availability of education and the direction of scholarly research remained subject to bureaucratic interests and official whim. In funding the university and appointing its faculty, the state considered above all the immediate, professional interests of its own civil service, and the candidate's wealth and family connections. Political corruption, intellectual lassitude, and bureaucratic calculation sapped the university of the will and capacity to transform itself.

Within the partially lit amphitheater of the Psychiatric Clinic, the first Viennese Freudians encountered a different intellectual atmosphere. Science as a humanist calling seemed to have endured in Vienna, sheltered in a location beyond the precincts of official culture. Here, young intellectuals driven by an unwanted sense of isolation and embitterment, aspiring to renewed contact with society, discovered a means through which they could fulfill their inward sense of mission. Here, the humanist striving for enlightened understanding and the Romantic seeking after the authentic self became combined in the search for psychological clarity. As demonstrated by the reconsideration of *Oedipus the King* in *The Interpretation of Dreams*, such a calling could also lead its followers toward a new vision of culture.

Those who pursued the serious study of psychoanalysis beyond Freud's lectures joined what both Max Graf and Isador Sadger called a "circle of friends."[30] The Psychological Wednesday Society strove consciously to preserve its character as a confraternity. Prospective recruits required sponsors within the group and received membership only after consultation among the members, it being agreed that no one suggested by Freud would be rejected. The group did not desire to register with the government as an official organization.

The circle gathered at Freud's home each Wednesday evening. After the presentation of the week's paper, discussion would follow until late into the night. As with his lecture course, Freud required that every member participate in the discussion. Members determined the order of speakers by choosing from a Greek urn slips of paper on which they had inscribed their names. The lot drawn, each member was expected to remain until the completion of the meeting. In its earliest years of existence, the society left the ideas discussed at meetings for the free use of its members in their own publications, labeling the policy "intellectual communism."[31] Finally, Freud himself envisioned "that a deeper psychological understanding would overcome the difficulties in personal contacts"[32] and strengthen the society's cohesion. From the Viennese circle of recruits, Freud sought a cadre for the movement. For their part, his closest Viennese disciples accepted the role of vanguard as an essential element of their vocation.

Hoping to revive the mission of the intellectual, the Viennese psychoanalysts sought to redefine psychological and cultural consciousness. For these first Freudians, the psychoanalytic movement melded nineteenth-century humanism, Romanticism, and science within the core of a new, twentieth-century intellectual calling. With Freud, they would shape that calling, applying the methods and aims of educators, artists, and scientists. A cultural vocation began to emerge from the new psychology first enunciated in *The Interpretation of Dreams*.

II

Alfred Adler explained one aspect of the new vocation in his first psychoanalytic essay, published in 1904 in the *Aerztliche Standeszeitung* and entitled "The Physician as Educator."[33] According to Adler, Freud's theory of childhood as expressed in *The Interpretation of Dreams*, and his "demonstration of the tragic conflicts which flowed from the anomalies of childhood experience" provided a basis "for influencing the general education of the people" and for forcing recognition of the "high significance of pedagogy."[34] In keeping with the traditional ideal of *Bildung*, he defined the educator as one who knew when and how to promote, inhibit, or channel the individual's constitutional predispositions. The physician's new knowledge of childhood development qualified him as such a teacher, one who could exert pedagogical influence by applying his psychological knowledge to the relationship between parent and child. In that way, the medical practitioner contributed not only to the child's health, but to his "guidance toward ethically valuable strivings, toward work, diligence, attention."[35] With David Bach,

Adler belonged to that wing of the Social Democratic movement which stressed social reform through education and cultural change. Through psychoanalysis, Adler joined the humanist's concept of *Bildung* to the Social Democratic effort to create new educational contacts—in this case, through the physician—among Viennese workers.

In 1905, the socialist periodical *Die Neue Gesellschaft* published Adler's next article, "The Sexual Problem in Education," which took for its starting point Freud's theory of the sexual instincts and their sublimation as set forth in *Three Essays on the Theory of Sexuality*. Infantile sexuality, Adler explained, conformed to an evolutionary program, as "sensuality and the longing for gratification force the individual to establish a relation to the external world through all its organs, in order to gather impressions and nourishment. Thus the sexual motives, together with the sensual mechanism of cells, serve to introduce the child to the objects of the external world, and to lead him into communication with culture."[36] In the process of education, however, the chief significance of sexuality lay in the transformation of sensual impulses into psychic energy: "The culture of the child stands and falls with the transference of the efficient capacity for work from the sensual conductor to the cultural load capacity of the cell complex. A considerable increase of sensual excitability, from which pure gratification becomes a lasting end in itself to the child, proves to be inhibiting to the path of transference and hinders the progress of culture."[37] Cultural life rested on "the capability to endure unfulfilled or momentarily unfulfillable wishes through constant power of the spirit, until a gratifying goal can be attained by putting into action one's entire psychic and physical power."[38] In a word, the sexual problem in education consisted in fostering the process of sublimation.

According to Fritz Wittels, the early ally of Karl Kraus, educational work had to be directed toward moral reform and sexual liberation. On 20 March 1907, Wittels's uncle, Isador Sadger, proposed him for membership in the Wednesday Society.[39] The following week he was accepted unanimously, and on 10 April, he attended his first meeting. Wittels had recently begun writing for Kraus's *Die Fackel*, his first contribution having been published in February 1907. His articles continued to appear in its pages until May of the following year. Wittels's first collection of essays, *The*

Sexual Need, published in 1909, included several articles from *Die Fackel*, printed there under the pseudonym, Avicenna. The theme of Wittels's writing and of his presentations to the Wednesday Society remained constant: the social and psychological harm caused by the suppression of sexuality.

Published originally in *Die Fackel* in February 1907, and reprinted in *The Sexual Need*, Wittels's essay "The Greatest Crime of the Penal Code (The Prohibition of Abortion)" explained that the state consciously sought to increase the danger and injury it already attached to sexual love by imposing severe penalties for abortion. Government could not, however, have maintained the law against abortions without the collaboration of other powers: "But in the state's prohibition of abortion those two supports stood behind it, whose representative it is: capital and the Church."[40] Capitalists demonstrated a hypocrisy more monstrous than that of religion, for they realized full well that the burden of the law fell only on the poor. "It is clear why the class state prohibits abortion," Wittels concluded. "The Church needs Christians, militarism needs recruits, capitalism needs coolies, they all need those who are defenseless."[41] In his essay on venereal disease, presented first to the Wednesday Society in November 1907, and published in *Die Fackel* the following month, Wittels argued that similar motives prevented the treatment and cure of that illness. Dishonesty and secrecy regarding the problem meant, in effect, that society exacted the disease as a price for individual happiness.[42] In other essays included within *The Sexual Need*, Wittels described what he considered to be the most harmful features of the bourgeois family. As well as advocating earlier sexual enlightenment of children and greater sexual freedom during adolescence, he proposed transforming the institution of monogamy to allow for liaisons, or "side marriage [*Ventilehe*]."[43] The chief focus of Wittels's essays, however, was the sexual suppression of women.

Wittels gave his views on female sexuality to the Wednesday circle in two presentations, originally published in *Die Fackel*, entitled "Female Assassins" and "Female Physicians."[44] In those essays, he adopted the dichotomy, emphasized by *Die Fackel*, between the essential spirituality of man, and the sensuality and naturalness of woman. As he told the society, the assumption underlying his interpretation of physicians and assassins was that "woman's sexuality permeates whatever she does or feels."[45] Wittels saw the political behavior of female assassins and the professional activity of female physicians as substitutes for sexuality, and, therefore, symptoms of hysteria. The ancient hetaera, or "child woman [*Kindweib*],"[46] represented to Wittels the fulfillment of woman's nature in the innocent gratification of all her sensual desires.

In reaction to his essay on female assassins, members criticized Wittels for his narrow understanding of revolution, and of the—male and female—revolutionist's ascetic ideal. Bach pointed out that Wittels had chosen to interpret "pseudo-revolutionary deeds."[47] The psychology of female assassins as Wittels had described it did not provide insight into the revolutionary impulse: "The discussion should have focused on the genuine Russian revolutionists who express the pathology of the atmosphere of an entire period and social class, and not [just] that of individuals who are of course tied to the ethical and sexual conditions of this class."[48] Adler asserted that Wittels had wrongly applied the psychological interpretation of revolutionaries by ignoring the phenomenon of revolutionary asceticism: "Above all, one must note the ascetic attitude toward life which most revolutionaries (men as well as women) have."[49] Hitschmann commented that he had expected to receive an explanation of the roots of individual heroism. The problem of revolutionary psychology, he indicated, lay in the transition from self-denial to acceptance of self-destruction.

Members of the Wednesday circle vehemently opposed Wittels's psychological characterization of female medical students. Paul Federn emphasized that the "importance of work and the concept of giving a meaning to life through work have to be taken into account in evaluating women's wish to study. The need to work is not rooted solely in social conditions, but is one of those instincts of man which have developed at a late period."[50] At a following meeting, Hitschmann described Wittels's ideas as "the fantasies of a youthful reactionary."[51] Freud and other members of the circle criticized the pamphleteer for distorting and misusing the theory of sublimation: Wittels's application of sexual psychology still betrayed his puritanical mentality. Thus, Max Graf stressed to him that "man's achievements also spring from sensuous sources."[52] Freud explained that "Wittels is quite correct in pointing to sexuality as the driving force of the wish to study; except that he neglects to differentiate between sublimated and crude sexuality, which, to him, are equivalent. But the displacement of sexuality onto the thirst for knowledge is at the root of every investigative endeavor."[53] In December 1908, at the final meeting devoted to discussing his proposals for ethical reform and sexual liberation, Wittels expressed his own moral rage and inward alienation. His self-defined calling remained that of the prophet: "It was not caution that made Wittels cast his demands in the form of a utopia," the minutes record his comments, "but the fact that he really was unable to visualize this situation."[54] He concluded that "things cannot go on as they are today. How to bring about a change, he does not know."[55] To Wittels's anger and sense of righteous isolation, Freud responded, as cited in the previous chapter, that

> we liberate sexuality through our treatment, but not in order that man may from now on be dominated by sexuality, but in order to make a suppression possible—a rejection of the instincts under the guidance of a higher agency. The *Fackel* stands for "living out" one's instinctual desires to the point of satiating them [*ausleben*]; we distingish, however, between a pathological process of repression and one that is to be regarded as normal. We try to replace the pathological process with rejection. This is also the only way open to society; society too must first revoke its suppressions, in order to be able to repudiate anew.[56]

In Freud's vision, the stance of the moral prophet did not belong to the psychoanalyst. Culture remained a demand consciously to be endured, a source of inward misery, but a condition of the sublime. For Freud and Viennese psychoanalysts, the psychology of art revealed most clearly and forcefully that duality: creativity originated in inner need.

III

In the first years of the movement, members of the Freudian circle began to demarcate the boundaries of art and psychology. David Bach first undertook that task briefly in a review of Freud's *The Psychopathology of Everyday Life*, which he entitled "While Writing" and which he published in the *Arbeiter Zeitung* in October 1904. Freud's theory of the unconscious demonstrated that "we live spiritually [*geistig*] through our second ego."[57] The artist distinguished himself from society by his power to transform and disguise the contents of his inner life. Self-analysis, on the other hand, "in the special meaning given by Freud," provided direct comprehension of "the motives of inner events [*die Gründe inneren Gescheh-*

ens]."[58] The difference between art and psychoanalysis lay in the fact that understanding art was "possessing self-understanding without feeling it, and practicing it without wanting to."[59]

Otto Rank's *The Artist* sounded the theme which the lonely diarist had found in both Nietzsche and Weininger: the development of art toward the creation of a new self. Now the psychological meaning of that process emerged at the forefront of his concern. In the summer of 1904, no more than a few months after Rank had finished reading Weininger's *Sex and Character*, Adler had given him a copy of *The Interpretation of Dreams*.[60] After reading the dream book, Rank made a thorough study of Freud's essays on sexuality and neurosis. In February 1905, he began his psychoanalytic study of art. The manuscript began as journal notes, with the title "Artist." As Rank progressed, he gradually lost interest in the journal itself. His last diary notes were dated 24 August 1905; he did not, however, transcribe any entries into his journal after 1 July 1905.[61] Work on the manuscript replaced the journal. Just as importantly, Rank had found a confidant in Adler, and soon also in Freud.[62] Ernest Jones recorded that Rank "presented himself to Freud with an introduction from Adler."[63] In his diary notes of 22 August 1905, Rank first mentioned a meeting with Freud.[64] At that meeting, Rank showed Freud the two sections of his manuscript, "The Sexual Foundation" and "Artistic Sublimation," which he had completed that month. With a new introduction on the principles of psychoanalysis, *The Artist* appeared in March 1907.[65]

The first section of the book reflected Rank's association with Adler—he heard Adler deliver the paper "The Sexual Problem in Education" to the Society of Abstinent Teachers[66]—and his own reading of Freud's work. Rank opened *The Artist* with a description of libido:

> But with the organism there also grow organic needs, which soon no longer find their gratification from within. This absence creates in the organism a kind of dissatisfaction, which soon builds into an inner excitation, a tension, and finally calls forth an urgent desire, a libido which aims at removing the excitation. The libido, therefore, is a reaction to an inner disturbance, a displeasure, for the elimination of which it is called into being. But with the removal of that displeasure, the first experience of pleasure occurs.[67]

In its effort to avoid displeasure, the libido served the instincts of self-preservation. The aims of those instincts, however, did not require all of the libido's energy, so that "the libido, which has become free, seeks independent gratifications. . . . Then the sensation of pleasure no longer appears as a result of the gratification of an organic need, but pleasure is sought and created solely for its own sake."[68] To that state of being Rank applied the term "pansexuality."[69] The competition for gratification between libidinal drives created the first resistances to complete satisfaction, resistances which were later strengthened by external suppression. The inevitable repression of the libido into the unconscious created psychic tension and the sensation of need [Not], the earliest and deepest source of human suffering.

As defined by Rank, culture represented humanity's effort to protect " 'psychic' equilibrium"[70] by channeling unconscious drives into disguised, nonsexual paths of fulfillment. The "withdrawal of sexuality"[71] served the purposes of repression; yet, as an alternative means of expression, cultural activity made possible "a progressive becoming conscious of the unconscious."[72] All cultural creations, including religion, mythology, and philosophy, originated in this Janus-like process of "artistic sublimation."[73] Efforts at sublimation gradually intensified suffering within the individual, ending finally in the cultural emergence of the poet [Dichter]. The poet experienced internal conflict most acutely, and therefore felt the greatest sense of isolation within the community, and the greatest urgency to give expression to the unconscious. By finding in art a release for himself, he offered a path of release to his audience; thus did the poet's self-cure become a collective cure.

In the period of history when humanity felt its greatest inner need, art achieved its highest expression. That stage, according to Rank, was reached in the nineteenth century and found its embodiment in the work of Richard Wagner. Wagner's effort to unite music with drama represented the last attempt in art to give full expression to the unconscious. The attempt failed, because "the greatest portion of 'recognition' is suppressed by the residue of illusion."[74] The significance of Wagner's work lay not in the regeneration of art, but in the final demonstration of the artwork's limits.

In the late nineteenth century, the role of art passed to science. The intensity of psychological repression now forced humanity to seek direct knowledge of the unconscious:

> For the progressive sexual repression in the developmental process of the human race ever more urgently demands the control, the becoming conscious, of the unconscious, and art is not capable of achieving this aspiration, since art itself originates only unconsciously, and only has its effect unconsciously as well; that is, it can only communicate to people indirectly the progress of consciousness. . . . True, the work of art is always produced in full consciousness, but just for that reason it must finally in this way convert into science, which wants to penetrate to the driving forces of art itself, and make everything conscious: for "real consciousness is knowledge of our unconscious" (Wagner).[75]

In the work of Henrik Ibsen the transition from art to science had already taken place: Ibsen's dramas, in which "the 'characters' are described, analyzed," represented aesthetic regression, but scientific progress.[76]

Science, however, did not complete Rank's vision. The program to bring unconscious material into consciousness had to create the conditions under which humanity would control the unconscious. Scientists assumed man's dependence on his drives. The individual who suffered from neurosis, however, "needed knowledge, mastery of the unconscious, for his cure."[77] As cultural repression reached its highest pitch of intensity, neurosis compelled individuals to seek knowledge of the psyche; thus, the "healing artist,"[78] who asserted conscious, intellectual control over his instinctive impulses, replaced the poet. Rank still stood as close to Nietzsche and Weininger as he did to Freud when he concluded *The Artist* with a description of that transformation which knowledge of the unconscious would produce: "Once, however, the complete revaluation of everything psychic has turned out successfully, then will the unartistic, asexual *Übermensch*, light and strong like a 'god,' stand in the midst of the game of life, and guide and control his 'drives' with a sure hand."[79] Thus, in Rank's vision, the path which led from art to psychoanalysis still promised deliverance.

IV

In the early work of Wittels and Rank one can still find the impress of their moral journeys to psychoanalysis. Within the Viennese psychoanalytic movement, however, redemptive and prophetic visions gradually gave way to a new vocation for psychological research and exploration. At the amphitheater and at the Wednesday Society, Freud conveyed his own notion of that calling, and the vision of culture and learning embodied within it. According to that vision, art not only allowed insight into the contents of the repressed, but gave expression to the human capacity to endure suffering.

In a passage from *The Interpretation of Dreams*, Freud briefly discussed how art gave evidence of the intensification of repression across generations:

> Another of the great creations of tragic poetry, Shakespeare's *Hamlet*, has its roots in the same soil as *Oedipus Rex*. But the changed treatment of the same material reveals the whole difference in the mental life of these two widely separated epochs of civilization: the secular advance of repression in the emotional life of mankind. In the *Oedipus* the child's wishful phantasy that underlies it is brought into the open and realized as it would be in a dream. In *Hamlet* it remains repressed; and—just as in the case of a neurosis—we only learn of its existence from its inhibiting consequences. Strangely enough, the overwhelming effect produced by the more modern tragedy has turned out to be compatible with the fact that people have remained completely in the dark as to the hero's character.[80]

Meditation on art led to speculation on the course of history. At a meeting of the Vienna circle in March 1909, Freud's more complete articulation of his perspective was presented and recorded:

> The entire development of humanity could also be characterized, from the psychological point of view, by a formula in which two elements stood out: on the one hand, it is a question of an enlargement of the consciousness of mankind (analogous to the coming into consciousness of instincts and forces hitherto operating unconsciously); on the other hand, progress can be described as a repression that progresses over the centuries. Our culture consists in this: that more and more of our instincts become subject to repression, for which there are beautiful illustrations, particularly in poetic productions (see Rank: "The Incest-Motif"). When placed next to each other, these two characteristics seem to be entirely contradictory to each other, for with the progress of repression, more and more should become unconscious, and not the other way round. But then comes the liberating thought that these two processes are the condition

for each other: the enlargement of consciousness is what enables mankind to cope with life in the face of the steady progress of repression. Freud believes that Rank expressed this idea in his *The Artist*. That would be the introduction of psychology into historical studies.[81]

Consciousness granted neither deliverance nor the power of prophecy, but confrontation with the sources of inward suffering. Through the images of art, that suffering achieved its sublime, visual representation—a wordless articulation.

For Freud, the Viennese aspiration to a psychology of art and creativity led also to an examination of the historical past, and of its tragedy. The Aeschylean spirit elucidated that history. In the poet's words, "Cry aloud without fear the victory of Zeus, you will not have failed the truth: Zeus, who guided men to think, / who has laid it down that wisdom / comes alone through suffering."[82]

FOUR

THE ARTIST AND
THE PSYCHOLOGIST

I

In two articles published in consecutive issues of the *Österreichische Rundschau* in 1906 and 1907, Max Graf declared psychoanalysis to be the first science of creativity. Like other members of the Wednesday circle, he identified the study of culture with the study of artists and their work. In artistic creations—specifically, in the creative image—one could explore the nature and progress of human consciousness, and the causes of inward suffering.

According to Graf, the emergence of a scientific psychology of the artist had until Freud been prevented first by "the belief in something mystical in the creativity of artists," and second, by "a mythology of the classical poets": "Removed from the earthly sphere, they wander in blessed heights, their corporeality dissolved, the deep lines, which human suffering, passions, and struggles had engraved in their faces, smoothed away."[1] Those conceptions of creativity changed, however, "when one subjects the fantasy of the artist to scientific analysis."[2] Like the dream, the artistic fantasy was capable of psychological interpretation. For Graf, Wilhelm Dilthey had already announced the "working program" for that type of analysis in the following passage from his study of Goethe in *Das Erlebnis und die Dichtung:* " 'The fantasy confronts us like a miracle,

67

like a phenomenon utterly different from the everyday activities of men, but it is however only a more powerful organization belonging to certain men, one grounded in the unusual strength of fixed, elemental processes; from this, mental life, *in accordance with its general laws*, builds itself into a form deviating completely from what is customary.' "[3] The motive behind the artist's fantasy, Graf continued, lay in the pressure of inner conflict: "An undaunted psychology of the creations of dramatists, which will form a part of the natural science of the artistic human being, will above all study the psychic conflicts of great tragedians, the nature of those conflicts, and the nature of their resolution."[4] The analysis of inward, emotional experience—*Erlebnis*—not the study of character, opened the way to psychological understanding of the artist.

Graf did not see art merely as one field for the application of psychology, but the true subject of a science of the psyche. "Just as the science of chemistry will hardly relinquish searching for the secret of living substance, if only to make use of this hope as an ideal working program," he concluded, "so the future science of psychology will not relinquish the hope of analyzing the origin of a poetic work, and seeking out behind the many-colored work of imagery, behind the representation of passions, the emotional life of the artist, that which oppresses him and burdens him, his inner struggles, and the resolution of his conflicts."[5]

In his second article, Graf explained that psychoanalysis, beginning with *The Interpretation of Dreams*, answered the requirements of a psychology of creativity. Dream formation provided the model of poetic invention. Artistic images derived from the richness and clarity of the artist's memory pictures. More than this, the repressed compelled the artist to create, to bring forms and images from the preconscious into consciousness. Suppressed impulses, traceable to rebellious, cruel, or erotic wishes from childhood, sought disguised fulfillment in poetic images.

The inward struggle between desire and flight only reached its last, decisive phase in the concluding acts of the creative process. The ego offered the same, furious resistance to the artistic transformation of unconscious impulses as it did to their direct expression. The final act of tragic drama reflected the completion of the creative process, for "when at the end of a tragedy, the hero dies, thus has the artist killed with the hero those unconscious affects which burdened him; he has robbed them of their effect. He feels one with himself, feels like a person recovered, and has performed on his own soul 'catharsis,' in which he has also allowed the spectator to take part."[6]

Among Viennese Freudians, the study of art raised significant questions concerning the aspirations of a psychological science of culture. The first question was one of method: To understand art and individual creativity, should the psychoanalyst concentrate on the personalities of artists or on their works? Second, Viennese psychoanalysts asked how and to what end artists themselves should apply psychological material and analysis in their imaginative work. Finally, by exploring the labors and aims of the artist, the Viennese defined more sharply the tasks and goals of the psychologist. Through the study of art, Freud and his recruits began to develop the psychoanalytic science of culture as *technē*, a craft with its own methodology, material, and obligations. Thus, the Viennese circle raised the question of the relationship between art and science, and confronted in a new light the tasks of each.

II

Within the Wednesday Society two schools of thought existed on the proper method for studying art and creativity. One school, represented by Isador Sadger and Wilhelm Stekel, settled its focus almost solely on the artist's personality. In short, its approach sought to spell out the points of identification between the artist and the neurotic. The second line of thought, defended chiefly by Freud and Graf, argued that artists could best be known through their works. The differences between those two methodological positions produced sharp controversy within the Viennese circle, beginning with the meetings of December 1907, the month in which Sadger presented his pathography of the Swiss writer Konrad Ferdinand Meyer.

Little is known about Sadger. He was born in 1866 to a German Jewish family in Galicia. The family moved to Leopoldstadt, where, like Freud, he attended the *Sperlgymnasium*. In 1890, he graduated from the university's school of medicine.[7] A specialist in nervous illnesses and hydrotherapy, Sadger first attended Freud's lectures in 1895.[8] In an article on hydrotherapy published in 1897, he briefly noted Freud's conception of hysteria as a "sexual defense neurosis," but the essay's purpose was to announce hydrotherapy as the "cure of the future" for diseases of the nervous system.[9] At the time the article was published, however, Sadger was also devoting his attention to the study of poets, presenting to the Jewish student organization, *Jüdisch-Akademische Lesehalle*, a lecture on the Romantic writer Heinrich von Kleist.[10] In 1898, "Ferdinand Raimund: A Pathological Study" appeared, followed in the next year by "Was Goethe a Pathological Phenomenon?"[11]

Sadger's essays on Raimund and Goethe intended to demonstrate the presence of "hereditary taint" (*Belastung*) in the poets' personalities. (In 1909, when Sadger rewrote his study of Kleist from a psychoanalytic perspective, he still included a description of those aspects of Kleist's behavior which he believed resulted from hereditary influence.) According to Sadger, pathology determined both the character traits and the distinctive creative rhythms of Raimund and Goethe. He found signs of hereditary degeneration in their inability to maintain an attachment to one person, place or activity, in their deep depressions, and in their violent mood changes. Tracing these phenomena to deficiencies in the brain's "sphere of bodily feeling,"[12] he classified those personality traits and behavior patterns under the category, "hereditary neurosis *[Belastungsneurose]*."[13]

Sadger introduced one psychoanalytic perspective into his picture of Raimund. Raimund's fear of rabies, which, according to Sadger, became the immediate motivation of his suicide, indicated a "highly important impression from earliest childhood."[14] Sadger related that Raimund's mother prophesied that her son would die from a bite if he continued to play with dogs and cats. The threat would have been meaningless, however, without there having been behind it "a story of a bite in earliest childhood with sexual overtones."[15] Still, whatever the strength of the phobia and the childhood impression, the intensification of fear to the point of the final "act of violence against the self" could have arisen only from "the soil of severe hereditary taint."[16]

Sadger continued to attend Freud's lecture courses after 1895, enrolling in 1903 for a fourth time. In November 1906, two weeks after Freud proposed his name for membership, Sadger attended his first meeting of the Wednesday Society. Throughout the years before the First World War, Sadger showed a remarkable capacity simultaneously to defend both the views of nineteenth-century psychiatry and the tenets of psychoanalysis. Writing to Jung more than a year after Sadger became a member of the Viennese circle, Freud characterized him as "that congenital fanatic of orthodoxy, who happens by mere accident to believe in psychoanalysis rather than in the law given by God on Sinai-Horeb."[17]

In 1908, Sadger published *Konrad Ferdinand Meyer: A Pathographical-Psychological Study*. The book and his presentation on it to the Wednesday circle in December 1907 concentrated on what Sadger considered signs of pathology in Meyer's life during the long period before he became a writer. Sadger traced the origins of each sign or instance to hereditary taint, and the unconscious erotic attachment between mother and son. Sadger focused solely on Meyer's childhood neurotic symptoms, his later inhibitions, his isolation, his "aversion to association"[18] (or frequent changes in occupations and interests), and his "extravagance of sensitivity."[19]

Members of the Wednesday Society rejected Sagder's reductionist method. "Stekel is horrified and fears that this work will harm our cause. Sadger has a formula with which he wants to explain the psychology of all writers [literally: poetic souls]; but the matter is not that simple. This is surface psychology."[20] "Federn is indignant. Sadger has not said a single word about the poet's sexual development, because one just does not know anything about it: therefore, one cannot write a pathography."[21] Graf stated the case for those who would have proceeded from the creation rather than the creator: "From a psychological study of a poet one can expect to learn something of the connection between the poet's personality and his work. Sadger has not paid enough attention to this essential point."[22] Nothing could be learned about the creative process from Sadger's approach: "A psychological study of poets should also enable one to discover the typical characteristics of artists who come to produce only very late in life."[23] According to Freud, the road to understanding the artist led through the artwork: Sadger's approach "is not the correct way to write pathographies; Graf has come closer to suggesting the correct way which must proceed from the works. . . . The enigma of this personality remains unsolved."[24] Emphasizing that the artist's creativity defined the true interest of psychoanalysis, Freud continued that "there is altogether no need to write such pathographies. The theories can only be harmed and not one iota is gained for the understanding of the subject."[25] He explained, "If one already knows a great deal about psychic mechanisms, then the pathological component can be investigated as a residual phenomenon."[26]

Provoked by Sadger's paper, Max Graf responded the following week with his own presentation—"Methodology of the Psychology of Poets"—explaining how psychoanalysis illuminated not only the artist's life, but also the artwork. "To what purpose," Graf began, "does one study the psychology of poets?"[27] Cesare Lombroso and the French school, which stressed the concept of *dégénéré supérieur*, sought out signs of pathology. Challenging that psychiatric perspective on art, psychoanalysis sought to comprehend more closely the creative mind itself: Freud

> has thrown light on the road to the unconscious, and thus has mightily furthered the understanding of the psychology of the poet. . . . He is a psychologist and has erected a unified psychological structure. . . . Lombroso looks at poets in the same way as he looks at a particularly interesting type of criminal. The French psychologists see in the poet only a neurotic. Professor Freud is interested in the human soul, the psychic organism. The first two therefore may write 'pathographies'; Prof. Freud writes psychological analyses, and everyone who has an analytic interest in poets must decide whether he wants to write a case history or a psychoanalytic portrayal. But he must not, as Sadger has done, constantly confound these two methods with each other.[28]

Once creativity, not pathology, became the focus, the problem of methodology could be more sharply defined: "The next question to be answered is: What shall be the point of departure for my reflections? The artist? His work?"[29] The cathartic function of artwork indicated the most effective method of approach. The work of art revealed repressed forces more fully than, for example, the artist's autobiography or records of his conversations. As Graf stressed, "all artistic creation is rooted in the repressed. But the repressed will offer resistances when the autobiographer is about to relate his most important experiences. Precisely the most significant questions therefore will remain unanswered. The artist overcomes his psychic inhibitions only by creating, and whoever wishes to know the poet must seek him out in his works."[30]

Yet, how could a Freudian analysis succeed with seemingly silent works of art, poetry, and literature? Within the artwork one traced the return of the repressed. In Graf's words, "I proceed from those motifs which I call typical ones; that is, those poetic motifs which recur in the artist's works. . . . The central themes of the poet's creations betray the innermost mechanisms of the poet's mind."[31] From artworks one progressed to the study of creativity. In that endeavor one had "to compare kindred personalities among the poets and artists, to establish *types of artists*. . . . The creative process of all artists discloses kindred features, and the ultimate goal of the analyses of artists, it seems to me, is finally to reach a 'theory of artistic creation.' "[32] Pathography had nothing to offer that endeavor, even in the case of minor artists: "Their creative process is changed, is destroyed, is inhibited by the illness. The purely medical analysis, the pathography, contributes little toward the understanding of the poet's creative process because it is concerned only with these inhibitions, and not with the positive creative forces."[33]

Rank seconded Graf's arguments. "For the time being," he commented, "we are not at all interested in the poet's experiences (his external life) but only in the way these experiences are worked over [and absorbed] (in his inner life)."[34] Adler stressed that "a poet's early work should be studied with special care; in connection, of course, with his later work."[35] Sadger, however, remained unconvinced: "He himself writes pathographies purely out of medical interest, not for the purpose of throwing light on the process of artistic creation, which, by the way, remains unexplained even by psychoanalytic interpretation. Graf's method is nothing but the age-old method of the literary historians who compare life and work, augmented by the key which Freud has put in our hand."[36]

With Graf, Freud emphasized that the application of psychoanalysis to the artist's works differentiated it from the psychiatric approach, which saw in the artist the source of a medical case history: "Every poet who shows abnormal tendencies can be the object of a pathography. But the pathography cannot show anything new. Psychoanalysis, on the other hand, provides information about the creative process."[37] Freud had expressed his interpretation of that process in a lecture delivered only days earlier, on 6 December 1907, at the publishing house of Hugo Heller, a member of the Wednesday circle.[38] The lecture, which appeared the following year as "Creative Writers and Day-Dreaming," described the process of fantasy formation common to daydreams and artistic creations. An event from the present awakened desire. With that desire there was revived a wish from the past, and joined to it the memory of an experience, usually from childhood, which had satisfied the wish. Calling on material from the present and on memories of the past, the writer now pictured once more an image in which the wish found fulfillment. The creative writer gained acceptance, and even a pleasurable response, for his fantasies, because his work "softens the character of his egoistic day-dreams by altering and disguising it, and he bribes us by the purely formal—that is, aesthetic—yield of pleasure which he offers us in the presentation of his phantasies."[39] That bribe, as Freud had first explained in *Jokes and their Relation to the Unconscious*, made possible the further release of unconscious energy, in the guise of artistic enjoyment: "Our actual enjoyment of an imaginative work proceeds from a liberation of tensions in our minds."[40]

Commenting on Graf's paper, Freud explained that Graf's approach presented the first "proposition" of a method for interpreting the creative process through the work of art: "(from the paper 'Creative Writers and Day-dreaming'): *creative writing* generally partakes of the same mechanism as the daydream: the 'dominant motifs' (Graf) are the desires which are dominant throughout the poet's life (Freud)."[41] The second methodological proposition Freud defined as *"the principle of the transposition of elements*, which is of special significance for the analysis of myths and legends. The relationship between the contents of the conscious and of the unconscious: the elements are the same, but the order is changed in many ways."[42] Finally, analysis of creative works required both "the definition of types in Graf's sense" and "special emphasis on the early works of the poet as Adler has suggested." Freud concluded, "With these resources one can attempt to draw conclusions about the process of artistic creation from the works."[43] With his study of Leonardo, Freud put the method into practice.

Graf provided his own demonstration of the methodology in his pamphlet, *Richard Wagner in "The Flying Dutchman": A Contribution to the Psychology of Artistic Creation*, published in 1911 as a pamphlet in Freud's series *Papers on Applied Psychology*.[44] Wagner's opera, Graf wrote, offered a suitable object for psychoanalytic interpretation for two reasons. First, the central motif of "struggle between the drive toward sensual pleasure [*Triebe zum Genusse*] and the longing for a principle of chaste, pure love" reappeared throughout Wagner's work.[45] Changes which Wagner introduced into the traditional story provided a second point of departure, as Graf explained: "It is, however, of great significance to determine where an artist makes use of material handed down without changing it, and where his own fantasy completes the work. One can accept that, especially in these supplementary additions, problems which occupy the artist with extraordinary intensity force their way into foreign material."[46] In this instance, Wagner modified the saga first to have the Dutchman successfully intrude between a woman and her betrothed, and secondly, to have him demand a sacrifice from the woman. Those changes altered the "bourgeois interpretation"[47] common to Romantic operas in which the woman chose correctly between a demonic tempter and a virtuous suitor.

The motif of the intruder, Graf argued, recreated the intrusion of Johanna Wagner's second husband, Ludwig Geyer, between the mother and her infant son. It assumed influence over Wagner's work, because in fantasy Wagner identified with Geyer as a rival to his own father. The motif of sacrifice, however, emerged directly from his unconscious, erotic attachment to his mother. The sensual side of that attachment combined with an idealization of women, modeled on the exclusive attention Johanna Wagner devoted to her son after his father died when Wagner was only six months old. The sacrifice of Senta at the end of *The Flying Dutchman* resolved the Oedipal conflict at the core of both motifs. The Dutchman's success in winning Senta represented a triumph of the son over the father, while Senta's sacrifice followed from the son's idealization of the mother in earliest childhood. Wagner's career disappointments and the collapse of his marriage awakened those conflicting desires expressed in *The Flying Dutchman*. As in his later works, Wagner created in this opera "a substitute for the experience of happiness [*erlebten Glückes*], the fulfillment of wish fantasies which life had not stilled."[48] The struggle between those wishes, which allowed for no inner peace in life, found its momentary psychological resolution in the work of art. Thus did Graf affirm the assertion which some years earlier he had put forth in his article on the science of creativity: "What else are the images of the drama other than visions, in which the inner struggles of the dramatist acquire shape [*Gestalt*]."[49]

III

As young cultural critics attacking the contemporary crisis of responsibility, Viennese psychoanalysts had called upon artists to point a direction out of the malaise. Creative work did not release artists from moral responsibility, but imposed new obligations. That principle applied equally to the artist's use of psychological material in dramatic creations. The artistic expression and resolution of psychic conflict had to confer meaning on inward suffering: anguish and longing demanded not only an empathetic art, but a purposive one.

From the Freudian perspective, the problem of responsibility in art began with aesthetic form. In 1910, Graf published *The Inner Workshop of the Composer*, a psychology of music composition in which he likened the artist to a master craftsman who works unconscious impulses and fantasies, the raw material of his trade, into conscious unity and order. That labor demanded an act of will: "One can say that this feeling of unity is related to the function of will, for in actuality the creators of great symphonic works were men of will power of the first order."[50] Furthermore, he maintained, such artists "alone possess the will power to control and to guide intellectually those masses of elemental, passionate vehemence."[51] Through the image of the artisan, Graf contrasted the ideal of classicism, which mastered and molded the passions, to the profound, but undisciplined energy of Romanticism. In its conclusion, however, the book directly targeted the amorality of "art for art's sake." According to Graf, if his own psychological study of creativity and artistic form could

> contribute, in an age of vain virtuosity, glittering spirit and fantasy-rich dilettantism, to pointing the way back toward the forceful earnestness of noble artistic work, which in all great epochs has risen to the heights from broad grounding in technical craftsmanship [*Handwerk*], it has fulfilled its goal. For the time of a natural scientific, descriptive aesthetic [*naturwissenschaftlich beschreibenden Ästhetik*] is past, and aesthetics must again remember its true calling: to point out the great laws of artistic creation, and hold up the ideal to the striving and struggling artist.[52]

Thus, a psychological aesthetics examined simultaneously the artist's emotional motives and his sense of purpose.

In *The Artist,* Rank described the creative process in similar terms, distinguishing it from other mental processes by which the repressed entered consciousness. "The artist (to have an art [*können*]) can free himself from painful feelings, when they press him, as distinct from the neurotic who cannot, but wants to, and the dreamer, who lets it happen. Thus, only a peculiarly tuned relation of psychic forces to each other, a kind of will power, differentiates the artist from the neurotic and the dreamer."[53] As described by Graf and Rank, aesthetic form provided an expression of the artist's unconscious relationship to his work—the function of will, or relation of psychic forces. At the same time, the choice of that form gave an indication of the artist's conscious definition of his task. Thus, the psychologist of art had to examine the technique applied in the artwork so as to locate and distinguish accurately the presence of unconscious motives and the assertion of moral aims.

An early Freudian analysis of the artist's technical style appeared in David Bach's review of Richard Strauss's *Elektra* for the *Arbeiter Zeitung* on 26 March 1909. Bach began his article by defining the artist's vocation: "All true art is moral; it works not on the emotions, on the nerves alone, but rather on the perception and the understanding, which it enlarges."[54] He challenged the ideology of "art for art's sake":

> Where this is concerned, the cry of those who already denounce the mere word "morality" as reactionary Philistine attachment, as endangering free art, changes nothing. In truth, there would be nothing more reactionary, also for that reason more dangerous to art, than this nothing-but-aestheticism. Certainly, art has its own laws which only the artist, no one else, has the right to change or create anew. After all, the fundamental conditions of all art should not be set aside. Autonomy of art is the condition of its existence. Self-legislation [*Selbstgesetzlichkeit*] admits in the very word the compulsion of a law, and in that lies, as a simultaneous given, morality in the higher sense, through which autonomy, conversely, is originally guaranteed.[55]

Paradoxically, those who saw "art as end [*Kunst als Zweck*]" were forced to seek new form and content outside of art, in the sphere of sensations. Such was the path followed by Richard Strauss, and what Bach considered the "unpleasant" effect and "offensiveness" of his music derived from reliance on the "sensational."[56]

Hugo von Hofmannsthal's operatic text demonstrated a similar evasion of the artist's calling. To make his point, Bach referred to Freud's theory of creativity: "In the characters [*Gestalten*] created by the poet inhere secret drives, which could only have been subdued through the art form, and thus have found manifestation through a diversion benefiting the poet and the world."[57] As for Hofmannsthal's Elektra, the audience saw "the psychology of that character reduced to an insurmountable perverse drive."[58] In portraying Elektra as a being consumed by instinct, Hofmannsthal removed the moral problem from her tragedy: "For an overpowering drive, no one is responsible. The meaning of the drama is lost. . . . Thus we have the instinctual drive as fate, and man with no possibility to shape his destiny. His downfall is physiological practicality, nothing more."[59] By contrast, in Sophocles' conception of Elektra, the heroine who herself thirsted for vengeance "acquires guilt." By resorting to psychologism—a variant of sensationalism—the modern dramatist Hofmannsthal renounced the mission of art: "It is permitted to the psychologist to demonstrate his theory on poets, but not to the poet to poeticize with slavish accuracy a theory of artistic creation."[60] Through creative invention, artists achieved for themselves, and offered to others, temporary liberation from inner suffering. Through craftsmanship, however, they constructed a meaning for that suffering. Thus did Bach, like others among Freud's followers, join the technical to the moral tasks of the artist.[61]

If artists were to provide both an emotionally cathartic and psychologically authentic treatment of their material, did the work of psychoanalysts have a bearing on that mission? The question occupied the center of Otto Rank's concern in *The Artist*. The book's conclusion asserted that the therapist represented the culmination of the development in civilization leading from art to science. Like Otto Weininger, Rank believed that the progress of consciousness would lead to the creation of a new type of moral individual—in Rank's words, the fully conscious "healing artist."[62] The scientist pursued direct knowledge of the unconscious. The healing artist, however, practiced psychical therapy, which surpassed both art and science in that it provided a means to govern the unconscious. As with Weininger's ideal of a "third self,"[63] the healing artist would become complete master of himself. Thus, the redemptive function of art passed to psychology.

Rank expected that the advance of psychological knowledge would eventually undermine the conditions for artistic creation. That conviction met challenges, however, during the discussion of his first presentation to the Wednesday Society, in October 1906. Rank's paper that evening briefly summarized the first draft of his book, *The Incest Theme in Literature and Legend*, finally published in 1912. Tracking the representation of Oedipal conflict from ancient mythology to contemporary literature, its "main objective was to show the correspondence of certain phenomena in myth and art with phenomena in the psychoneuroses."[64]

In discussion, Adler interpreted the effect of psychoanalytic knowledge on the future of art: although artistic activity would suffer, the expansion of consciousness would open paths to other cultural advances. Thus, he maintained that

> the significance of art for the development (cultural and spiritual) of a people has been overrated until now. Investigations such as those made by Rank do not encourage the development of art; if continued, such investigations could even become dangerous to the mentality of people [*Volksgeist*]. The creativeness of artists would be inhibited if too much were brought to consciousness. The artist would become incapable of creation; this, of course, implies the destruction of art. On the other hand, a loss in this direction might be compensated for by the progress in other fields which might result from expansion of the sphere of consciousness.[65]

Rejecting Adler's conclusions, several members responded that unconscious impulses, especially repressed sexual desires, would provide constant impetus to art. Adolf Häutler, a member of the Wednesday circle until November 1908, stated that position most forcefully. "Häutler," the minutes record, "is strongly opposed to the view that artistic creativity could ever be weakened. So much will never become conscious as to impair a normal individual's power of imagination. Much will always remain obscure in the human mind, hence one of the driving forces of creative writing will never cease to exist; such an end could only come about if all sexual energies were obliterated. Were this to occur, it would bring with it the demise not only of art but of many other human endeavors as well."[66]

Rank himself remained unmoved. The minutes state that "he cannot help but stick to his conviction that art must perish when the unconscious is made conscious. Against Häutler he asserts that artists are the ones who attain the highest degree of consciousness among their contemporaries, and that therefore it is *in them* that such transition takes place."[67]

The debate over the impact of psychoanalysis on art was joined again during a meeting of the society devoted to Wilhelm Stekel's analysis of Gerhardt Hauptmann's play *Griselda;* the meeting was held on 31 March 1909, five days after the appearance of Bach's review of *Elektra.* Hauptmann's play derived from Boccaccio's tale of "patient Griselda," the peasant woman who, on becoming the wife of a count, was forced to suffer extreme tests of her devotion. The count forbad Griselda to see their two children and finally banished her from their home, allowing her to return only as maid to his prospective bride. When the count saw that Griselda endured this treatment without complaint, he revealed to her that it was meant as a test of her love, and he restored her to her rightful place. Finally, he disclosed to her that the young woman whom he had supposedly chosen as a new wife was in fact their daughter.

Stekel's paper contrasted Boccaccio's version with Hauptmann's contemporary reworking of the legend. In Hauptmann's play, the count appeared as a neurotic, dominated by sadistic and masochistic impulses. Stekel pointed out, "In the second act, we learn about the Count's peculiar mode of living, which is strikingly reminiscent of the penance that neurotics impose upon themselves in order to atone for some wrongdoing."[68] Emphasizing the count's neurosis, Hauptmann ensured that the "father, too, is twice referred to as a peculiar man."[69] Hauptmann's count revealed a marked masochistic strain in his erotic life, "for he is always searching for the powerful woman."[70] He finally chose as his wife, however, a woman whom he could overpower: he "recognizes that this awakening of her masochistic streak is the surest way to her love."[71] Griselda's pregnancy causes her husband to become "sad and moody;"[72] he is overcome by jealousy toward her physician. In conversation with the doctor, the "Count now admits to him that he hates the child, because it will take his wife's love away from him, etc. He hates the still unborn child 'as if he had had a bloody strife with him in another world.'"[73] After his son is born, the count is possessed by murderous ideas. He has the child sent to relatives. Stekel concluded: "Only after Griselda has returned to her former life—that is, after she has left him—does his love reawaken; he then becomes reconciled with her and [gives up] his hatred for the child."[74] In contrast to Boccaccio's story, Hauptmann's version stressed the father's jealousy toward his son as a future rival: "The sado-masochistic character of the neurotic is extraordinarily well portrayed. We also see that jealousy is intimately connected with sadism. Jealousy is, one might say, sadism that has been turned against one's own person, and yet [at the same time continues to] seek out opportunities to torment the loved person."[75]

In discussion, Freud spoke first. He was familiar with Hauptmann's work in general, but in this case relied on Stekel's summary of the play, as he "knows the drama only from this paper."[76] According to Freud, dramatists wrongly used psychology when they transformed their work into case histories. Such an approach both undermined the artist's mission and weakened the bond between himself and the public:

> The naked brutality with which he develops his dramas is as repulsive in *Griselda* as it is in the others. Freud has perceived no poetic beauty in the drama; the hero is a mad dog who belongs in a lunatic asylum. Since Hauptmann created the hero, the poet must be reproached for not knowing how to present psychological problems in a way that might take hold of us. As Bach very rightly pointed out in a *feuilleton* in the *Arbeiterzeitung* just a few days ago, on the occasion of the performance of *Elektra*, the art of the poet does not consist of finding and dealing with problems. That he should leave to the psychologists. Rather, the poet's art consists of obtaining poetic effects out of such problems; experience shows that these problems must be disguised if they are to produce such effects; furthermore, that the effect is by no means diminished if one merely suspects what the problems are and none of the readers or listeners can make out clearly what the effect is. Thus the poet's art consists essentially in covering over. What is unconscious ought not, without more ado, be rendered conscious; of course it must become conscious to a certain degree—that is, to the point at which it still affects us, without our occupying ourselves with it in our conscious thoughts. At the point where this becomes possible, art leaves off. We have the right to analyze a poet's work, but it is not right for the poet to make poetry out of [*poetisieren*] our analyses. Yet, this seems to be a sign of our times. The poets dabble in all possible sorts of sciences, and then proceed to a poetic working up of the knowledge they have acquired. The public is fully justified in rejecting such products.[77]

Freud cautioned his followers not to be misled by the contemporary artist: "Bribed by the poet's psychological treatment of the problem, we ourselves may become more lenient in our criticism."[78]

Rank looked in Freud's comments for confirmation of his own concerns. The minutes record his reaction:

> As far as the problem of modern poetic art is concerned, Rank can only agree with the Professor's remarks; he himself had earlier indicated, in his *Artist*, that when the unconscious is made conscious art ceases to exist. However, this is by no means a sign of a deficiency of artistic skill in Hauptmann's case; rather, it is an inescapable sign of the development of our times, which documents the deterioration of art as consciousness advances (Hofmannsthal, Wedekind, etc.). The poet can cope with his personal conflicts only if he brings them to consciousness as far as is possible, but then he is not in a position to analyze them in universally valid human terms; they remain all too subjective, and it is understandable that the public must reject them.[79]

Freud, however, did not come to the conclusion that art would yield to psychology. In response to Rank, he singled out the work of Ibsen as justification: "The correct evaluation is to be found only through a comparison of Hauptmann with Ibsen. Surely Ibsen is not the more abnormal personality of the two. Ibsen, with his self-containment, unity, and simplification of problems, along with his art of concentration and concealment is a great poet, whereas Hauptmann is the neurotic who portrays himself alone."[80] Freud concluded the meeting, "There is no reason to see in this a sign of the decline of art. . . . This is an isolated phenomenon which [historical] development will soon be on its way to bypassing."[81]

According to Freud and Bach, the artist's choice of form and conscious perception of responsibility sustained the mission of art. Psychologism provided an artificial substitute for that genuine relationship between the artist and his work, which found an expression in aesthetic form and which produced an unconscious bond between the artist and audience. Neither did it allow for moral confrontation between the artist and the spectator. The artist remained caught within his own complexes. As Freud said of Hauptmann the dramatist, he "invariably depicts only himself and never the problem."[82] For both Freud and Bach, in classical tragedy, poets not only portrayed human suffering in a form that could be withstood by themselves and their audience, but brought to that suffering a sense of meaning. Contrasting Hofmannsthal's tragedy of Elektra to the works of the ancient tragedians, Bach—now expressly following "the eminent philologist, Wilamowitz," and not that classicist's Dionysian critic, Nietzsche—emphasized that Greek tragic cycles "were held together not through the legendary material alone, but through the moral idea—always in the sense of the artwork, not of moral clericalism—which the poet could exhibit in the material. Only through the idea in their artwork could the Attic poets distinguish themselves from each other, for the material was common to all. But the modern interpreter thoroughly expelled the idea from it. He abandons the artwork; and nearly himself as a poet."[83] To Freud's mind, however, contemporary artists had not yet lost their calling. Morality remained a foundation of artistic creativity, morality now understood as that conviction which permitted endurance of inward suffering. Perhaps that perspective explains Häutler's enigmatic comment during the October 1906 discussion of art and psychoanalysis: "As long as mankind is capable of passing judgment, there will be poets."[84]

IV

If artists could not resort to psychologism and still preserve the mission of art, could Viennese psychoanalysts resort to similar reductionism and expect to sustain their own cultural analysis and criticism? Interpreting art and creativity raised the question of their aims and obligations as psychologists. In the study of culture, Freud's Viennese followers thus debated and defined their own craft. The discussion emerged within the circle itself, but also received impetus from without, as the Freudians confronted criticisms leveled by their erstwhile ally, Karl Kraus.

Kraus directed his criticisms chiefly at the works of Wilhelm Stekel and Isador Sadger, whose interpretations of artists had aroused controversy within the Wednesday Society itself. In 1909, Stekel published *Poetry and Neurosis: Foundation for the Psychology of the Artist and the Artwork.* When Stekel wrote that "every poet is a neurotic," he meant not only that poets experienced intense "psychic conflict" between cultural inhibitions and unconscious wishes, but that every poet suffered from hysteria, or the conversion of repressed sexual impulses into physical symptoms.[85] He saw the artist's work as an extension of his neurosis, or more specifically, a sublimated expression of the impulses bound within his illness.

In this book, Stekel sought to demonstrate his theory through Franz Grillparzer's drama, *A Dream Is Life*. In Grillparzer's play, a young Persian, Rustan, planned to leave the farm of his uncle, Massud, and desert his uncle's daughter, Mirtza, who was in love with him, to fulfill his ambition of becoming a soldier with the king of Samarkand and one day marrying the king's daughter, Gylnara. A nobleman, Osmin, provoked Rustan to the decision, and Rustan's slave, Tsanga, encouraged him to act on it. On the night before his departure, a dream came to him: while traveling to the capital, Rustan sees the king attacked by a large serpent. From a nearby cliff, an old man descends to slay the serpent and save the king's life. At Tsanga's urging, Rustan claims credit for the deed, and the king rewards him with his daughter's hand in marriage. To preserve his secret, Rustan kills the old man. Through further betrayals and murders, including that of the king himself, Rustan comes to rule the kingdom. His crimes, however, are finally exposed by both a mute wanderer and a witch. While attempting to flee, Rustan faces death in the figure of Tsanga, now revealed as the Devil. At that moment, however, he awakened from the dream, determining in that instant to remain with his uncle and Mirtza. According to Stekel, the drama was written by an obsessional neurotic. At the core of the play, he argued, lay the doubts and reproaches characteristic of such patients.

In October 1908, Stekel had presented his interpretation of the play and playwright to Freud's circle, describing what he believed to be the correspondence between figures in the drama and persons from Grillparzer's life. Grillparzer's first love, Stekel pointed out, was his cousin, as Mirtza was to Rustan. Tsanga embodied the suppressed unconscious, while at the same time shared characteristics with Grillparzer's brother, Karl. Stekel identified Osmin with Grillparzer's other brother, Kamillo. Because the old man reminded Rustan of Osmin, he provided a second representation of Kamillo, as well as a demonstration of Grillparzer's feeling of rivalry toward that brother. Grillparzer's father appeared as generous in the figures of Massud and the king, but, like the brother, also as a rival in the figure of the old man. Finally, Glynara assumed the place of Grillparzer's mother. Concluding his presentation, Stekel interpreted the correspondence between the action in the drama and the unconscious impulses against which Grillparzer fought in his neurosis:

> The wish fulfillment of the first act of the dream is this: he renders a great service to the king (father and mother), and kills father and brother. The old mute Caleb, who accuses him of murder, is again the murdered father. The old witch personifies his mother, who thus also appears in two figures. In this a fantasy of rape is also indicated. In Osmin's report, which the King reads, Mirtza is directly identified with Glynara. It shows Rustan's homosexual tendencies when he orders Tsanga to stab him in the back with his dagger. Rustan then dies on the same bridge on which his father died. Tsanga is transformed into the Devil, the tempter. Finally, a feeling of release takes hold of Rustan when he feels that it is all nothing but a dream, that he hates no one, and that, with regard to murder, he can have a free conscience.[86]

Sadger's *Heinrich von Kleist: A Pathographical-Psychological Study*, published in 1909, also focused on the presence of neurosis in the poet. As in his study of Meyer, Sadger made little use of the artist's work. Rather, he examined what he considered to be pathological traits in Kleist's chain of erotic attachments and inevitable separations. Hereditary influence remained as a factor contributing to the poet's erratic behavior and dark moods, but now it played a strictly subordinate role. Yet, from Sadger's point of view, the significance of examining the pattern of Kleist's life lay in connecting it to a deepening pathology. In Sadger's analysis, Kleist's personal relationships appeared as a repetitive, nearly indistinguishable series of associations. Through Sadger's explanatory lens, one saw the unconscious in Kleist produce a cycle of compulsive desire and inevitable dissatisfaction, and finally lead him to the idea of death as the only act of true devotion. Thus, Kleist's sudden marriage to Henriette Vogel ended in a suicide pact.

Sadger's *From the Love Life of Nicolaus Lenau* appeared in the same year as did the study of Kleist. Published in the *Papers on Applied Psychology*, the book showed new restraint in Sadger, who limited his conclusions about the presence of pathology in Lenau and restricted his focus to the most significant attachment in Lenau's life, his friendship with Sophie Löwenthal. Yet, Sadger studied Lenau with the same interest in neurotic formations that he had applied to Meyer and Kleist: from his perspective, poetic works still did not deserve a central place in an analysis of the poet's life.

Freudian discussions of art drew the attention and scorn of Karl Kraus. Like Viennese psychoanalysts, Kraus feared that art at the turn of the century had sacrificed its moral purpose. In his view, however, psychological investigations of creativity made more severe the crisis of contemporary culture. Instead, the moral spirit thrived on the creative chaos of the psyche. As in the sphere of sexual ethics, so the Krausian paradox applied in the domain of art: complete moral responsibility allied itself to complete freedom. His severe criticisms of psychoanalysis in the pages of *Die Fackel*, beginning in 1908, seem to have been the first in print directed at Freudian studies of creative genius.

Like other culture critics who joined with Freud at the time, Kraus had initially seen in the Freudian explanation of humor an insight into the creative process. From Kraus's early perspective, the appearance of Freud's theory had exemplified the mystery of creativity: the free-floating creative impulse had chosen to reveal itself through rationalistic psychology. As Kraus wrote in July 1907, "F. has demonstrated the relationships between jokes and dreams. It is not his fault, if among the treasures which he has extracted from the unconscious, now and again a sapphire turns up."[87] And again, in December 1907: "Recently they toasted neurological knowledge at a banquet for physicians, and he, whom one does not have to follow on the tortuous paths of dream interpretation in order to recognize in him a scholarly investigator among after-dinner speakers, was not present. This is only as it should be. Of what use is Stanley in a society which has not uncovered a dark continent, but has simply transformed Europe into one."[88]

In June 1908, Kraus began objecting to what he saw as a coldly clinical and irreverent approach in psychoanalysis:

> There is a medical tendency, which applies the technical terms of surgery to what pertains to the soul. It is like every intellectual analogizing between apparently remote spheres, a joke, and probably the best of which materialism is capable. Now if the doctor wants to scratch out the subconscious [*Unterbewusstsein*] of a female patient, or if emotional abscesses are cut out, such attempts are based on an associative flash of extraordinary wit [*höchst witzigen Einfall*], and one which must have far greater certainty of its irresistibility than have the surgical interventions of a mental doctor carried out without the narcosis of suggestion. For my part, I think it would be better not to have a whimsical method of treatment

diminish the true value of this ingenious discovery of the origins of mental illnesses, which redounded to the honor of its discoverer.[89]

Not content with being the mere vessel of the creative mind, psychoanalysis sought to intervene in its workings: "The transcendental faith in miracles had the advantage of being decorative. Faith is missing in rationalistic miracles."[90] The theory of the unconscious had initially undermined rationalist hubris. Now, in psychoanalysis itself, determinist impulses threatened to overwhelm the Freudian sense of humility. As Kraus wrote,

> The psychiatrist is to the psychologist as the astrologer is to the astronomer. The astrological factor has always played a role in psychiatric science. At first our actions were determined by the positions of the heavenly bodies. Next our destiny's star was in our own breasts. Then came the theory of heredity. And now it is absolutely decisive whether the infant is fond of his nurse, in which case he finds his star of destiny in her breasts. Childhood sexual impressions are certainly not to be underestimated, and praise is due the researcher who cleared away the belief that sexuality begins with the completion of one's *Maturas*. But one should not exaggerate anything. If the times have passed when science practiced abstinence from knowledge, one should not on that account yield to the pleasure of sexual researches without any inhibitions. "My father," sneers Gloucester's bastard, "compounded with my mother under the dragon's tail, and my nativity was under *Ursa major*; so that it follows I am rough and lecherous." And still it was more beautiful to be dependent upon the sun, the moon, and stars, than upon the fateful powers of rationalism."[91]

According to Kraus, the scientist's lack of moral reverence had begun to reveal itself in the psychoanalytic approach to art. Citing a conversation with one of Freud's followers, who pointed out to Kraus the unconscious sexual impulses within Goethe's "The Sorcerer's Apprentice," he wrote, "Physicians of the nervous system who pathologize the genius should have their skulls knocked in with his collected works. . . . But in the face of those others, the modern psychiatrizers, who test the work of giants merely for the presence of sexuality, one should simply laugh out loud."[92] As for interpreting the creative genius of Goethe: "He wrote 'The Sorcerer's Apprentice' and did not know what it signified. And one had believed all along that the unconscious of a Goethe would always be more conscious than the highest consciousness of a sexual psychologist."[93]

Jolted by the appearance of Sadger's studies of Kleist and Lenau, Kraus resumed his criticisms in April 1910. "The new psychology dared to spit at the mystery of genius," Kraus exploded. "If the matter does not rest with Kleist and Lenau, I will keep watch at the door, and will send the medical peddlars, whose cry 'Anything to treat?' is now heard everywhere, into the wastelands. Having extended the limits of irresponsibility, its teaching would now like to narrow the personality. As long as the business sticks to private practice, the individuals concerned can defend themselves. But we will remove Kleist and Lenau from the surgery."[94]

Kraus absolved Freud from the sins of his disciples. The abuses of psychoanalysis he attributed to Freud's followers, whom he likened to the apprentice in Goethe's poem: "Finally Professor Freud returns. 'Master, my misery is great. The spirits, which I summoned, I cannot get rid of.' The Professor sees how the student has compromised his teaching, and decides to make an end of the gross misconduct. It was high time. Into the corner with everything that looked like a broom and must have signified something else! 'Be done with you. / For as spirits, / No one except your old master, for his ends, / Will summon you.' "[95]

At the meetings of his society, the master used the discussions of art to steer his disciples away from that reductionism so furiously denounced by Kraus. In his own responses to Stekel and Sadger, the Professor emphasized that psychoanalysts did not study artistic creations to collect the psychological material supplied by artists, but to interpret the significance which they gave that material in their work, the nature of the artist's work demanding that the Freudian discriminate between levels of psychological meaning. After the presentation on Grillparzer's *A Dream Is Life*, Freud responded that Stekel's "analytic method is too radical; everything he finds in Grillparzer can be found in every neurotic, as well as in all normal persons. It is not enough to demonstrate [the existence of] these complexes, which, as we know, must be present; the problem is rather to demonstrate their psychic localization."[96]

When Sadger presented his study of Kleist to the Viennese circle in May 1909, Freud reminded those present of the distinction between a clinical sketch and a psychoanalytic portrait of the artist. "Why is it," he is reported to have asked, that, even though Sadger makes assertions that must be accepted as correct, his communications feel strange to us, sometimes even offensive? That is the enigma that Freud would like to try solving. The first reason lies in the fact that in such a psychological analysis of a creative writer one does not find any point of contact with our image of the man's personality, and that is why the analysis seems strange. One simply cannot do justice to a personality if one stresses only its abnormal sexual components and does not make an effort to establish their close ties with the individual's other psychic forces. In that case, as has been said here, one might just as well have written a pathography not of a creative writer, but of anyone else you could think of, someone unknown to us who—by the way!—left a number of works of creative writing. . . . The general public is right in rejecting this type of analysis—and this refers in part also to Stekel (*A Dream Is Life*). In such elementary analyses all finer distinctions of structure manage to get completely lost, and so does the understanding of the poet. One just cannot ignore the value of the object employed in such research. For a mere demonstration that every human being typically has these basic emotions, our poets are too good.[97]

The artist, Freud thought, did not provide material for clinical case histories.

Calling to mind his analysis of the playwright Hauptmann, Freud indicated to his followers how an understanding of the artist's craft illuminated the application of psychoanalysis. "Sadger," he maintained, "must also be reproached for having a special predilection for the brutal. However, our task is not arbitrarily to speak new truths, but rather to show in what way they can be arrived at. A certain degree of tolerance must go hand in hand with a deeper understanding, especially of unconscious phenomena, if life is to remain at all bearable."[98] Freud imparted psychoanalysis here as *technē*—a craft—the correct practice of which, as with all crafts, not only demanded devotion to method, but also awareness of human needs. As such, it belonged to a commonalty with art, conceived perhaps as a Renaissance artist comprehended it—as *arte*, or skill.

In December 1909, Freud presented a paper to his followers entitled "A Fantasy of Leonardo da Vinci"; in the following year, he published in the *Papers on Applied Psychology* his biographical study of the artist and scientist. Responding in part to the discussions within the Viennese circle, the essay not only offered a psychological interpretation of the images in Leonardo's creative work, but explored as well the conflict in Leonardo between his

commitment to painting and dedication to research. A psychoanalytic biography of the painter, Freud's study of Leonardo da Vinci
also reflected upon the relationship between art and science.

FIVE

IMAGES IN ART
AND BIOGRAPHY

I

In his presentation to the Vienna Psychoanalytic Society on the psychology of poets, Max Graf instructed his fellow researchers that "not everyone is fit to pursue the psychology of artists—that is to say, the psychology of the most complex, the most sensitive souls, and whoever undertakes such a task must first ask himself whether he is fit for it; that is, whether he himself knows how thoughts, images, emerge from the unconscious and are transformed into conscious material. In short, he alone shall approach the artist who is himself artistically inclined."[1] Graf returned to the point in his concluding remarks, admonishing that "Prof. Freud's technique alone cannot unravel the mysteries of creative writing unless it is used with Prof. Freud's artistic sensitivity."[2] The music critic certainly meant to remind fellow members of the society of the singular insight and skill—usually associated with the artistic vocation—necessary for the application of psychoanalysis to the mental life of poets. Such comments, however, suggested, if only obscurely, that psychoanalytic biographers had to combine in themselves not only the skills, but, to some extent, the identities of artist and psychologist.

While writing his first psychoanalytic biography, Sigmund Freud too found in the task a sense of identity between the artist and psychologist. On 11 November 1909, in the early stages of the project, he wrote to Carl Jung that "a noble spirit, Leonardo da Vinci, has been posing for me—I have been doing a little ΨA of him."[3] Freud painting an image of Leonardo: if only in metaphor, psychoanalytic science is joined to Renaissance art. Yet, the metaphor provides a point of departure: it is an explicit statement of an identification with Leonardo, and that identification is grounded in the craft of the portraitist.[4]

The comment to Jung, however, was not the first time Freud drew a comparison between his own method and that of Leonardo. In an address delivered to the Viennese College of Physicians in December 1904, Freud sought to emphasize the distinction between the use of suggestion in therapy, and the psychoanalytic approach:

> There is, actually, the greatest possible antithesis between suggestive and analytic technique—the same antithesis which, in regard to the fine arts, the great Leonardo da Vinci summed up in the formulas: *per via di porre* and *per via di levare*. Painting, says Leonardo, works *per via di porre*, for it applies a substance—particles of colour—where there was nothing before, on the colourless canvas; sculpture, however, proceeds *per via di levare*, since it takes away from the block of stone all that hides the surface of the statue contained in it. In a similar way, the technique of suggestion aims at proceeding *per via di porre*; it is not concerned with the origin, strength and meaning of the morbid symptoms, but instead, it superimposes something—a suggestion—in the expectation that it will be strong enough to restrain the pathogenic idea from coming to expression. Analytic therapy, on the other hand, does not seek to add or to introduce anything new, but to take away something, to bring out something; and to this end concerns itself with the genesis of the morbid symptoms and the psychical context of the pathogenic idea which it seeks to remove.[5]

In comparing the approaches of Leonardo and Freud, we must keep in mind that contrast.

Freud, of course, found the comparison of the arts in Leonardo's notes to his manual on painting—never published in Leonardo's lifetime—in which the artist not only explained in detail the techniques and aims of his craft, but expounded and justified the claim of painting to be included among the Renaissance sciences. Fortunately, in his notebooks we have fragments of his ideas for the book, which his devoted pupil and literary heir, Francesco Melzi, first organized into the "Book on Painting by M. Leonardo da Vinci, Florentine Painter and Sculptor," and which in later editions and translations has become known to us as the *Trattato della Pittura* (*Treatise on Painting*). There we have what is left to us of his thoughts on painting not only as an art, but as a science.

Between the Viennese Professor who likened his work as a scientific biographer to the craftsmanship of Renaissance art and the Florentine master who sought for the rising art of painting a place among the sciences there is an intellectual symmetry. What follows is an exploration of that symmetry. Freud's understanding of psychoanalysis during the early years of the movement can be illuminated by Leonardo's conception of painting as a science. Further, it will be useful to examine the metaphor in Freud's letter to Jung for what it reveals not only about his notion of the relationship between art and psychology in these years, but also about his conception of culture.

II

Leonardo's concern to have painting accepted as one of the sciences evidenced the increasingly prominent, but as yet uncertain, intellectual and social stature of the visual arts in the age of the Renaissance. Still more, it epitomized a tendency toward what Erwin Panofsky called the "decompartmentalization" of cultural activity during that period.[6] The strict division between liberal and mechanical arts, between intellectual and technical pursuits, came under question, as individuals sought to narrow that divide through self-education, collaborative work, or the creation of informal academies.[7] Leonardo—the artist, investigator, and engineer—embodied with unequaled intensity and unparalleled achievement a wider social and cultural phenomenon.

If Leonardo and others made an attempt—foreign to the modern mind—to bridge the division between artistic and scientific endeavors, there existed also during the Renaissance an understanding of art and science that differed significantly from what is accepted in our own day. Renaissance culture did not ascribe the distinction between artistic and scientific activities to the opposition between unfettered imagination and controlled experimentation. As E. H. Gombrich has written of Leonardo, "when we hear him praised (and in a way quite justly) as a man who had uniquely combined the two disparate branches of human creativity which we call 'art' and 'science', we might do well to reflect that he would scarcely have understood this form of adulation; indeed it could not have been expressed in the language of his time. To his contemporaries 'art', *arte*, meant skill, much as we still use the concept in 'the art of war' or the 'art of love', while 'science', *scientia*, meant knowledge."[8] Associated specifically with theory, and the search for rational laws and principles, the sciences defined the substance of the seven liberal arts—grammar, rhetoric, dialectic, arithmetic, geometry, astronomy, and music. By educational and social convention, their scientific nature separated those studies from the mechanical arts—painting and sculpture among them—which derived from the exercise of a manual craft.[9] Yet, according to Leonardo, as well as other Renaissance artists and educators, painting had developed into a craft demanding recognition as a true science, and therefore deserving a place among the liberal arts. Comparing Leonardo's attitude to modern views, Gombrich again emphasized their wide divergence: "Maybe there is hardly another aspect of Leonardo's outlook more remote from the preconceptions of our age than this insistence on the rationality of artistic procedures."[10]

In his notebooks, often in fragments reminiscent of those that survive of the pre-Socratic philosophers, Leonardo recorded his reflections on art and science, reflections which were of several kinds.[11] In the *paragone*—comparisons of the painter's craft with poetry, music, and sculpture—he unfolded his conception of painting, explaining why it was he ranked that activity supreme among the arts.[12] Further, he gave detailed instruction and advice on the techniques of that craft, most importantly the use of light and shade, and the mastery of perspective. Among his chief aims, finally, was to demonstrate the standing of painting as a science. For Leonardo, the relationship of painting to experience, "the common mother of all the sciences and arts,"[13] justified its elevation to the sciences and its preeminence among the arts. Specifically, the supremacy of the visual sense in apprehending nature, and the ability of the painter to convey that understanding by applying the laws of mathematics gave painting a unique status. According to Leonardo, the activity of painting—combining the immediacy of sense experience with the application of rational principles—exposed the error of distinguishing so-called mechanical knowledge from scientific learning. As Panofsky explained, Leonardo embodied the movement toward "the elimination of the barriers which in the Middle Ages had separated the 'liberal arts' from the 'mechanical' ones—theoretical insight, which was supposed to be a matter of the pure intellect, and practical pursuits, including the representational arts, which were supposed to be a matter of mere sensory perception and manual skill."[14]

For Leonardo, the process of visualization provided one of the crucial links between painting as an art and as a science, painting as a liberal, as well as mechanical, pursuit. What, therefore, did it mean to visualize the world? First and foremost, it meant to ground oneself thoroughly and continuously in experience. All that deserved the name of science, wrote Leonardo, "penetrated through the senses as a result of experience."[15] Experience humbled the prideful scientist and raised the lowly craftsman:

> They say that knowledge born of experience is mechanical but that knowledge born and ending in the mind is scientific, and that knowledge born in science and ending in manual operations is semi-mechanical, but to me it appears that those sciences are vain and full of error that have not been born of experience, mother of every certainty and which do not likewise end in experience; that is to say, those that have neither at their beginning, middle or end passed through any of the five senses.[16]

Of all the senses, sight, according to Leonardo, gave the richest, most direct, most nearly universal experience of the world; as he wrote, "the eye has no need for translators from various languages, as have words, and it gives immediate satisfaction to human beings in no other way than the things produced by nature herself."[17]

Visualization freed the painter from dependence on authority. Relying on his own observations, the painter need not become a slave to tradition: "The painter will produce pictures of little excellence if he takes other painters as his authority, but if he learns from natural things he will bear good fruit."[18] Freedom from authority allowed painting to aspire to universality in its art, an aspiration Leonardo demanded of each painter, writing "you cannot be good if you are not a master universal enough to imitate with your art every kind of natural form, which you will not know how to do unless you observe them and retain them in your mind."[19] He advised that painters never be without small notebooks in which to sketch their observations of nature and humanity, and that such notebooks never be discarded. Expressing one of his most deeply held convictions—and strongest fears—he reminded painters that "those who take as their authority any other than nature, mistress of the masters, labour in vain."[20]

To visualize nature based on experience and direct observation helped join painting as an art to the activity of science. For Leonardo, however, all science had also to rest on the foundation of mathematics; in fact, "there is no certainty where one can neither apply any of the mathematical sciences nor any of those which are connected with the mathematical sciences."[21] In painting, perspective, and the geometric laws upon which it was based, provided those mathematical principles of order and certainty.[22] Together with an understanding of how light and shade delineated surfaces, knowledge of the laws of perspective gave a rational framework within which to organize visual experience.[23] As an artist, however, the painter made known an idea of nature and the world removed from that of the other mathematical disciplines, for "the quality they cannot express is the beauty of the works of nature and the adornments of the world."[24]

Joining art and science, skill and knowledge, the painter represented nature to humanity without need of language. Such representational art, relying exclusively on visualization, rose above music and sculpture in the fullness, immediacy, and genuineness of its effects. The beauty and order of nature found authentic expression in painting. In his notebooks, Leonardo sought to describe the quality of that authenticity, a source both of aesthetic enjoyment and intellectual insight. We read: "Painting immediately presents to you the demonstrations which its maker has intended and gives as much pleasure to the greatest of senses as anything created by nature";[25] "The poet is not able to present in words the true configuration of the elements which make up the whole, unlike the painter, who can set them before you with the same truth as is possible with nature";[26] "Do you not know that our soul is composed of harmony, and that harmony cannot be generated other than when the proportions of the form are seen and heard instantaneously?"[27] Represented in painting, the truths of nature required no proofs: "Painting does not speak, but is self-evident through its finished product."[28]

Panofsky pointed out that such an approach to painting contributed not insignificantly to what we today would accept as science. Referring to Leonardo's anatomical drawings, the art historian reminded us that "in the observational or descriptive sciences illustration is not so much the elucidation of a statement as a statement in itself."[29] Thus, Panofsky concluded that during the Renaissance "the tangibilization of science . . . was complementary to an intellectualization of all mechanical professions, pre-eminently the arts."[30]

For Leonardo, painting allowed humanity to glimpse that hidden necessity of nature which forever remained beyond complete human comprehension. Human beings could trace the paths of cause and effect in experience, and formulate their laws, but the necessity which bound all nature and humanity lay beyond our grasp. "Nature does not break her law," Leonardo wrote, "nature is constrained by the logical necessity of her law which is inherent in her."[31] That conviction inspired Leonardo's art and science. As Martin Kemp has explained, "What has been sensed is that his artistic productions are more than art—that they are part of a vision embracing a profound sense of the interrelatedness of things."[32] Painting not only directed the gaze to the sensible beauty of nature's works, but gave a visual, untranslatable impression of their profound necessity. Thus, whatever the achievements of art and science, painting contained within itself the intimation of a mystery.

The common ground between the artist and scientist that Leonardo had helped prepare began to crumble even in his own day. Toward the end of the Renaissance, as Panofsky described, the perception of the painter as a creator rivaling nature helped popularize the notion of the artist as a genius tormented by that daemonic madness which Plato had associated in antiquity with the prophet and poet. Art gradually became defined by creative vision and inspired invention, as science became ever more closely identified with quantifiable and classifiable knowledge.[33] Artists and scientists—or perhaps more accurately, late Renaissance theorists of art and science—regarded each other with ever greater social and intellectual suspicion.

III

Again, we are seeking here merely to illuminate one aspect of Freud's conception of the psychoanalytic movement. As noted, in the course of writing his biography of Leonardo, Freud identified metaphorically his own activity with that of Leonardo's as a portraitist. Throughout his notebooks—in the *paragone*, in his instructions on technique, in his reflections on experience and nature—Leonardo himself carefully explained and fervently defended his conception of painting as both art and science. That conception, it is being argued here, can shed light on Freud's own understanding of psychoanalysis and culture at the time he turned his attention to interpreting the figure of Leonardo.

We do not know when Freud first became interested in Leonardo's life and work, nor along what path. Was it Leonardo's art—perhaps a reproduction of a single painting—or tales of his scientific endeavors that originally captured Freud's curiosity and imagination? Did his interest take a decisive turn in 1885 during his study with Jean-Martin Charcot in Paris, where we know Freud visited the Louvre? There, however, the sculpture of the ancients—at least on his first visit—drew his attention, as he wrote to Martha Bernays: "yesterday I went to the Louvre, at least to the antiquities wing, which contains an incredible number of Greek and Roman statues, gravestones, inscriptions, and relics. I saw a few wonderful things, ancient gods represented over and over again, as well as the famous armless Venus de Milo to whom I paid the traditional compliment. . . . For me these things have more historical than aesthetic interest."[34] Could his attitude have been the same when he finally approached the Mona Lisa and the *Virgin and Child and St. Anne*, about which he would write so movingly in his biography of the artist? Or when he viewed the *Virgin of the Rocks*, whose secret, he once confessed to Ernest Jones, he could not unravel?[35]

We do have an indication of the frame of reference within which he may have first interpreted such paintings. In 1874, Freud had written to his friend, Eduard Silberstein,

> They (the theologians) have long been puzzled why the good Lord +++ required six days for his work of creation, when he could have completed it in a second. All previously advanced exegeses do not hold up; I alone have the correct explanation. He wanted to show mankind that in any task it is essential to observe a rational order and logical sequence of

steps; had God created everything in a second, this important lesson would have been lost on humanity in its striving toward godliness. The self-same order must also be reflected in our letters, but it must not be artificial or lifeless, rather that of a work of art, whose parts are not merely distinct, but also closely interrelated.[36]

We cannot, of course, know Freud's reactions when he first encountered in the Louvre those paintings which came thirty-five years later to figure so prominently in his first—and last—effort at biography. We can only take note that he chose as his subject a painter, that painter in whom science mixed as greatly as art.

Freud read Dmitri Merejkowski's historical novel based on Leonardo's life, and in 1907, in response to a questionnaire from Hugo Heller, counted it among what he would classify as good books.[37] Had he already chosen Leonardo as the subject of a psychological biography when he opened the novel, or did Merejkowski's work help determine Freud's decision? The conservative Russian author saw in Leonardo's art and pursuit of knowledge a subliminal message of the Spirit to the modern world, Leonardo's sacrifices to be redeemed as the Spirit became more fully manifest. Freud's Leonardo, however, was denied redemption.

The life of Leonardo which Freud completed in 1910 represented in part a meditation on the uneasy relationship between art and science, a theme of active concern within the Viennese psychoanalytic movement. That theme now became woven into the fabric of Leonardo's biography. The disharmony between art and science, Freud argued, ultimately prevented fulfillment of Leonardo's own aspirations as an artist. As contemporaries of the painter had noted, the majority of Leonardo's artworks remained incomplete, or failed to survive. A life of Leonardo, as written by Freud, not only had to devise an approach to the ethereal images of his art, but at the same time ask after "the factors which have stamped him with the tragic mark of failure."[38]

Freud's study of Leonardo reflected the view within the Viennese psychoanalytic circle that changes in art accompanied, or even preceded, changes in science; but whereas the scientist could productively apply the insights of art, the artist's work suffered from too close reliance on the results and intentions of science. From this perspective, Freud chose Leonardo for his subject as an ideal type of both the artist and scientist, thus setting Leonardo's personal biography within the context of a wider cultural opposition between those two figures. Yet, one must be careful when describing Freud's view of that opposition both within Leonardo and the intellectual world at large. In the biography, Freud himself traced the development and consequences of Leonardo's ambition to join art and science. Initially, Leonardo joined his scientific interests to his art by concentrating on the understanding of light, shading, and perspective as essential to painting, on which Freud commented dryly: "It is probable that at that time he already overrated the value to the artist of these branches of knowledge."[39] The demands of art, as Leonardo understood them, intensified his pursuit of science, as Freud wrote: "Still constantly following the lead given by the requirements of his painting he was then driven to investigate the painter's subjects, animals and plants, and the proportions of the human body, and, passing from their exterior, to proceed to gain a knowledge of their internal structure and their vital functions, which indeed also find expression in their appearance and have a claim to be depicted in art."[40] Finally, Leonardo's "investigations extended to practically every branch of natural science, and in every single one he was a discoverer or at least a prophet and pioneer."[41] In consequence, without ever foreseeing such a result, he sacrificed his art:

> What interested him in a picture was above all a problem; and behind the first one he saw countless other problems arising, just as he used to in his endless and inexhaustible investigation of nature. He was no longer able to limit his demands, to see the work of art in isolation and to tear it from the wide context to which he knew it belonged. After the most exhausting efforts to bring to expression in it everything which was connected with it in his thoughts, he was forced to abandon it in an unfinished state or to declare that it was incomplete.[42]

Freud concluded his depiction: "The artist had once taken the investigator into his service to assist him; now the servant had become the stronger and suppressed his master."[43] That suppression conformed to the second pattern in Leonardo's life: his ascetic existence and "cool repudiation of sexuality"[44] in a time when sensuous living and experience asserted itself against anchoritic contemplation and self-denial.

Art and science remained unreconciled, but not, in Freud's telling, dissociated. How, therefore, did his biography of Leonardo explore the meaning of what was discordant? We must turn to Freud's interpretation of a memory from Leonardo's childhood.

IV

Freud's study of Leonardo appeared in May 1910 as the seventh volume of the *Papers on Applied Psychology*. Freud founded and edited the series, and contributed its initial volume, *Delusions and Dreams in Jensen's "Gradiva,"* his analysis of dreams in a work of fiction. In subjecting fictitious dreams to interpretation—dreams taken from Wilhelm Jensen's short story, "Gradiva: A Pompeian Fantasy"—he sought not only to confirm principles of dream formation, but elucidate the process of literary creation. In confronting objections to such an approach, his justification of it may allow us to think of Leonardo: "Real dreams were already regarded as unrestrained and unregulated structures—and now we are confronted by unfettered imitations of these dreams! There is far less freedom and arbitrariness in mental life, however, than we are inclined to assume—there may even be none at all. What we call chance in the world outside can, as is well known, be resolved into laws. So, too, what we call arbitrariness in the mind rests upon laws, which we are only now beginning dimly to suspect."[45]

Freud's study of Jensen's short story, however, brings Leonardo to mind for another reason. The pivotal element in the story and its dream was the ancient bas-relief of a young woman, given the name Gradiva by the story's central figure, a German archaeologist. That visual representation provided the link between the formation of the dream and the story's conclusion. When Freud turned to biography, the problem of visual representation remained at the forefront: he chose as his subject not one of the many literary figures whom he and other psychoanalysts admired—as his Viennese followers had done—but a painter. And like Leonardo himself, Freud explored not only the laws and means of the construction of images, but their unconscious necessity.

Freud's *Leonardo da Vinci and a Memory of His Childhood* relied on visual representations in two ways: first, in Freud's explorations of Leonardo's memory, itself a discrete, visual image; and in his interpretations of the painter's art. The memory, according to Freud, provided means through which to discover the psychological roots of the conflict in Leonardo between artistic creativity and scientific investigation, and the inward reasons for the suppression of the former. That image, however, also indicated an approach to Leonardo's paintings, the true object, as Freud had explained to his

Viennese disciples, of a biography of the artist. The laws and processes of nature, as Leonardo himself would have agreed, had to be confirmed in the work of art. Thus, through an interpretation of the memory, Freud followed the process of psychological repression and instinctual sublimation originating in Leonardo's earliest childhood first to the creation of his most celebrated paintings, and finally to their sacrifice on the altar of science.

In his notebooks, Leonardo recorded his single memory from childhood as a distinct visual impression; Freud cited the German translation: "It seems that I was always destined to be so deeply concerned with vultures; for I recall as one of my very earliest memories that while I was in my cradle a vulture came down to me, and opened my mouth with its tail, and struck me many times with its tail against my lips."[46] Despite the strength of the impression, it was unlikely that this image came from memory; instead, Freud wrote, it had to be considered a fantasy transferred into early childhood. Such fantasies took shape from authentic motives and experiences from the past, but, like dreams and historical legends, came to awareness in altered form, their content of truth hidden from view or distorted out of conscious recognition.

As a result of the process of repression, the psychological motives of Leonardo's fantasy became condensed into a single image. That image, Freud would show, referred to the circumstances surrounding his birth and early childhood. Leonardo was born in a village outside of Florence, the illegitimate son of a young peasant woman, Caterina, and Ser Piero da Vinci, a Florentine notary. According to Freud, the fantasy, a representation of the situation of the infant sucking at the mother's breast, recreated the solitary child's first impression of pleasure. Why, however, had Leonardo's mother been represented by a vulture? Referring to the ancient Egyptians' practice of symbolizing motherhood in the form of a vulture, and their belief that all vultures were female, impregnated by the wind, Freud theorized that Leonardo had become aware of that belief through the teachings of the Church fathers, who had cited it in connection with the doctrine of the virgin birth. Leonardo's encounter with this belief awakened in him the memory of his own childhood, "which was transformed into the phantasy we have been discussing, but which meant to signify that he also had been such a vulture-child—he had had a mother, but no father."[47] The experience at the core of the fantasy was Leonardo's perception of his father's absence, and his seclusion with his mother in earliest childhood. "An inevitable effect of this state of affairs," Freud concluded, "was that the child—who was confronted in his early life with one problem more than other children—began to brood on this riddle with special intensity, and so at a tender age became a researcher, tormented as he was by the great question of where babies come from and what the father has to do with their origin."[48]

The representation of the vulture's tail in Leonardo's fantasy had a dual significance. First, it indicated more exactly the period of origin of his childhood researches. In Egyptian mythology, the vulture-headed mother goddess possessed a phallus. That mythological representation, Freud explained, corresponded to an infant boy's original assumption that both sexes possessed the male genital. When through his own observation a boy learned otherwise, he did not question his assumption, but concluded that women had suffered the fate of castration as punishment. An infant's reflections followed a period in which a large portion of sexual curiosity attached to the observation of the bodies of both sexes. Leonardo's fantasy confirmed that his libidinal attention had very early found an object in his mother: "We can now provide the following translation of the emphasis given to the vulture's tail in Leonardo's phantasy: 'That was a time when my fond curiosity was directed to my mother, and when I still believed she had a genital organ like my own.'"[49] The second significance of the image of the vulture's tail in Leonardo's mental life, Freud argued, derived from the component of homosexual feeling which through sublimation would become a dominant, but idealized, feature of the artist's erotic psychology, as expressed, for example, in his tendency toward deep, emotional attachment to his students.

The prominence in Leonardo's fantasy of the sensation against the mouth could be traced not only to the scene of the infant at the mother's breast, but also to the kisses which Leonardo's mother, left only with her son, devoted to the child. In the case of an artist, the recollection of such a powerful erotic relationship could be expected to find expression in the artist's work. One such manifestation, Freud believed, appeared in the enigmatic smile of the Mona Lisa, combining as it did contrasts of reserve and seduction, tenderness and sensuality. Such a smile adorned the figure of Mary in the *Virgin and Child and St. Anne.* The encounter with Mona Lisa del Giocondo had awakened in the artist a dormant memory: "This memory was of sufficient importance for him never to get free of it when it had once been aroused; he was continually forced to give it new expression."[50] Thus, the mnemonic image of the desolate, loving mother, Caterina, found its way into Leonardo's work, not only in the portraits of women, but also of youths, perhaps most notably John the Baptist, whose portraits Leonardo surrounded with "a mystical air into whose secret one dares not penetrate."[51] As Freud noted, in the latter paintings, the figures

> do not cast their eyes down, but gaze in mysterious triumph, as if they knew of a great achievement of happiness, about which silence must be kept. The familiar smile of fascination leads one to guess that it is a secret of love. It is possible that in these figures Leonardo has denied the unhappiness of his erotic life and has triumphed over it in his art, by representing the wishes of the boy, infatuated with his mother, as fulfilled in this blissful union of the male and female natures.[52]

Art momentarily overcame the sensation of inexpressible loss contained within Leonardo's memory.

Leonardo's scientific activity, however, followed a pattern laid down by the child's relationship to his father. Leonardo's rejection of the authority of the ancients, Freud maintained, carried into science the rebellion of the son. Furthermore, his reliance not on the support of authority, but on the observation of nature as the source of truth derived from the original unimpeded satisfaction of his curiosity toward his mother: "Only Leonardo could dispense with that support; he would not have been able to do so had he not learnt in the first years of his life to do without his father. His later scientific research, with all its boldness and independence, presupposed the existence of infantile sexual researches uninhibited by his father, and was a prolongation of them with the sexual element excluded."[53] Leonardo's rebellion extended to religion. In that regard, art and science joined in the same tendency. Just as Leonardo's scientific researches challenged assumptions of the Church, his art transformed sacred figures into representatives of intrinsically human emotions. In what concerned Leonardo's personal convictions, "the reflections in which he has recorded the deep wisdom of his last years of life breathe the resignation of the human being who subjects himself to Ἀνάγκη, to the laws of nature, and who expects no alleviation from the goodness or grace of God."[54]

In the final section of the study, Freud summarized the dynamic of repression and sublimation which underlay the inhibitions of Leonardo's artistic work and sexual life, but which also gave powerful impetus to his scientific researches. The sexual curiosity of his early childhood opened the way for the sublimation of much of his sexual impulse along the path of seeking knowledge. The early expression of his erotic drive in the relation of the infant son to his mother suffered complete repression, until in adolescence, Leonardo found an outlet for it in his art. The wave of repression which overtook his adult sexual activity, however, also reasserted itself against the artistic expression of that early libidinal component of his past. Thus, the sublimation of his sexual instincts into the investigative urge finally conquered the inclination toward artistic creation. In Leonardo, the passion for science now replaced commitment to painting. Only later in life, when he encountered a woman who reawakened in him the long forgotten memory from earliest childhood, did he experience the revival of that commitment. A deeper layer of instinct again sought expression: "With the help of the oldest of all his erotic impulses he enjoyed the triumph of once more conquering the inhibition in his art."[55]

Concluding his study of Leonardo, Freud described the goals and limits of psychoanalytic biography. It could not, he explained, give an account of the source of the capacity for sublimation, and so the ultimate foundation of artistic creativity lay beyond its scope. It could, however, explain the transformation of instincts, and in that way show "the connection along the path of instinctual activity between a person's external experiences and his reactions."[56] Toward that end, Freud emphasized, one could not underestimate the significance of the child's early experiences and impressions, however artfully disguised or hidden from view.

In Leonardo, science, as the striving for greater consciousness of nature, triumphed over art owing to a specific process of repression and sublimation. There remained, however, no doubt of the persistence of a separate function for art. Investigation did not triumph completely, as painting continued to be that means through which Leonardo fulfilled his earliest and deepest longing.

V

At this point, let us look at certain threads of Freud's psychological study in the light of Leonardo's own ideas. In this way, we can consider how Leonardo's views on painting may help elucidate Freud's own conception of art, science, and culture in the early years of the psychoanalytic movement. For justification we may recall that the artist aspiring to science and the psychoanalyst aspiring to the art of biography found common ground in the domain of images.

For Leonardo, the painter had to subject his artistic technique consciously and assiduously to the laws of nature. In fact, the more securely the painter anchored his artwork in those laws, the more singularly effective would be its light and shading, the more eloquent its perspective, the more powerful and uncommon its impression on viewers. With science and art so conceived, Freud similarly sought to construct a biographical portrait from laws of psychology, writing at the very outset of his study of Leonardo that psychiatric research into the lives and works of great figures "cannot help finding worthy of understanding everything that can be recognized in those illustrious models, and it believes there is no one so great as to be disgraced by being subject to the laws which govern both normal and pathological activity with equal cogency."[57] And he could also have described how the noble subject of that study kindly posed for him as if for a fellow craftsman.

According to Leonardo, painting deserved the name of science because visualization itself helped to free the painter from authorities of the past, and embolden the spirit of observation. Further, as the most substantial expression of the laws of nature, the intellectual and sensual fullness of the visual image conferred that immediate and authentic sense of knowledge which Leonardo considered the core of science. There exists perhaps a parallel here between Leonardo and Freud. For Freud, the dream image provided, in his famous phrase, the royal road to knowledge of the unconscious. A technique—psychoanalysis—could, by giving new attention to the image itself, and the dreamer's associations to it, begin to undo the distortions within the dream and allow insight into its psychological construction. Thus, as Freud explained in the early years of the movement, it became possible to discover the laws and content of unconscious mental processes. The psychological theory and method on which the Freudian movement had been built applied equally to images created from memory, fantasy—or art. Thus the choice of Jensen's *Gradiva* and, as we have noted, Leonardo as Freud's first subjects for applied psychoanalysis.

In their own callings, therefore, both Leonardo and Freud emphasized imagery as one of the necessary points from which analysis of nature and the mind had to proceed. For both, the image appeared as an individualized embodiment of general laws of nature, laws perceptual and psychological. In visual or mnemonic representations the artist and biographer located the presence of the universal in the manifestations of the particular, an undertaking which both Leonardo and Freud defined as scientific. Thus, the artist who aimed to make of painting a liberal, Renaissance discipline and the psychoanalyst who aimed to make of psychology a cultural science based their endeavors on the search for laws which governed the creation, reproduction, and recalling of images.

Leonardo's thought, one cannot forget, also stressed that the immediacy and the authenticity of knowledge as conveyed by visual imagery had their origins in experience. In the visual discovery and the physical representation of images, the artist thus returned from the universal to the particular. In Panofsky's phrase, the artist rendered knowledge tangible. In this sense, too, painting, according to Leonardo, rightfully claimed recognition as a science. Such a conception may be usefully applied to Freud's notion of psychoanalysis as a new scientific field. As Freud's explanations of his early work indicated, by removing psychological repression—or removing the distortion of mental images—psychoanalysis sought to render the unconscious tangible: to identify within a deeper layer of the psyche a more authentic image—reproducible in biography—and to give a particularized account of universal psychical motives. To confer on the unconscious that quality of experience which Leonardo believed was elicited by the art—and science—of painting Freud himself likened to the work of a sculptor. For Freud, Leonardo's childhood memory provided the material with which the biographical sculptor could carve the image of a mother's smile; and, like all sculpted portraits, that image contained within itself further, inchoate depths. Unlike the single, stone image buried with the sculptor's marble—or confined within the ruins of the ancient past—imagery from the unconscious derived from a protean source.[58]

We must acknowledge, however, the limits of our comparison between the artist and biographer, the first of which is the general necessity in psychoanalysis for translating images into words. Further, in the specific case we are considering, Freud wrote his biography of Leonardo as a study of the conflict between art and science in his subject's life and work. As Yosef Hayim Yerushalmi has pointed out, that conflict, as Freud saw it, was not specific to Leonardo, but indicative of an essential opposition.[59] Poets and researchers might recognize similar truths, but their approaches and aims necessarily drove a wedge between their pursuits. That division between art and science traceable to the end of the Renaissance and culminating in the nineteenth-century opposition between the Romantic poet and trained investigator was not only ingrained within Freud's professional training, but, as Yerushalmi has stated, essential to his definition of psychoanalysis as a new science. Freud was at pains to distinguish the psychoanalyst from the artist possessed by "divine madness," daemonic inspiration, or even simple inventive intuition. In other words, he carefully and consistently distanced the figure of the psychoanalyst from that model of the artist which emerged toward the close of the Renaissance with the revival of the notion of genius. Psychoanalysis originated as, and remained, a body of knowledge and a theory of the mind built upon the foundation of an interpretive method confirmable in experience, and teachable as a technique of research and therapy.

In applying Leonardo's ideas to Freud's work, we have, then, been applying older notions of art and science, but with the hope that they might still cast some light on our subject. To be sure, Leonardo's conception of painting as a science applied to visual images, whether from nature or art, which have no counterpart among those psychological phenomena which were Freud's chief concern. We are reminded here of the issue with which Freud grappled throughout his career: how to visualize the structure and content of the unconscious. In *The Interpretation of Dreams*, he introduced a topographical description—a landscape, if you will—of the unconscious and conscious mental regions, and the preconscious boundary between them. Such a description proved necessary in order to envision the depth of psychic forces together with their dynamics. During his career, as is well known, Freud also frequently applied visual analogies available from archaeology to offer an image of the psychic stratification of the mind and the survival of the unconscious in mental life. In these instances, the visual not only functioned as metaphor, but also organized and transmitted unfamiliar information and insight. Leonardo had transformed the visual image into an essential bridge between old sciences and new, and such it became in its own way for Freud, as both a graphic metaphor and a conduit of knowledge.

Finally, as we have seen, Freud's biography itself drew attention to Leonardo's respect for *Ananke*—necessity—as essential to his view of nature. In his conclusion, Freud revisited that point so as to propose a final context within which to see Leonardo's life and work. That context came not from modern psychology, but the Italian Renaissance. Bringing his study to a close, Freud returned Leonardo to his time, asking the reader to consider psychoanalytic biography from within the worldview of that day. According to that view, *Necessità* and *Fortuna*, immovable, hostile, or capricious, confronted humanity, widening the scope for human action and agency, but exacting sacrifice and retribution. Leonardo, Freud had stressed, came to recognize in the force of necessity the operation of the laws of nature. But what of the role of fortune in human affairs, specifically in the life of Leonardo himself? "But may one not take objection to the findings of an enquiry which ascribes to accidental circumstances of his parental constellation so decisive an influence on a person's fate," began Freud's concluding thoughts on Leonardo.[60] "I think one has no right to do so. If one considers chance to be unworthy of determining our fate, it is simply a relapse into the pious view of the Universe which Leonardo himself was on the way to overcoming when he wrote that the sun does not move."[61] Destiny is joined to chance, "chance which nevertheless has a share in the law and necessity of nature, and which merely lacks any connection with our wishes and illusions."[62] Mindful of how Leonardo himself once gave expression to his inspiration as both an artist and a scientist, Freud in closing observed, "We all still show too little respect for Nature which (in the obscure words of Leonardo which recall Hamlet's lines) 'is full of countless causes ['*ragioni*'] that never enter experience'."[63] Thus, Freud drew the reader's attention to the Renaissance conception of science and the world, not only to assist a closer psychological understanding of Leonardo, but to elucidate the psychoanalytic approach to biography.

That approach, as we have seen, emerged in part from the debates over art and science that took place within Freud's Viennese circle. In fact, Freud expressed through his biography of Leonardo his conviction, enunciated to the members of the Vienna Psychoanalytic Society, that the artist who turned to science did so to the peril of his art. Yet, Freud argued, both to the society and in his study of Leonardo, that within the wider culture the psychology of art would not interfere with aesthetic creativity and production. The laws of necessity and the workings of chance would, as had always been true, continue to rule over the destiny of art.

Of equal importance to Freud, the study of Leonardo demonstrated how the application of psychology to art confirmed psychoanalysis as a new science of the mind and culture. Not merely in his psychological portrait of Leonardo, but also through his own analysis of the content of visual representation, Freud offered psychoanalytic technique as a method of cultural science. Further, through the analysis of mnemonic images, he identified pathways between inward experience, artistic creativity, and biographical events. Here we should recall that the first psychoanalytic journal for the study of the humanities and social sciences, founded within the Viennese movement, received the title *Imago*. The concept imago would—to borrow a term from the art historian, Aby Warburg—refer to the afterlife of a psychological image in the world of external events. And just as Freud redefined the boundaries of applied psychoanalysis through his study of Leonardo, so in the first issue of *Imago* he would reconceive the psychological exploration of culture through *Totem and Taboo*. In the life of Leonardo, the image emerged from inward fantasy and memory to express itself in painting. In the life of society as presented in *Totem and Taboo*, it emerged from a communal and historic event, and survived in mimetic form across generations. From the Renaissance studio to the ancient amphitheater, from Mona Lisa's secretive smile to the mask of tragedy, the way led from the exploration of individual creativity to the study of society.

Before turning to the Freudian analysis of community, however, we should perhaps consider once more Max Graf's reflections on the psychology of poets. In discussing the application of psychoanalysis to the artist, was Graf perhaps reviving that older notion of art as the exercise of a craft, and of science as the discovery and enunciation of knowledge? Listening to Graf's presentation, perhaps Freud was reminded of such notions. We cannot, of course, know whether such was the case, any more than we can know what Freud may have thought when he first saw Leonardo da Vinci's paintings in the Louvre, those paintings which later became the subject of his Renaissance biography. Perhaps, however, while working on his study of the life and work of Leonardo, he took solace in remembering that he was not the first to defend a new, practical technique as a scientific advance, and not merely an art.

SIX

DRAMA AND COMMUNITY

I

In March 1912, the first issue of *Imago* left the printer. From its conception and organization to its production and distribution, *Imago* remained a venture of the Viennese psychoanalytic movement. Otto Rank and Hanns Sachs served as editors, Hugo Heller's firm published it, and Sigmund Freud held the position of director and general editor. Perhaps most significantly, in its subtitle, *Zeitschrift für Anwendung der Psychoanalyse auf die Geisteswissenschaften*— Journal for the Application of Psychoanalysis to the Cultural Sciences—the journal gave embodiment to the impulses and aspirations of the cause in Vienna.

The creation of *Imago* had followed two years of unsettling turmoil within the Vienna Psychoanalytic Society itself. Throughout 1910, the differences between Freudian and Adlerian psychology continued to grow such that the society was forced to confront the division in a series of meetings early the following year. In the summer of 1911, the schism became complete with Freud's demand that Adler resign as editor of the first psychoanalytic journal, *Zentralblatt*, and Adler's decision to form a psychological society devoted to his new theories.

The troubles in Vienna, however, were soon followed by tremors from Zurich. In September 1911, Freud read the first part of Carl Jung's *Wandlungen und Symbole der Libido*, finding in it, despite nascent misgivings, reasons to confirm his judgment that Jung should succeed to the leadership of the international psychoanalytic movement. The second part of Jung's work, however, produced a radically different impression. Reaching Freud in September 1912, it initiated the final break between the two.

There can be little doubt that after Hanns Sachs first approached him with the idea to found a journal for applied psychoanalysis, Freud came to regard the project as an important consolidation of the movement. In fact, so much so that in November 1911 he wrote to Jung requesting his support for the new journal: "For it is another of the possessions that I hope to pass on to you one day."[1] At the time of that letter, Freud was completing his first essays on totemism, essays which he yet believed would find strong support in Jung's own research into collective psychology, and which he intended as his own contribution to the new publication of the Viennese circle.

In 1913, having contributed to *Imago* four essays on early forms of religion and society, Freud published the essays together as *Totem and Taboo*, in this way bringing to its culmination the psychoanalytic study of culture prior to the First World War. In *Totem and Taboo*, Freud returned to that historical interest which had led him in the Louvre to concentrate his attention first on the museum's ancient sculptures, rather than on the art of the Renaissance masters. Specifically, he now sought to apply that program for historical study which he had enunciated some years earlier when to his Viennese circle he had described the process of history as the deepening of psychological repression accompanied by the advance of conscious recognition. With *Totem and Taboo*, Freud determined to trace through psychoanalysis the origins and earliest acts of that process.

Grounded to a significant degree in the initial Viennese approach to culture, *Totem and Taboo*, it must also be remembered, marked a new direction. Through biography, Freud had depicted the return of a repressed image in the smile of the Mona Lisa, interpreting in the work of art the sublime visual residue of a profound inward experience. With *Totem and Taboo*, Freud explored in communal organization and behavior the residues of a primal, historical action, a deed whose unconscious meaning survived within both the individual and the community through the psychological impulses which had generated it, and through its mimetic reenactment in ritualized forms. The imitation of an action: civilization originated as a drama in history. For Freud, the study of the image led to the study of that drama; along this path, the Viennese Freudian movement began to move from the examination of art to the examination of society. By shifting the focus of inquiry, Freud introduced to the movement a new psychoanalytic investigation of culture. From the perspective of *Totem and Taboo*, culture expressed the drama of community lost and regained.[2]

II

In March 1910, the Nuremberg psychoanalytic congress called for the creation of an international organization. Branch societies would be chartered and affiliated through an International Psychoanalytic Association, whose president, as Freud had planned, would be Jung, and whose administrative headquarters would be Zurich. In October 1910, the Vienna Psychoanalytic Society constituted itself, in accordance with the decision taken at Nuremberg and the requirements of Austrian law, as a chapter of the new association.[3] In the same month, its meetings moved from Freud's home to the College of Physicians in the heart of the old city.[4] Further, the members voted at that time that the society institute a series of monthly lectures on psychoanalysis open to colleagues and the public.[5] During the year, 1910-11, the group's general membership reached thirty-two, its highest number before the war.[6] Yet, even as the Viennese gradually expanded their contacts with the outside world, they suffered a crisis of internal unity.

In 1910, the opposition between the psychological theories of Freud and Adler became irreconcilable. As we have seen, Adler's first articles on childhood education described how a cohesive ego emerged from the sublimation of desire, and how libidinal impulse mediated relations between the ego and the external world. Now Adler emphasized the will and aggressive assertion, even desperation, of the ego itself as the motive force of psychological development, to the extent that he characterized repressed desire, or impulses of longing, as mental fictions. By the fall of 1910, neither

Freud nor Adler had expectations of combining their views within the movement.

The true extent of the difference between Adler and Freud began to appear in Adler's essay, "Psychic Hermaphroditism in Life and Neurosis," which he presented to the Vienna Society in February 1910, and published in the journal *Fortschritte der Medizin* in the same year.[7] In his presentation to the society, Adler stated that children, male and female, experienced their dependence, personal deficiencies, and inhibitions of will as signs of inferiority and identified such traits as feminine. They endeavored to compensate for them through a will to dominate, which Adler labeled in both men and women the masculine protest. That protest not only could take the form of aggression, ambition, or competitiveness, but also neurotic defensiveness and sensitivity. Neurosis, arising from the struggle between the feeling of inferiority and overcompensation, could be interpreted as an exaggerated or compulsive reaction of the masculine protest. In his response to the paper, Freud replied that Adler's formulation not only disguised instinctual dynamics of neurosis, but suffered from a narrowness of language: "But the concepts of 'masculine' and 'feminine' are of no use in psychology and we do better, in view of the findings of the psychology of the neuroses, to employ the concepts of libido and repression."[8] What Adler described in his presentation as a masculine protest, Freud commented, referred to "the striving to fulfill a wish, and this striving is a matter of libido, is active."[9]

By the fall of 1910, the opportunity for reconciliation between Freud and Adler had passed. In the inaugural issue of the psychoanalytic journal *Zentralblatt*, Adler published the first in a series of articles questioning not only the libido theory, but also the theories of repression and the Oedipal complex. For Freud, the period of watching and waiting had come to an end. In November 1910, the society's minutes record, "Hitschmann moves that Adler's theories be for once thoroughly discussed in their interconnections, with particular attention to their divergence from Freud's doctrine, so that there may be achieved, if possible, a fusion of the two views, or at least a clarification of the differences between them."[10] Neither Freud nor Adler, however, saw such a discussion as a means of reconciling their views. Rather, they both perceived it as necessary to establish their own positions. "Adler," the minutes state, "declares his readiness to discuss the question, but thinks that Hitschmann's wish cannot be so easily fulfilled."[11] "Prof. Freud," they continue, "would like to modify the motion to the effect that only one aspect of Adler's views be discussed—one that does not seem to him to have been clarified, i.e., the relationship of the 'masculine protest' to the doctrine of repression, which in Adler's writings plays no role."[12] Freud's proposal was accepted, and in January and February 1911, Adler delivered two papers to the society based on his most recent publications.

The first two articles which Adler published in the *Zentralblatt*, "The Psychic Treatment of Trigeminal Neuralgia" and "On the Masculine Attitude in Female Neurotics," specifically called into question the libido theory. The first article reaffirmed that neurosis resulted from "a feeling of inferiority, compensated by the masculine protest."[13] In the characterology of neurotic children, Adler explained, defiance, obstinacy, and craving for attention existed together with anxiety and fearfulness. Both sets of traits appeared because the yearning to triumph, or "urge to dominate [*Herrschsucht*],"[14] expressed itself in the child as the desire to avoid feelings of humiliation and loss of self-esteem. To "safeguard"[15] against possible humiliation, the child became overly sensitive and mistrustful. Thus, neurotic character traits, in children and adults, represented both overcompensation and safeguarding. In Adler's view, the libidinal urges of childhood now appeared as exaggerations of instinctual activity, or even false desires. On the one hand, such urges developed as forms of compensation. From a different perspective, however, the instinctual wish expressed in the unconscious fantasies in children and neurotics represented a "fiction"[16] meant to produce fears and inhibition. The unconscious, fictitious wish came into being because it "serves the main object of the neurotic, which is to safeguard himself."[17]

Adler's second essay described the relationship in women between sexual desire and the masculine protest. In the case of one patient, the woman's feeling of inferiority had manufactured in childhood the unconscious "fiction of extremely strong libidinous strivings."[18] That invention presented "her image as that of a passionate and at the same time weak-willed girl, a depraved creature, blindly following her sexual drive,"[19] and generated in her a fear of playing the roles of wife and mother. Against this unconscious fantasy "she always defended herself with her fears and with her neuroses."[20] By way of her symptoms, Adler wrote, the patient became a dominating figure in her home. The case, Adler believed, demonstrated how neurosis arose both as a direct expression of the masculine protest, and as a device protecting the individual from feelings of inferiority.

In Adler's view, psychoanalysis had also misinterpreted the meaning of the Oedipal complex in the formation of neurosis. In a third article for the *Zentralblatt*, he maintained that the Oedipal attitude in children represented, on the one hand, an expression of the masculine protest, and on the other, a caution intended to protect the individual. Unconscious Oedipal fantasies in his patients expressed both a claim to unbounded sensuality, and a warning to secure themselves against it. Referring to the Oedipal relations of child to parent, Adler concluded, "These forms of experience [*Formen des Erlebens*], which Freud described in the clearest, most certain manner, have no driving force in themselves."[21]

The debate over Adler's views took place over four meetings in January and February 1911. The January meeting focused on the role of sexuality in neurosis. As Freud requested, the following meetings, held on three evenings in February, centered on the issue of repression. During the discussions, the debate moved from the theory of neurosis to the interpretation of culture and the aims of the movement.

In his presentation of January, 1911—"Controversial Problems of Psychoanalysis: 1. Sexuality and Neurosis"—Adler finally discarded the libido theory. He maintained that sexuality could not be considered a motive force of neurosis. The minutes record that "he sees a distortion of the libido in neurosis and in civilization, and it is because of this distortion that the libido cannot in any way be regarded uniformly as the driving factor, but must rather be seen as compounded with and artificially nourished by the masculine protest, and hence felt in an exaggerated way, either tendentiously overvalued or else reduced in value."[22] The sexual instinct, Adler maintained, did not originate as polymorphously perverse libido. He told the meeting, "Whatever libido the neurotic shows us is not genuine. Incest fantasies, for instance, far from being the core complex of the neurosis, serve the sole purpose of nurturing the subject's own belief in the superior strength and criminal tendency of the libido, thereby making it possible for him to avoid any other sexual relationship."[23] Neither could the aggressive instinct be seen as a primary, moving force, as it too derived from the masculine protest. And in the therapeutic situation, the patient's transference "is 'arranged' [*arrangiert*] as a transference of love, but as such has no genuineness. The patient is constantly in complete rebellion against his physician; the transference is the excuse and starting point for getting down to the battle."[24]

Little discussion followed this presentation. Freud, in fact, offered no response. The confrontation awaited the paper of 1 February 1911, in which Adler gave his views on the concept of repression. The discussion following this paper, which extended to two further meetings in February, ended with the first factional split within the psychoanalytic movement.

Adler's paper, "The Masculine Protest as the Central Problem of the Neurosis," asserted that the "propelling factor" of neurosis was not repression, but the "irritated psyche."[25] Adler traced the source of irritation to the ego, defining the ego instinct as "the sum total of all exertions, as a posture directed against the outside world, as a wanting to be important, as a striving for power, for dominance, for being 'on top.'"[26] In the course of adapting instincts to the external world, the ego altered them in such a way that their "gratification, and with it the quality and strength of an instinct, is at all times variable and therefore unmeasurable. The libidinal tendencies make for just as little conclusion as to the strength and composition of the sexual instinct."[27] The repression of instincts encountered in neurosis occurred due to "the increased pressure of the masculine protest," while resistance during treatment derived from the patient's desire to "devalue the physician."[28] Therapy had to proceed by making the patient aware of "the character traits of protest."[29]

In the course of the presentation, Adler also turned his attention to cultural development, noting that the presence of "protest-tendencies" throughout history had been confirmed by the acceptance of "the idea of the struggle for existence."[30] He denied the link between culture and repression as described by psychoanalysis, arguing that the Freudian explanation of cultural development was a tautology: "All repression occurs under the pressure of civilization; but where does our culture originate? Answer: From repression."[31] Adler concluded his paper by reminding the society of his argument that the ego's will power constructed instinctual desires: "One can no longer speak of a complex of libidinal wishes and fantasies; even the Oedipus complex will have to be understood as one component phenomenon of an overstrong psychic dynamic, as one stage of the masculine protest—the point of departure from which it is possible to gain more significant insights into the characterology of the neurotic."[32]

Freud responded first, and immediately removed all doubt as to his position on Adler's theory, informing the circle: "This is not psychoanalysis."[33] Addressing himself to the presentation, Freud stated that Adler's perspective would at first gain support within the movement. "Instead of psychology," he observed, "it presents, in large part, biology; instead of the psychology of the unconscious, it presents surface ego psychology. Lastly, instead of the psychology of the libido, of sexuality, it offers general psychology. It will, therefore, make use of the latent resistances that are still alive in every psychoanalyst, in order to make its influence felt."[34] Adler's system sacrificed the movement's aim of an autonomous psychology. Freud told the meeting that "our endeavor is precisely to keep psychology pure, free from any dependence—whereas Adler subjects it to biological and physiological viewpoints."[35] In sum, Adler constructed his theories from the perspective of the ego, which denied unconscious motives and rejected the demands of sexuality. "The core of neurosis," Freud emphasized, "is the ego's fear of the libido, and Adler's expositions have merely strengthened this view. It is the ego that is afraid of the libido, the libido is just as great as are its disturbing effects."[36]

Adler's theory, Freud stressed, disavowed psychoanalysis as a cultural movement. Referring not only to applied psychoanalysis, but the movement as a whole, he commented that "by adopting the new terms, we would have to suffer the loss of those terms that indicate our program and which have established our connection with the great cultural circles. The [concepts of] *suppression of instinct* and *overcoming resistance* have aroused the interest of all alert and educated people."[37] In the final meeting devoted to discussion of Adler's presentation, Freud finally responded to Adler's criticism of the psychoanalytic theory of culture, emphasizing once more how the suppression of instinct had intensified throughout history:

"Repression takes place in the individual and is demanded by the claims of civilization. What then, is civilization? It is the precipitate of the work of repression carried on by all preceding generations. The individual is required to carry out all the repressions that have already been carried out before him."[38] In *Totem and Taboo*, Freud would trace those processes to the historical act which set them in motion.

Throughout the debate over Adler's ideas, members of the Vienna Psychoanalytic Society defended the concept of instinctual repression as the foundation of depth psychology. Rudolf Reitler referred the meeting to his refutation of Adler in the *Zentralblatt*, which was to appear the following month. In that article, he emphasized that psychic conflicts in neurosis originated in the struggle between "instinctual impulses which derived from infantile sexuality"—and which could not be characterized as either masculine or feminine—and the "cultural ego consciousness."[39] Reitler observed, "Both the feeling of inferiority and its counterpart, the 'masculine protest' are a characterological product of the psychic illness, however, not its cause."[40] Adler's insight "extends itself merely along the surface, without penetrating into the depths."[41] Victor Tausk put forward the question: " 'Who is protesting?' Obviously it is someone who is becoming suppressed, and this can indeed be only an instinct."[42] Paul Federn commented that Adler had attributed to the ego an urge belonging to "the ungratified libido."[43]

According to Eduard Hitschmann, Adler's system reflected the progress of repression in contemporary culture. "In denying the power of the sexual, by pointing out that sexuality no longer plays a prominent role in civilized man, Adler overlooks the fact that it is precisely this condition that must lead to a neurosis."[44] Maxim Steiner believed that Adler's theory represented a renewed effort at suppression at the moment of rebellion: "Since his valuable study on organ inferiority, Adler has deviated more and more from Freud's doctrine; his turning away from sexuality, which is reminiscent of the early Christians, seems downright anachronistic today, when we, in a kind of Renaissance, are trying to link up with the sensual joys of the ancients."[45]

Wilhelm Stekel could not accept Adler's abandonment of the theory of repression, but explained that he too had now adopted a different conception of instincts and the Oedipus complex. "Behind the sexual element stands a second instinct, which Adler calls 'aggression' and he himself calls 'criminality.' The primary factor to him is no longer love, but hate; excess of love is nothing but overcompensation for primary hatred."[46] Adler's system was, according to Stekel, "simply a structure built on Freud's foundation."[47]

The minutes record Freud's final stance: "Prof. Freud considers Adler's doctrines to be wrong and, as far as the development of psychoanalysis is concerned, dangerous."[48] Stekel's response, he explained, ignored the situation: "While Stekel asserts that he does not see any contradiction between Adler's views and Freud's doctrines, one has to point out that two of the persons involved do find this contradiction: Adler and Freud."[49]

The members of the society still resisted a formal split in their original ranks. Over Freud's objection and despite the criticisms expressed at previous meetings, the group passed a resolution which "would refuse to acknowledge any incompatibility."[50] According to Ernest Jones, after the society's meetings concluded for the year, Freud asked Adler to withdraw as editor of the *Zentralblatt*.[51] Writing to Jung, Freud explained that only after he urged J. F. Bergmann, the German publisher of the journal, to remove him, did Adler relinquish the editorship, submitting his resignation from the society at the same time.[52] During the summer, Adler founded a new circle, the "Society for Free Psychoanalytic Investigation," later renamed the "Society for Individual Psychology." In the fall, the Vienna Society passed a resolution declaring membership in Adler's organization to be "incompatible with membership in the Psychoanalytic Association."[53] The first break in the unity of the cause had now been acknowledged.

III

Independently of the controversy surrounding Adler, in 1910 and 1911 Freud's original circle underwent further significant, if less visible and painful, changes. Perhaps as early as the society's discussion of his book *The Sexual Need*, in 1908, Fritz Wittels felt at odds with the movement's rejection of the role of moral vanguard. His resignation was announced in October 1910.[54] David Bach had attended the first international congress in Salzburg in 1908, and published his review of *Elektra* in March 1909. He participated, however, in only two meetings of the Vienna Society in 1909 and

1910. Freud announced Bach's official resignation in October 1911.[55] Finally, the year 1910 saw Max Graf gradually withdraw from the work of the movement. Graf's book on the psychology of creativity appeared in 1910, and his psychoanalytic pamphlet on Wagner in 1911. In 1909, Freud had asked him to accept as his next project an essay on "the theme of 'Mozart and his Relationship to Don Juan.' "[56] Graf, however, did not pursue the idea. After the fall of 1910, he attended meetings of the society on only three occasions. During 1913, he resigned from the gatherings.[57] Perhaps some insight into his motives can be gained from his reaction years earlier to the first discussions on restructuring the society: "These proposals to reorganize stem from a feeling of uneasiness. We no longer are the type of gathering we once were. Although we are still guests of the Professor, we are about to become an organization."[58] According to Graf—perhaps according to Bach and Wittels as well—the members' sense of commitment to a cause did not survive the transformation of the society.

Yet, even as the circle lost these writers, it acquired new members from the younger generation of culture critics, students whose education—or self-education—had included an introduction to psychoanalysis. Having attended Freud's lectures at the amphitheater for two years, Hanns Sachs finally introduced himself to Freud in 1910, and joined the society in October of that year.[59] Soon thereafter he suggested to Freud the creation of a journal for applied psychoanalysis. In June 1911, when Freud wrote to Jung introducing Sachs to him, the project had begun, with Sachs and Otto Rank as editors.[60]

The founding of *Imago* provided a new Viennese base from which to expand the cause. The new journal not only offered a consistent venue for the psychoanalytic study of culture, but a point of entry into the movement. Alfred von Winterstein, who joined the society in October 1910, soon contributed to *Imago* his first psychoanalytic work. In November 1911, Theodor Reik became a member of the circle while still a student of literature and psychology at the University of Vienna. In his second semester at the university, summer 1908, Reik had attended Friedrich Jodl's "Fundamentals of Psychology."[61] During a lecture on Wilhelm Wundt's laws of empirical association, Jodl "mentioned offhandedly, with a keen ironic smile, that there was one instructor in our city who asserted that there was a type of forgetting that did not follow Wundt's laws, but the laws of a psychic process he called repression."[62] Reik gave no more serious attention to Freud's ideas than had Jodl in his lecture until he came across a copy of *The Interpretation of Dreams*. Upon completing the book, Reik "in the following week read everything that Freud had published."[63] During the next two years, Reik sat in on Freud's lectures, and finally introduced himself to Freud. With *Imago* in preparation, Freud advised Reik to begin his career not as a psychoanalytic physician, but as a psychoanalytic researcher.[64]

In the autumn of 1911, when Reik joined the Vienna Society, Freud was attempting to bring the search for a publisher for *Imago* to a close. He had first approached Franz Deuticke in Leipzig, publisher not only of the psychoanalytic *Jahrbuch*, but the *Papers on Applied Psychology*, which Deuticke had taken over from Hugo Heller in 1908 after Freud had become dissatisfied with Heller's firm.[65] In October 1911, Deuticke rejected a periodical for applied psychoanalysis as too great a financial risk. During the remainder of the month, Freud received refusals from J. F. Bergmann and two prestigious medical publishing concerns, J. A. Barth, and Urban and Schwarzenberg.[66] Freud finally turned to Heller. On 12 November 1911, he wrote to Jung that "I have made no headway with the new non-medical journal. Heller won't publish it either. But I still don't want to abandon the plan."[67] Heller, however, changed his mind; on 14 November, Freud wrote Jung the news: "It gives me pleasure to inform you that the new ΨA journal was founded yesterday by Sachs and Rank as editors, Heller as publisher, and myself."[68] Two days later, he wrote again to Jung, asking to be relieved as a reviewer for the *Jahrbuch*, as "I am consumed by the new project."[69]

Throughout the initial stages of preparation, Freud, following Stekel's suggestion, referred to the new journal as "Eros and Psyche."[70] Before the first issue was sent to the printer in January 1912, however, he accepted Sachs's proposal, *Imago*, and under that title the journal appeared on 28 March 1912.[71] Freud explained his reasoning to Jung: "we need a handy name that doesn't sound too literary."[72] The creation of *Imago*, according to Freud, secured the nonmedical foundation of the movement, and he advised Jung that the "'secularization' of ΨA is of no great moment now that we are bringing *Imago* into existence."[73] Yet, writing to Ernest Jones,

Freud expressed his concern for the survival of a psychoanalytic cultural science: "I am glad you take an interest in *Imago* which I fear will not have so easy a career as the other organs have met with."[74]

Within the psychoanalytic movement, Jung had introduced the Latin term *imago* in the first part of his *Wandlungen und Symbole der Libido*, published in 1911.[75] There he described how in the mental life of the individual "an erotic impression, to which conscious acknowledgment is denied, usurps an earlier and discarded transference and expresses itself in that."[76] That early transference, which now became revived, Jung termed the imago. In religious and mythological thought, he wrote, "the idea of the masculine creative deity is a derivation, analytically and historically psychologic, of the 'Father-Imago.'"[77] Jung noted that the Swiss writer Carl Spitteler had already indicated the significance of the imago as a "psychologically conceived creation" in his novel of the same name.[78]

In his memoirs, Sachs recalled that Spitteler's novel had inspired him to choose the title *Imago*.[79] In an article on the Swiss author which he contributed to the new journal, he clarified the link between the Viennese *Imago* and that of the novelist. In his essay, Sachs defined imago as a "memory image [*Erinnerungsbild*] preserved in unconscious fantasy"[80]—what, as we have seen, Freud had explored through the bas-relief of Gradiva and the smile of the Mona Lisa. Spitteler had demonstrated the influence of such a "model [*Vorbild*]" in the life and art of his novel's hero:

> *Imago* is the story of a love returning from repression, which first appears disguised as avoidance and contempt, then struggles for expression through dreams and through 'conversion into the somatic,' until it makes its way again into consciousness. But the uniqueness of the book is not the description of the battle with resistance—splendid, by the way, in all details—rather the fictional realization [*Gestaltung*] of the idea that for the individual mired in inner conflict the love object is no longer exclusively the beloved person, but with and beyond that person, those figures which the individual's fantasy has itself produced after its own image of the beloved. . . . Victor, the hero of the novel, forms out of all his thoughts and wishes figures which acquire independent life for him—a madman then, if he were not a poet.[81]

In January 1912, Freud first employed the term imago in his own writings to help clarify the phenomenon of transference in analytic therapy. The libidinal cathexis which the patient transferred

onto the therapist, Freud explained, invariably built upon an unconscious "prototype" or imago from childhood. Thus, "the cathexis will introduce the doctor into one of the psychical 'series'
which the patient has already formed."[82] The construction of the
transference conformed to the pattern of the psychoneuroses, in
which "libido whether (wholly or in part) has entered on a regres-
sive course and has revived the subject's infantile imagos."[83] Later
in 1912, in an essay on the psychology of love, Freud further defined imago as a "model"[84] upon which individuals chose their love
objects.

Thus, the meaning of the word imago referred both to the psychological inventiveness of images and the influence of a prototypical model, according to which model individuals unconsciously
patterned their relations to others. Through that concept the Viennese psychoanalytic movement began to redirect itself from art to
society, from the phenomenon of inward creation to that of outward mimesis. In the interpretations of Freudian cultural science,
the unconscious imago not only initiated an emotional revival or
recathexis of a mnemonic fragment, but also acquired mimetic
form. The unconscious prototype became, so to speak, the subject
of mime: individuals enacted psychological images in the attitudes
and relationships which they adopted toward the external world. In
the creations of the poet, the love life of the individual, or the
transference of the patient, that internally generated prototype
provided a foundation for the mimetic portrayal and reliving of an
emotion. In his study of Leonardo, Freud had drawn attention to
the mnemonic and artistic expression of an imago from the life of
the painter. Now the Viennese project associated with the new
journal would in part track the wider cultural influences and enactments of such images. That project required a nonliterary title not
only to assert its scientific basis, but to emphasize the diverse creative and mimetic roles of mnemonic fragments. For Freud, the
journal would become the forum in which he would extend the notion of mimesis beyond the reexperiencing of an emotion to include the imitation of a particular, historical action. Thus did the
Freudian interpretation of art gradually open a path to the exploration of society and the communal past.

Indeed, in the journal's inaugural issue, Rank and Sachs described an ambitious intellectual program for *Imago*, stating that

"all constructions [*Gestaltungen*] which mankind created as the expressions of immortal wishes and affects" comprised the subject matter of the cultural sciences [*Geisteswissenschaften*].[85] Psychoanalysis explored the common ground of those sciences: the relation of such formations to psychological life. In exploring culture through its images, however, Freudianism arrived at the problem of interpreting society itself. So Hanns Sachs concluded in a lecture which he delivered in February 1912, the month before *Imago* was to appear, to the Viennese Sociological Society, a circle founded and led by Max Adler and other Social Democratic scholars for the discussion and formulation of social theory.[86] Entitling his presentation "The Meaning of Psychoanalysis for Problems in Sociology," Sachs indicated that psychoanalytic investigation had become essential to exploring "those sociological problems tied to the beginnings of social organization"[87]: What were the original motives of unity among men? What were the principles of organization and authority in the first communities? Finally, what was the first desire to be renounced for the community? Such were the questions addressed by Freud in *Totem and Taboo*, which he had already determined to publish in *Imago*.

IV

Before turning to *Totem and Taboo*, we must first consider how at this time Freud's Viennese followers applied psychoanalysis to the study of culture, and themselves put *Imago* to use. Not surprisingly, in the pages of the new journal they reinvestigated the crisis of responsibility. In his first contribution, Sachs confronted that crisis by examining one of the ideals of *Bildung*, specifically, the humanist feeling for nature—in his words, an essential modern "criterion of the cultural development of the personality."[88] His analysis of that ideal charted not only the advance of psychological repression, but also a simultaneous retreat from the moral aspirations of liberalism.

The feeling for nature, Sachs began, could be traced to the ancient world, where, from the animistic to the classical period, it was expressed in the personification of natural objects and the emotions attaching to them. Such projections of the ego came into being through the transference onto the external world of repressed narcissistic libido—that portion of libido which Freud had described as having originally been directed toward the self. The share of libido which attached to personified natural objects made itself felt as a conscious conviction in their reality.

The transformation of the feeling for nature marked one of the stages in the making of the modern mind, a transformation which, according to Sachs, "signifies a reorientation [*Umschwung*] in almost every field of educated Europe's intellectual activity," beginning with Rousseau, and extending from the *Sturm und Drang* and Romantic period to contemporary naturalism.[89] "The ancient world values the object toward which the feeling for nature is directed, not the feeling itself," Sachs wrote, "the modern values the feeling, and the object is indifferent to it."[90]

The modern attitude came into being as "a consequence of the heightened repression."[91] Value had been withdrawn from sexual drives, and once forced below, could transfer safely to nonsexual objects. The return of repressed impulses, however, could be found in the overvaluation of the feeling for nature, and its attachment to more objects. That modern feeling bore a direct connection to political and intellectual upheaval at the turn of the nineteenth century. When individuals "had to learn to be virtuous, atheistic, and free," libido that thus became detached from traditional religious and social objects "had to find application elsewhere if it were not to destroy the entire mechanism of culture."[92]

The contemporary mind objectified or generalized the feeling for nature itself. Unlike the ancient attitude, which found in nature the embodiments of human desires, that generalized reaction or *Stimmung* refused to discriminate among its objects, thus debasing the expression of individual passion. In Sachs's words, when "persons of only somewhat similar emotional disposition confront the identical natural drama, they will find themselves in the same emotional situation, because the sensations which they have projected onto nature have shed their individual characteristics."[93] "What once seemed to the human race more substantial than any reality," he continued, "what was to it higher and more holy than earthly hates and loves, today has sunk to the level of a plaything, which the soul may seize only at that moment when the cares of the day have been set aside."[94] In contrast, the ancient response to nature provided the "possibility of fundamental abreaction."[95] The problem of the feeling for nature, Sachs concluded, exemplified the moral and psychological condition of his day:

> In singular contrast to the esteem accorded the feeling for nature stands the fact that all important social functions were withdrawn from it; between the official valuation of an affect in a specific cultural milieu, and its real significance for it, there exists absolutely no connection. . . . Therein the feeling for nature gives us a small section from the picture of our time, which cannot do enough toward the care and admiration of emotional life, but hardly anywhere grants it full scope.[96]

For Sachs, the modern feeling for nature had originally embodied the sublimation of impulse necessary to *Bildung*, that concentration of passion necessary to the development of individuals "virtuous, atheistic, and free." By the end of the nineteenth century, however, that feeling produced among the educated bourgeoisie a uniform recreation, a diffuse emotional response which masked the repression of instinct. The progress of suppression had undermined the aspiration toward the sublime, the humanist union of moral responsibility and intense passion. Here, we find in Sachs a concern not only for the repression, but also the corruption, of feeling. Perhaps here we find as well, if only indirectly, Freud and Kraus still united in a single cause.

In Alfred von Winterstein, who published his "Psychoanalytic Observations on the History of Philosophy" in *Imago*, one can see how the demand of his generation for a Nietzchean revaluation of values inspired the Freudian science of culture. As Winterstein explained, philosophic systems gave intellectual form to images from the unconscious, and thus represented systems of psychological valuation. In analyzing those psychical systems, he focused particular attention on idealist philosophies. From the perspective of cultural history, the movement toward idealism received impetus from the "thrust of repression"[97] which overtook the cult of Dionysos and fostered Orphic rites of purification. According to Winterstein, however, "service to Dionysos and the asceticism of the great reformers in reality aimed at the same goal. For there are two possibilities for finishing with the sexuality which burdens one: either one represses his libido or one rids oneself of it through continuous transference onto external reality."[98] Philosophies which exalted the "valuation of pure intellectual reality"[99] drew on those quantities of libido which the individual had detached from the external world and fastened to conscious thought processes. Yet, materialist thought, which emphasized physical reality and sense experience, also demonstrated the continued advance of repression by seeking, as did idealism, "to abolish [*aufheben*] the difference between the psychological and the physical."[100] Winterstein noted further that philosophic constructs reflected the psychical process of their origins, for example: "Genuine 'worldviews' are perhaps merely the creations of this visual type, to which the poetic type is so closely related."[101] In the case of "visualizers [*Schauern*]," he suggested that "a regression takes place from thoughts to images, while the poet, conversely, seeks to obtain from images a connection in thought."[102]

Psychoanalysis had a "purely negative"[103] task in relation to philosophic systems. As a "purely psychologically oriented science," it treated "the content of intellectual knowledge [*Erkenntnisinhalt*]" as "psychic evidence," and sought only the "individual and general conditions of origin" of such awareness: "an assessment from the point of view of a theory of knowledge is far from its intention."[104] Following Nietzsche, Freudianism examined philosophic ideas in light of the psychic needs they answered, or the personal conditions of life they created.[105] Such an examination required recognition of "a psychical unconscious," what "Freud calls, in the sense of a value—not existential—judgment, the genuine psychical reality."[106]

In his book on Arthur Schnitzler, published in 1913, Theodor Reik explored the crisis of values and the sense of moral betrayal as fundamental components of generational tension in Vienna. Schnitzler depicted the rebellion of the sons against the fathers of Austria's liberal era. A vague, deeply-rooted longing, or "instinctive life-impulse [*Lebensdrang*]" impelled his rebels.[107] Yet, the father-imago as depicted by Schnitzler demonstrated that the revolt against the fathers also contained a moral protest against compromised liberalism.[108] The novelist exposed sham liberalism, which, "glossed over by a thin layer of liberality and humanity, made a deep bow to the old order of things."[109] The bitterness of the sons surfaced in the image of the father as betrayer of liberal ideals.

Still, Schnitzler's work evidenced the emotional ambivalence which Viennese youths felt toward their elders. One of the chief subjects of his novels became those liberals and freethinkers who, caught in Vienna after the triumph of reaction in the 1870s, continued to preserve a commitment to principle, but failed to comprehend the "ultimate meaning [*letzte Konsequenzen*]" of the lost battle.[110] The inward suffering of such figures never led them to attain clarity, yet their fates demanded compassion. As in Viennese life, so in Schnitzler's writings: love toward the fathers competed with rage.[111] And in Reik's writing, there remained a concern for the possibility of generational reconciliation such as he had found expressed in the work of Beer-Hofmann.

Reik's interpretation of Schnitzler, like the essays of Sachs and Winterstein, infused psychological analysis with a persistent sense of moral crisis. The same sense of crisis also emerged from Otto Rank's chief psychoanalytic contribution before the war, *The Incest Theme in Literature and Legend*. Published in 1912, the book explored the universality of the Oedipus conflict in mythology and art. Building upon Rank's earlier work on the artist, it also traced the progress of repression and the expansion of consciousness in cultural development. Rank, however, no longer saw individual redemption as the final aim of art, nor did he as firmly believe that the psychologist would as a matter of course displace the artist. Instead, he saw the task of art as creating forms of expression corresponding to humanity's advance in consciousness.

Rank's periodization of cultural history into the primitive era, the era of mythology, and the era of art reflected his continued focus on the transformations of aesthetic consciousness. In the primitive era, he wrote, mankind knew fewer inner constraints on Oedipal impulses, but, as Freud had pointed out, that period also saw the creation of the first prohibitions and punishments for incest. The era of mythology marked the further suppression of Oedipal drives. Humanity projected those drives onto gods, heroes, and kings, dissociating itself from Oedipal wishes, yet permitting their undisguised fulfillment in myth. The instinctual gratifications given expression in collective fantasies mirrored the renunciations demanded of the individual.

During the mythological period, instinctual repression intensified, as illustrated by the treatment of the Oedipus legend itself. The myth of Oedipus became the first legend to represent both aspects of the incest complex—sexual desire toward the mother and hostility toward the father. The portrayal of the erotic source of the son's rivalry with the father expressed an advance in conscious-

ness. That the family members acted unwittingly, however, conformed to the aims of repression. The oldest form of the myth reflected a rudimentary stage of suppression, constructed as it was
from the standpoint of the son, who murdered or castrated his
father, and carried out the rape of his mother. The second form of
the legend, constructed from the perspective of the father, evidenced the advance of repressive forces. The father cast out his infant son, whose crime became justified as the fulfillment of an oracle; this patriarchal treatment of the myth required that the son
himself execute against his own person the punishment for the
crime. The final mythic version of the Oedipal legend, according
to Rank, completed the victory of the father. Although the son replaced his father at his mother's side, and was rewarded with a long
marriage and children, the hero suffered retaliation from his own
sons, who rebelled against him exactly as he had rebelled against
his own father.

From the final phase of mythological creation there emerged
the era of the artist, whose works gave expression to unconscious,
Oedipal wishes only in completely masked form. The condition
that family members not recognize each other as such marked the
starting point of artistic representation. At a further stage, the son's
desire became displaced onto a stepmother, or the conflict between
father and son appeared unmotivated, far removed from erotic rivalry. Succeeding poetic transformations left that rivalry unre-
solved, or allowed the complete triumph of the father over the son.
In the final phase of poetic development, best illustrated by Shakespeare's *Hamlet*, patricidal impulses once more came to light, but
the drama ended with the son rescuing or avenging the father.

With the psychic repression of the modern aesthetic era, however, there began to develop in response to that repression a movement toward greater consciousness. Ibsen's plays focused on ethical
or psychological struggles, but traced their origins to the family
complex. The dramas of Hauptmann, or Hofmannsthal's *Elektra*,
gave unconcealed expression on stage to the sexual impulses and
violent urges of the incest fantasy. The advance of individualiza-
tion, embodied in art, reflected the intensification of suppression,
but also the rebellion of consciousness.

Rank continued to believe that cognitive understanding of unconscious impulses led in his own day to a decline in the form and

significance of art. Psychological consciousness had usurped the role of poetic sublimation in the release of repressed impulses. "In this organic process of increasing expansion of consciousness, the psychoanalytical movement, which proceeded from the systematic expansion of consciousness to the therapeutic goal of treating specific individuals who have become neurotic, plays a highly catalytic role."[112] In Rank's view, the Freudian movement emerged at the limits of poetic creation. Once more, however, humanity required a new art.

In the view of those Viennese psychoanalysts associated with *Imago*, the Freudian science of culture responded to a crisis of moral and philosophic consciousness. Therein survived the anti-corruptionist sensibility. Initially concerned with the psychological conditions of creativity as embodied in the artist's struggle with repression, Viennese Freudians now examined as well the advance of repression and consciousness in the life of the collectivity. The progress of suppression in history, as well as in the individual, revealed itself in the moral, intellectual, and aesthetic dimensions of the current crisis. Explorations of philosophy, literature, and myth uncovered the dynamic of deepening resistance and growing consciousness in society as a whole. According to Freud, in the series of essays he contributed to *Imago*, the demands of repression and the resulting transformations of consciousness could be traced to that historic act and primal drama which brought into being communal life itself.

V

Freud's own ideas for the application of psychoanalysis to history and social theory originated at the same time as did *Imago*. In February 1911, less than a year after the appearance of his study of Leonardo, he wrote of his project to Jung, "For some weeks now I have been pregnant with a larger synthesis, and hope to be delivered of it this summer."[113] Conceiving of his project as a study of the origins and psychology of religion, Freud began in the summer of 1911 what became his first essay on totemism. That work and Jung's study of religious psychology, he believed, would reinforce each other.

The first part of Jung's volume on religion and mythology, *Wandlungen und Symbole der Libido*, appeared in the inaugural issue of the psychoanalytic *Jahrbuch* for 1911 and reached Freud in August.[114] In that essay, which Freud read the following month, Jung explored the role of libido in the origin of religions. Religious deities, he emphasized, arose from the father- and mother-imagos of childhood. Libidinal energy became detached from the parents and transferred to figures of divinity. Despite the success of that suppression, religion still treated sexuality as a danger, responding with two types of defense. One model, embodied in Christianity, imposed moral controls. The second, represented by ancient Mithraism and Renaissance sensibility, emphasized transference onto nature.

For Jung, religion ultimately depended on the process of "introversion"[115]—the withdrawal of libido from external objects and its application to objects in the unconscious. Yet, the concept of divinity also derived from the nature of libido itself, as demonstrated by the ancient worship of the sun. Symbols of the sun represented libido both as a power destructive of the individual, and as a source and active force of life. The sun-hero, who died and rose again, embodied that two-sided meaning.

Upon reading the first part of *Wandlungen und Symbole der Libido*, Freud wrote to Jung that "my conclusions are known to you."[116] Jung, he believed, was "aware that the Oedipus complex is at the root of religious feeling."[117] In the original preface to his essay on totemism, the first article published in *Imago*, Freud stressed the importance of Jung's work to the journal's project: "From the very beginning, psychoanalytic research has indicated similarities and analogies between its conclusions from the mental life of individuals, and those of collective psychology [*Völkerpsychologie*]."[118] According to Freud, a unique place belonged to Jung, who first pointed out that "the fantasy formations of certain psychologically ill patients (dementia praecox) coincided in the most striking way with the cosmogonies of ancient peoples."[119]

In September 1912, Freud read the second part of Jung's study.[120] Its publication led to the final breach between the two.

In his second essay, Jung distanced himself from the Freudian concepts of libido and the Oedipus complex. Libido, he wrote, did not have a primarily sexual meaning, but instead referred to an energy of life, or of will. That energy united urges of self-preservation and procreation. According to Jung, unconscious incestuous impulses did not derive from sexual desires, but represented the individual's wish to return to the mother and revive himself at the source of life.

Applied to religion and mythology, Jung's new interpretation saw in the life and death of the hero a symbol of return to the primal source of libido, a symbol of rejuvenation. Because libido sought to restore itself at its origins, it became fixated on the fantasy of incest as a representation of reunion with the mother. Religious symbolism detached libidinal energy from that fantasy and spiritualized it. In this way, Jung explained, religion and myth restored the personality's dynamic forces, making them serviceable to the individual.

In Jung's view, the incest prohibition expressed anxiety and resistance toward the tendency of libido to withdraw from external objects to its original source. The son created a personification of that prohibition in the figure of the father. At the same time, religious mythology depicted the son with attributes of the father, because he gave birth to himself a second time through his heroic ordeals.

With the publication of *Wandlungen und Symbole der Libido*, Jung attempted to reintroduce the problem of redemption into psychoanalytic psychology. Interpreting the search for spiritual renewal as the most compelling force of psychic development, he described cultural history as the story of mankind's striving after deliverance. By drawing psychoanalysis away from a focus on instincts and repression, he sought to unite psychological science with that striving.

Freud had begun his own studies of the origins of religion under the assumption that they would serve as a companion to Jung's work. They became instead a counterattack. When the *Imago* articles were republished as *Totem and Taboo*, they appeared with a new preface. Describing his approach as one of "applying the point of view and the findings of psycho-analysis to some unsolved problems of social psychology [*Völkerpsychologie*]," Freud sharply distinguished his procedure from that of "the writings of the Zurich school of psycho-analysis, which endeavour, on the contrary, to solve the problems of individual psychology with the help of material derived from social psychology."[121]

Freud also explicitly opposed his technique for the exploration of social psychology to the approach of Wilhelm Wundt, "which applies the hypotheses and working methods of *non*-analytic psychology to the same purposes."[122] Thus, Wundt had traced totemic worldviews and taboo practices to primitive notions of the soul and ancient demonic fears. Distancing himself from the folk psychology of Wundt, as well as from Jung's investigations of myth and symbolism, Freud turned instead to the work of James Frazer and the British anthropologists, whose findings provided much of the material for interpretation in *Totem and Taboo*. The researches of Frazer, William Robertson Smith, and others offered not only data, but a methodological perspective which Freud himself now sought to integrate with psychoanalysis. In its approach to culture, the British school of anthropology emphasized the examination of communal rites and ceremonial customs; it stressed the observation of action—or more precisely, in most cases, the records of such observation. Without adopting that school's instrumentalist interpretations, Freud adhered to its focus not only on the religious and social purposes, but also the emotional functions of ritual enactments.[123]

In 1913, through the firm of Hugo Heller, Freud published as *Totem and Taboo* the four essays which had appeared in *Imago* under the heading, "On Some Points of Agreement Between the Mental Lives of Savages and Neurotics."[124] Tracing the progress of repression in religious and social development, *Totem and Taboo* delved further into the past than had previous psychoanalytic studies. In religious images and social organization, the repressed left fragmentary signs of the original social contract, and clues to its permanent influence in communal life. From a study of religion, *Totem and Taboo* became an interpretation of the origins of community, thus bringing to culmination the work of the Viennese psychoanalytic movement before the First World War.

For Freud, the link between religion and society lay in the psychology of the Oedipus complex. The first essay of *Totem and Taboo*, "The Horror of Incest," which appeared as the first article of *Imago*, discussed the presence of that complex in the phenomenon of totemism. The totemic system joined religious and social functions which in later historical development became separated into distinct institutions. It is worth quoting in full Freud's definition of totemism. The system depended on clan structures, each of which is named after its totem. What is a totem? It is as a rule an animal (whether edible and harmless or dangerous and feared) and more rarely a plant or a natural phenomenon (such as rain or water), which stands in a peculiar relation to the whole clan. In the first place, the totem is the common ancestor of the clan; at the same time it is their guardian spirit and helper, which sends them oracles and, if dangerous to others, recognizes and spares its own children. Conversely, the clansmen are under a sacred obligation (subject to automatic sanctions) not to kill or destroy their totem and to avoid eating its flesh (or deriving benefit from it in other ways).[125]

A clan member's "relation to his totem is the basis of all his social obligations: it overrides on the one hand his tribal membership and on the other hand his blood relationships."[126]

According to Freud, the feature of immediate interest to psychoanalysis was totemism's close association with exogamy. In almost every case, totemic systems preserved *a law against persons of the same totem having sexual relations with one another and consequently against their marrying.*[127] The tie between totemism and exogamy demonstrated the existence of an especially strong horror of incest within primitive cultures. The prohibition of incest focused not simply on those with ties of blood, but on all those united by kinship through membership in the clan. Violation of that prohibition required communal punishment, "as though it were a question of averting some danger that threatened the whole community or some guilt that was pressing upon it."[128] The motive for such strict exogamy could be traced to the struggle against unconscious impulses. Psychoanalysts, Freud concluded his first essay, "have arrived at the point of regarding a child's relation to his parents, dominated as it is by incestuous longings, as the nuclear complex of neurosis. . . . It is therefore of no small importance that we are able to show that these same incestuous wishes, which are later destined to become unconscious, are still regarded by savage peoples as immediate perils against which the most severe measures of defence must be enforced."[129]

Freud's second essay, "Taboo and Emotional Ambivalence," explored the phenomenon of taboos as distant precursors of modern methods of social and religious control. Taboos possessed three interrelated meanings. In the first place, they referred to objects or conditions carrying a dual connotation of sacred or consecrated, on the one hand, and uncanny, dangerous, forbidden, or unclean, on the other. Second, the notion of taboo bore a connection to the idea that "certain persons and things are charged with a dangerous power, which can be transferred through contact with them, almost like an infection."[130] Thus, it included "everything, whether a person or a place or a thing or a transitory condition, which is the vehicle or source of this mysterious attribute."[131] Finally, the concept referred to "prohibitions arising from the same attribute."[132] Such prohibitions treated the object of taboo as unapproachable and were "mainly directed against liberty of enjoyment and against freedom of movement and communication."[133] Those who violated the prohibitions and came into contact with an object of taboo became themselves prohibited, as if they had acquired the dangerous charge. Taboo prohibitions and punishments had the character of being self-evident and automatic.

The ambivalence toward taboos, expressed by the dual attitude of veneration and horror, resulted from the conflict between an unconscious impulse and conscious prohibition. In the case of obsessional neurosis, the strength of the prohibition conformed to the persistence of the unconscious desire. As the aims of that desire shifted to substitutes, the prohibitions themselves shifted objects. Taboos arose from the same process. They derived from the prohibition of activities dating from the primordial past, the inclination toward which remained in the unconscious. The dangerous force of taboos arose from "the power of reminding a man of his own prohibited wishes and the apparently more important one of inducing him to transgress the prohibition in obedience to those wishes."[134] The violation of taboos required an act of renunciation as the means of atonement. Such a demand, Freud stated, "shows that renunciation lies at the basis of obedience to taboo."[135]

Verification of this explanation could be found in the taboo practices surrounding kings and the dead. The taboos attaching to the king aimed at providing protection of his person, while simultaneously guarding his subjects from him. The dual attitude of solicitude and mistrust demonstrated that beneath conscious veneration there persisted unconscious hostility. The same emotional position characterized a child's attitude toward the father. The presence of hostility, concealed beneath feelings of tenderness, offered the prototype of ambivalence. The identical configuration explained taboos surrounding the dead and their mourners. Such taboos centered on the belief that spirits of the dead turned hostile toward the living. Those spirits or demons, however, were the projected images of hostile feelings toward the deceased, feelings which remained unconscious to survivors beneath their pain and sense of loss.

Freud contrasted the societal meanings of taboo to the personal mechanisms and prohibitions characteristic of neurosis. For violations of taboos the community meted out punishment, if such punishment had not followed automatically. The motive for common action derived from the temptation to follow the violator's example: "In order to keep the temptation down, the envied transgressor must be deprived of the fruit of his enterprise; and the punishment will not infrequently give those who carry it out an opportunity of committing the same outrage under colour of an act of expiation. This is indeed one of the foundations of the human penal system and it is based, no doubt correctly, on the assumption that the prohibited impulses are present alike in the criminal and in the avenging community."[136] Social feeling itself arose from a combination of sublimated erotic impulses and egoistic motives of self-preservation. Where neuroses appeared, social instincts had not successfully replaced the attachment of the sexual instinct to its original aims and objects. The neuroses represented "asocial" phenomena, differing from social institutions in that they "endeavour to achieve by private means what is effected in society by collective effort."[137]

In his third essay, "Animism, Magic and the Omnipotence of Thoughts," published in *Imago* in the first issue of 1913, Freud examined animism as the first cosmology, tracing its derivation from the practice of magic. The use of magic in primitive societies reflected a belief in the omnipotence of thought, a belief characteristic of the early narcissistic stage of personal development, in which the ego, drawing libido to itself, attributed absolute power to its wishful impulses. In the case of neurosis, symptoms arose in response to what was thought or wished in the unconscious, not experienced in reality. Through a similar psychic mechanism, the practice of magic claimed for wishful impulses control over external reality. Animism, however, reflected a step toward greater psychological renunciation: "Whereas magic still reserves omnipotence solely for thoughts, animism hands some of it over to spirits and so prepares the way for the construction of a religion."[138]

Renunciation also offered the possibility of inward resolution, particularly significant "where a conflict has arisen between different impulses all of which are striving towards omnipotence—for they clearly cannot *all* become omnipotent."[139] A new stage in the progress of repression, animism offered the first intellectual worldview to attempt a conscious reconciliation of the struggle between unconscious forces.[140]

The final essay, "The Return of Totemism in Childhood," appearing in *Imago* in August 1913, enunciated Freud's theory of the origin of religion and community. The question of the relationship between totemism's religious and social functions provided its starting point. The relation of clan members to their totem defined the religious aspect of the totemic system, essential to which were both the idea of common descent from the totem figure and the prohibition against killing the totem animal. The clan structure as a system of social organization depended on the sense of kinship between all clan members, and on the institution of exogamy. Thus, the essential questions raised by the phenomenon of totemism, Freud asserted, "concern the origin of the idea of descent from the totem and the reasons for exogamy (or rather for the taboo upon incest of which exogamy is the expression), as well as the relation between these two institutions, totemic organization and prohibition of incest."[141] Those questions required that a "satisfactory explanation should be at once a historical and a psychological one. It should tell us under what conditions this peculiar institution developed and to what psychical needs in men it has given expression."[142]

The beginnings of a historical explanation of exogamy Freud found in Charles Darwin's theory of primitive social organization. According to Darwin, humanity survived in small bands, or hordes, in which the oldest and strongest male kept possession of several women and strictly guarded his rights to them. The older, dominant male protected his claims by driving younger males from the horde. Thus, Freud elaborated, "the practical consequence of the conditions obtaining in Darwin's primal horde must be exogamy for the young males."[143]

The psychological needs expressed by totemism could be explored in the return of totemic features characteristic of animal phobias in children. Such phobias showed the displacement onto an animal of fears relating to the father. To the son, the father appeared as Oedipal rival, opposing the male child's sexual desires and threatening punishment for those desires. The son's wish to take the place of his father, however, came into conflict with his feelings of affection and admiration. In consequence, the boy, although identifying with the animal of his phobia, exhibited ambivalent emotions toward it. The same features of identification and ambivalence characterized totemism. Thus, there existed justification to see in the totem animal the figure of the father. "If the totem animal is the father," Freud argued, "then the two principal ordinances of totemism, the two taboo prohibitions which constitute its core—not to kill the totem and not to have sexual relations with a woman of the same totem—coincide in their content with the two crimes of Oedipus, who killed his father and married his mother, as well as with the two primal wishes of children, the insufficient repression or the re-awakening of which forms the nucleus of perhaps every psychoneurosis."[144]

The link between the two meanings of totemism and exogamy — the historical and the psychological—gained confirmation from William Robertson Smith's hypothesis of the totem meal. According to Smith, the original form of religious sacrifice called for the killing of the totem animal. Every member of the clan joined in the act and shared the guilt for it before their god. The clan killed and consumed the sacrifice as an act of identity with each other and with their deity. The "sacramental killing and communal eating of the totem animal,"[145] Freud himself stressed, provided an occasion for both festivity and mourning. The nature of the totem sacrifice agreed, therefore, with the psychoanalytic assumption that the totem animal had attracted to itself the ambivalence originally directed toward the father.

On the bases of the psychoanalytic interpretation of the totem, the Darwinian theory of the primal horde, and the hypothesis of the totem meal, Freud offered a historical and psychological explanation of the origin of totemism. The brothers, who had been exiled from the horde, joined together, and, returning from banishment, slew the father and devoured him. The primal crime brought an end to the patriarchal horde. In unity the brothers achieved what they could not have accomplished individually. Through the act of devouring the father they sought to identify with him, as well as incorporate a portion of his strength: "The totem meal, which is perhaps mankind's earliest festival, would thus be a repetition and a commemoration of this memorable and criminal deed, which was the beginning of so many things—of social organization, of moral restrictions and of religion."[146] Ritual became an externalized memory image, an image preserved in the form of action. Not only the primal impulses of humanity, but traces of the deed itself survived in ceremonial activity and gestures. Thus did the reenactment of individual unconscious emotion and the imitation of the historic event combine in mimetic performance.

Society and religion developed from the renunciations which the brothers imposed upon themselves following the crime. Their ambivalence reasserted itself, and in a spirit of remorse and deference, they "revoked their deed by forbidding the killing of the totem, the substitute for their father; and they renounced its fruits by resigning their claim to the women who had now been set free. They thus created out of their filial sense of guilt the two fundamental taboos of totemism, which for that very reason inevitably corresponded to the two repressed wishes of the Oedipus complex."[147]

Totemic religion, grounded in the prohibition against killing the totem, derived from the brothers' effort at allaying their sense of guilt and at achieving reconciliation with the father through his substitute. Later religions depended upon both the feeling of guilt, and the attempt to appease the father through acts of obedience.[148] Totemic social structure reflected a combination of reactions generated by the primal crime. The prohibition against incest and the practice of exogamy first came into being as deferred obedience. Those taboos, however, sought also to eliminate the original sexual motive of the crime, and in that way prevent a "struggle of all against all"[149] among the brothers. Finally, the encouragement of social feeling safely revived the brothers' solidarity in the original act of rebellion: "Society was now based on complicity in the common crime."[150]

With increasing severity, sacred and communal institutions repressed not only primordial impulses, but also knowledge of the role that such motives had played in the origin of social and religious life. Despite the ever more strenuous efforts at suppression, within ancient religion and community there continually reappeared the repressed impulses and circumstances of the primal crime. Society fell under the influence of the longing for the father, and the wish on the part of the brothers to assume his role. The democratic equality of the brother clans gave way to patriarchal societies. The institution of the family recreated the primal horde, restoring to the father many of his primordial rights. With the institution of kingship, the state modeled itself on the principles of paternal authority, completing "the revenge taken by the deposed and restored father."[151]

In religion, the longing for the father and need for atonement resulted in the creation of male deities. Animal sacrifice to those deities continued to represent the historical source and psychological motives of religious practice. The "historical stratification" of events leading to the founding of religion received expression in the figure of the father as both god and sacrificial victim: "The two-fold presence of the father corresponds to the two chronologically successive meanings of the scene."[152] Further, that dual presence expressed the son's permanent ambivalence. "The importance which is everywhere, without exception, ascribed to sacrifice," Freud wrote, "lies in the fact that it offers satisfaction to the father for the outrage inflicted on him in the same act in which that deed is commemorated."[153] The memory of the first sacrifice remained with all later religions, despite efforts at its eradication. In fact, Freud stated, "at the very point at which men sought to be at the farthest distance from the motives that led to it, its undistorted reproduction emerged in the form of the sacrifice of the god."[154] Both the rebelliousness of the son and the weight of his guilt returned nearly undisguised within religion.[155]

Finally, Freud saw in the primal crime the explanation of the central problem of art: the origin of the suffering and guilt of the tragic hero. In Greek tragic drama, the hero suffered as the representative of the primal father. His guilt was, in fact, "the guilt which he had to take on himself in order to relieve the Chorus from theirs."[156] The chorus—the embodiment of the company of brothers—followed the hero's fate, and mourned his punishment: Greek tragedy portrayed the hero as fulfilling the crime for which the brothers bore original responsibility. Thus, Freud modified Nietzsche's vision of ancient drama as the Apollonian enactment of

Dionysian instinctual struggle: to the tragic miming of Oedipal impulse, he joined the masked recreation of the historic event.

In *Totem and Taboo*, Freud traced the origins of community and religion to the enactment of a drama, the reproduction in disguised or altered forms of the primal, historic action, a mimesis manifesting itself in diverse ways through social and sacred practices. The tragic example of Oedipus *tyrannus* allowed a construction of the violent, mournful scene which initiated that drama: "the beginnings of religion, morals, society and art converge in the Oedipus complex."[157] Thus, not only a historical, but also a dramatic sensibility compelled Freud to the conclusion that in fact, as Goethe had apprehended, "'in the beginning was the Deed.'"[158] The drama of civilization proceeded not only through the reliving and expiation of an emotional impulse, but through the imitation of a historical deed in the form of communal action across generations.[159]

Freud's application of individual psychology to society and religion contained two theories of historical transformation. The first, as we have seen, established the basis of a theory of historical change: the development of humanity had been ruled by the advance of repression, counteracted by the gradual expansion of consciousness. That conception of the evolution of culture led Freud and the Viennese psychoanalysts to apply psychology within a linear historical framework. The second principle, however, supported not a theory of progress, but, in the uncovering of the return of the repressed, a historical law of recurrence. Challenging liberalism's certainty of the steady advance of moral and intellectual reason, *Totem and Taboo* warned—one might say with anticorruptionist determination—not only of the continuous struggle between psychological suppression and enlightened recognition, but also of the weight of history within the suppressing forces.

Viennese anticorruptionist critics had also included those who conceived of history as a process of punishment and redemption. From Zurich, Jung had reintroduced that conception into the psychoanalytic movement, emphasizing the regenerative potential of myth and ritual, and the spiritual, no longer instinctual, energy of libido. In *Totem and Taboo*, Freud reasserted that neither the vicissitudes of libido nor the processes of history could be understood as paths toward moral or spiritual redemption.[160] The expansion of consciousness meant not the certainty of final deliverance, but the recognition of dramatic necessity.

As Freud described the process of civilization, throughout the evolution of history, in communal and religious institutions as well as in aesthetic production, the individual's unconscious impulses joined with mimetic cultural creations to preserve the memory of the primal crime and its aftermath. Disguised or distorted imitations of that decisive act, and the pathos and painful expiation to which they gave expression, became decisive means through which humanity recovered itself from the violence of the horde. The human community developed a dramatic as well as a psychological cohesion, the source of both artistic creativity and social unity. Reconstruction, however, never remained secure.[161]

It may be recalled that anticorruptionism, which had bound together the Viennese participants in *Imago* even before they had joined Freud's circle, included among its adherents those who saw history neither as the irresistible progress of moral reform nor as the scene of redemption. Anticorruptionist prophets warned of the abyss which imperiled society. Essays in *Imago* revealed that psychoanalysts continued to believe that they lived in a time of moral crisis. They did not, however, accept the apocalyptic vision of Viennese prophets. The origins of community did not contain a promise of deliverance, nor did they convey a prophetic message; instead they opened the enactment of a drama, a historical drama determined by the core complex of individual psychology, the conflict of Oedipus. Through a science of culture, consciousness discerned the recurring patterns of that drama in the return of the repressed. The sublime images of inward longing and momentary peace, toward which he had first devoted his attention, Freud now saw reflected in the dramatic cycle of community lost and regained, a cycle whose crises had until 1914 never completely denied the promise of recovery.

SEVEN

THE MOMENT OF RECOVERY

I

Soon after the publication of *Totem and Taboo*, Freud wrote for *Imago* a new essay on Renaissance art, "The Moses of Michelangelo," asserting his conviction in the power of visual art to convey, through a single, unified image, the dramatic content of culture. His analysis of Michelangelo's sculpture of Moses joined—momentarily—the psychoanalytic study of artistic creativity to Freudian social psychology. The image derived force and meaning from the drama in which Moses had partaken: in a moment of crisis for himself and his people, he recovered himself, triumphing over explosive impulses of rage. By interpreting the instant fixed by Michelangelo as a moment of self-possession, not disintegration, Freud found in the prophet a figure of pathos, etched sharply against the background of a still inconstant and fragile society.

In August 1914, the dramatic cohesion of culture shattered. For Freud, the pattern into which he had been able to place the image of the artist's Moses had broken, and that drama so passionately concentrated within the sculpture lost its meaning for him. Six months into the war, writing again for *Imago*, he confessed the sweeping disillusionment and unusual sense of disorientation which had overcome him.[1] "The Moses of Michelangelo" proved to be

Freud's last study of painting or sculpture. After 1914, he never re-turned to plastic images or visual representations as subjects in themselves.[2] The years of war drove him back to a consideration of the nature of community, without, however, that previous measure of confidence in the triumph of the sublime.

Yet, the theme of the prewar essay—the recovery of self and society—remained with Freud in the first years of the peace. In *Group Psychology and the Analysis of the Ego*, published in 1921, his concern centered on the moment in which community struggled to reconstruct itself. In the aftermath of the war, Freud saw society fragmented into isolated groupings, each a revenant of the primal horde, seeking after new leaders, but rejecting those with the inter-nal command and self-knowledge of Michelangelo's Moses, and turning instead to figures anxious for the role of Nietzsche's super-man. It was as if Freud confronted the moment at which the drama of culture had begun to unfold.

During the war and its aftermath, Freud's Viennese followers also began to interpret that drama, now through the cultural sci-ence outlined in *Totem and Taboo*. In four essays written from 1914 to 1919, Theodor Reik examined religious rituals as distorted or disguised imitations of those actions taken by the brother band, the reenactment of which permitted both the return and the control of primal impulses.[3] As the starting point of religious and social or-ganization, ritual, in Reik's view, conferred on civilization a primal dramatic structure and content. In the turmoil of postwar Vienna, Paul Federn recognized that same structure and content in the po-litical struggle to create the Austrian First Republic out of the wreckage of Habsburg rule. In his pamphlet *On the Psychology of Revolution: The Fatherless Society*, published in 1919, he perceived in the effort to establish a new, fraternal community the re-creation of that primordial stage in history following the destruction of the first patriarchy. Concerning themselves with the construction of brotherhood, and the sources of its instability, Reik and Federn, like Freud, focused psychoanalytic cultural science on the process of recovery.

Among the Viennese, however, Freud remained most deeply impressed with the fluid, open-ended nature of that process. The uncertainty surrounding the moment of recovery plagued him. At the end of war, in that dramatic instant repeated throughout history, the question whether community would be regained once more forced itself upon consciousness. The fragmentation of society in the wake of the First World War gave disquieting answers. For Freud, however, psychoanalysis demonstrated its continued relevance as a science of culture in its ability to confront the problem of reconstruction. From a meditation on the theme of individual recovery in Michelangelo's Moses to a critique of postwar society: such was the evolution of Freudian cultural science in Vienna from the approach of war to its unsettling aftermath.

II

In December 1913, Freud, after several occasions of solitary contemplation before the statue at the Church of San Pietro in Vincoli in Rome, and after much hesitation, wrote his analysis of the Moses of Michelangelo. In the following year, it appeared—anonymously—in *Imago*. Beginning with Ernest Jones's biography, interpretations of the essay have rightfully noted how its subject and timing were strongly determined by the schisms with Adler and Jung. Identifying with the figure of Moses, the founder of psychoanalysis saw his own movement threatened with disintegration owing to the inability of his followers to sustain their new commitments. Recently returned from Rome and newly embarked on research into art historical interpretations of the statue, Freud himself was the first to acknowledge such a connection, writing to Sándor Ferenczi in October 1912, "According to my mood, I would sooner compare myself with the historical Moses than with the one by Michelangelo, which I interpreted."[4] That loyal Viennese followers wished publication of the essay carried considerable weight with Freud, who wrote to Karl Abraham that "it is only because of editorial pressure (Rank and Sachs) that I have consented to publish it at all."[5]

The work of Marthe Robert and the more recent commentary on Freud's essay by Yosef Hayim Yerushalmi emphasize the extent to which Freud at the time saw in Michelangelo's Moses the figure of his own father, and identified himself with the crime and guilt of the religious apostates. Recounting his observations of the statue at the Church of San Pietro in Vincoli, Freud in fact recorded the following admission: "Sometimes I have crept cautiously out of the half-gloom of the interior as though I myself belonged to the mob upon whom his eye is turned—the mob which can hold fast no conviction, which has neither faith nor patience, and which rejoices when it has regained its illusory idols."[6] In her study of Freud's Judaism, Robert drew attention in Freud's portrayal of Moses to the turmoil closing in on the patriarch, and the sense of guilt which would soon overtake the younger rebels. Noting that Freud worked on "The Moses of Michelangelo" in the same years as *Totem and Taboo*, she stressed how in both, as well as in *Moses and Monotheism*, "the 'Oedipean' drama, which at the time of the *Traumdeutung* was merely an expression of infantile desires that could not be fulfilled, became the monstrous reality at the base of all history, the immense crisis, fraught at once with crimes and with progress, by which Freud himself, for all his science, was now literally shaken."[7] Yet, in tracing the affirmations and ambivalences in Freud's Jewish identity, Yerushalmi has cogently and movingly argued that Freud would also have recalled in the statue of Moses a father who had controlled his anger, and who, in an exquisitely and painfully sublimated manner, had communicated his religious hopes for his son through *melitzot*, biblical and Talmudic literary allusions.[8]

Our concern here is to indicate how "The Moses of Michelangelo" combined for Freud themes from the study of Leonardo with the ideas of *Totem and Taboo*. The artistic image, in its unity and immediate presence, remained his focus. To discern the creator's aims and aesthetic vision, and the reasons for their emotional impact upon the viewer, continued to be the object of his analysis. Now, however, Freud elaborated a new direction of questioning, a new step in the psychoanalytic technique for studying the artistic creation: a search for the action of which the visual image was a part. In doing so, Freud built upon a classical foundation, for, as E. H. Gombrich pointed out, "Michelangelo's statue is approached in the same way in which Winckelmann or Lessing approached the *Laocoön Group* or Goethe the *Last Supper* by Leonardo. The beholder wants to know why Moses sits in exactly this posture, what had gone before, to explain it, and what would follow."[9] Comparing Freud's essays on Leonardo and Michelangelo, Richard Wollheim observed that "if the Leonardo essay concerns itself with expression in the modern sense—that is, with what the artist expresses in his works, or with Leonardo's expressiveness—then the Michelangelo essay is concerned with expression in the classical sense—that is, with what is expressed by the subject of the work, or the expressiveness of Moses."[10] Freud did not seek in Michelangelo's statue an expression of the inner life and experiences of the sculptor; instead, he searched in the stone figure for a deed from the life of the lawgiver. With understanding of the act, he could return to the artist's inward intent. The essay thus came to represent the contemplation of a sublime instant from a historical and psychological drama.

To explain that instant Freud first turned to art historical interpretations. Traditionally, art historians and cultural commentators perceived in the figure of Michelangelo's Moses an aspect of the confrontation between the religious leader and his people. According to most interpretations, the sculpture embodied that instant when Moses, filled with anger and despair at the betrayal of his leadership and his cause, prepared to release his moral outrage. Other commentaries, however, saw in the statue a figure who first exerted his uncommon moral strength toward controlling his rage; the angry confrontation with his people followed upon Moses' initial struggle with himself, a struggle Michelangelo carved in stone.

Joining those critics who detected in Michelangelo's statue the signs of a struggle for self-control, Freud maintained that even they had not attended closely enough to the carved image of Moses itself, and thus had perhaps misread the drama in which Michelangelo had placed it. Freud asserted that the method developed by Giovanni Morelli for deciding the author of unattributed or misidentified paintings could provide new understanding of the sculpture. Morelli's technique concentrated on supposedly insignificant details within an image to determine the identity of its creator; Freud proposed to apply that approach to interpreting the scene from which Moses' image had been taken.[11] The way in which Moses' right hand rested amid the strands of his beard, and the manner in which his right arm pressed against the stone tablets indicated to Freud that the Moses of Michelangelo's vision, enraged and despairing in the extreme, recovered himself.[12]

The image of Moses, however, was an image extracted from a drama, or more specifically, for Freud, it embodied the final moment of a completed action. To confirm his interpretation, Freud included his own diagram of the scene, whose conclusion Michelangelo had immortalized in art. In a series of three drawings, Moses is first seated, concentrating intently on an inward purpose, holding the Tablets of Law securely with his right arm. In the second scene, he grips his beard in a reflex of rage at the betrayal he has just seen among his people, at the same time losing his hold on the tablets. In the last moment, he regains his composure, once more securing the tablets with his right arm, as his right hand remains in contact with his beard, the image of Michelangelo's Moses, a figure whose instinctive vehemence, but also inward command, allow him to protect the Law. Those commentators who had seen in the sculpture Moses' struggle for self-mastery, yet concluded that, despite all efforts, he had lost that struggle, had overlooked the precise positions of the hand, arm, and tablets, and thus placed the image inaccurately within the overall action. Freud pointed out that "they would have been correct if they had been describing not the statue itself but the middle stage of our reconstructed action. It almost seems as if they had emancipated themselves from the visual image of the statue and had unconsciously begun an analysis of the motive forces behind it, and that that analysis had led them to make the same claim as we have done more consciously and more explicitly."[13]

Freud recognized that the drama of Moses as he re-created it did not, of course, conform to the life of the lawgiver in biblical tradition; rather, it enacted a Renaissance ideal as Michelangelo may have conceived it. By constraining his impulses at the instant of confronting his people, Michelangelo's Moses acquired a composure of will and constancy of purpose attainable in no other way. In the vision of the Renaissance artist, the prophet's "giant frame with its tremendous physical power becomes only a concrete expression of the highest mental achievement that is possible in a man, that of struggling successfully against an inward passion for the sake of a cause to which he has devoted himself."[14] Within the context of that scene, one can envision Moses as Michelangelo portrayed him: an embodiment of "sublime repose."[15]

Repose which betrayed a mystery: the artistic problem which had drawn Freud to the study of Leonardo remained present within his analysis of Michelangelo's Moses. In the case of Michelangelo's sculpture, however, Freud sought an answer to that mystery not in the inner life of the artist, but in the connection between the image and its dramatic context. Freud approached the image of Moses not as a visual screen of the artist's memories or impulses, but as a fragment of action—in his words, "the remains of a movement,"[16] and, as he noted, an action "not meant to record any particular moment in the prophet's life."[17] Rather, the image and the surrounding scene belonged to the act of recovery, a renunciation of vengeance which allowed Moses to regain both himself and the Law. Through sculpture Freud found in the visual arts that which characterized drama—the imitation of an action; in the case of Michelangelo's Moses, a gesture toward recovery and ultimate composure, a gesture which represented the moment at which Moses submitted himself to universal Law, before that Law had taken root among his people: an action of sublime containment which created of the sculpture an image of pathos.

For Freud, the image of self-restraint, embodied in Michelangelo's visionary statue, only derived its full meaning from the dramatic action in which it shared a part. As noted above, Freud himself recreated the scene prior to that final moment of decision which Michelangelo had preserved in stone, a scene depicting the instant at which the lawgiver saw the betrayal by his people and before he regained his self-control: "when he saw the spectacle he lifted his foot preparatory to starting up, let go the Tables with his hand and plunged it to the left and upwards into his beard, as though to turn his violence against his own body."[18] An aggressive rage directed against the self: this—perhaps earliest—adumbration of Freud's theory of the psychological origins of the super-ego completed the drama of the statue. In the scene as constructed by Freud, Moses' first motion of recovery was to channel the anger which he felt toward his community inward, a movement that revealed not only his passion for the Law, but his attachment to—his identification with—his people. Thus did the pathos of the Jewish prophet give full expression to the historical and psychological dilemma of recovery.[19] Divided—nearly beyond endurance—by devotion to the Law's universal commands and concern for his people, the prophet gained temporary repose only through a painful sublimation, the final act of which Michelangelo had etched in stone. To observe the self-imposed calm of the figure meant to contemplate its tragic achievement.

III

August 1914 began a process of social disintegration within which all actions—real, ritualized, and sublime—lost their traditional meanings and customary outcomes. As Freud described in "Thoughts for the Time on War and Death," published in *Imago* in 1915, the European war not only destroyed bonds which had once seemed permanent between societies, but broke ties between individuals themselves, and between citizens and their communities. In lament, he wrote that "the great nations themselves, it might have been supposed, would have acquired so much comprehension of what they had in common, and so much tolerance for their differences, that 'foreigner' and 'enemy' could no longer be merged, as they still were in classical antiquity, into a single concept."[20] Furthermore, within each nation, the "individual citizen can with horror convince himself in this war of what would occasionally cross his mind in peace-time—that the state has forbidden to the individual the practice of wrong-doing, not because it desires to abolish it, but because it desires to monopolize it, like salt and tobacco."[21] The collapse had become general, and with it followed disenchantment and disorientation. Freud's "Thoughts for the Time on War and Death" revealed the deep uncertainty about recovery and the extreme caution toward collective action which would characterize his immediate postwar social psychology.

After 1914, Freud never returned to the interpretation of visual art, as if he had lost that feeling for images whose emotional power over him had once been so remarkable. Perhaps his distance from the great products of the European tradition reflected one portion of that emptiness which followed the experience of the war, and which accompanied Freud through the remainder of his career. But in seeking an explanation, we should also bear in mind the point to which he had brought his own studies of painting and sculpture before the war: with the uncertainty of recovery, the background of coherent action against which he had begun to interpret works of art fell away. The immediate postwar years saw the beginnings of Freud's search for a new pattern of action—a new drama—within civilization, a pattern without which the highest creations of individuals would remain unapproachable. In that search, the relation between inward experience and the behavior of the collective became his chief focus.

In *Totem and Taboo*, Freud examined the psychological roots of social life through the study of ritual, the most dynamic and telling example of which was the ceremony of the totem meal: that dramatic reenactment of the primal crime and its aftermath gave forceful, if masked, expression to the inward impulses and historical deeds which bound the earliest human community. We have argued that the dramatic nature of ritual ceremony and observance suggested to Freud a new approach in the psychoanalytic exploration of culture, and that he extended that approach to interpret objects of art as themselves imitations of action. Within the Viennese psychoanalytic circle, Theodor Reik took up the new perspective in a series of investigations, studies which he began on the eve of the war and completed in the first year of the peace. The first, an interpretation of couvade, Reik presented to the Berlin Psychoanalytic Society in April 1914, and published in *Imago* the same year. The companion study on puberty rites was presented to the Vienna Society in January 1915; it appeared in *Imago* soon thereafter. His essay on the Kol Nidre ceremony, however, Reik read only privately to Freud. In January 1919, he delivered the final paper, examining the tradition of the shofar, to the Vienna Society, publishing the four studies together later that same year. Thus, throughout the war years, Reik continued to explore in the dramatic enactments of ritual the pattern of community lost and regained.

In the preface to the 1946 American edition of his book, Reik recalled from the spring of 1913 a meeting with Freud at which the latter spoke of the likeness between psychoanalytic method and Morelli's procedure in art criticism, impressing upon the young, Viennese Freudian the importance of, in Reik's words, "the remnants of observation."[22] At the same meeting, Reik informed his teacher that he was turning his attention to the psychoanalytic study of religious ritual. In the introduction to the 1919 German edition of his study, Reik explained that the advantage of ritual as an object of study derived from its "character of *action*," a quality which allowed it to be "more profitably investigated psycho-analytically than the ideas, commands, prohibition [sic], dogmas and complicated sentiments, which have later become the chief content of religion."[23] For Reik, the ritual act possessed a unique psychological immediacy, but, equally important, as action—or more accurately, as a remnant of action—ritual included tangible signs of a wider dramatic pattern.

In his study of couvade, Reik introduced that theme which would remain constant in his early works on religion: specifically, ritual as an emotionally compelling, but psychically reworked fragment of action preserved from the historical drama of communal life. The chief form of couvade in tribal religions prohibited a father from killing or eating certain animals on the birth of his child, prevented him, in other words, from carrying out what were "substitutive actions."[24] The emotional significance of such actions on the part of the man derived from feelings stirred unconsciously into motion on his becoming a father, the moment at which in the unconscious the rebellious impulses toward his own father received new confirmation and force. The revival of those impulses engendered an instinctive fear of retaliation, reinforced by the psychologically buried fear of a son who, coming into the world with a like feeling of rivalry toward his own father, would serve as an instrument of retribution. The substitutive actions, against which the practice of couvade was directed, pointed to buried Oedipal hostility as the motive for the ritual: in allowing the individual to overcome that hostility, the prohibitions of couvade provided him with the means of inward atonement.

For Reik, ritual held significance not only as an expression of individual psychology, but as a fragment of dramatic action. From such fragments one could, he believed, reconstruct the earliest era of community, in the case of the remnants left behind in couvade, the momentous transition in human society from the violence of the patriarchal horde to the stability of the brother clan. The practice of couvade, Reik argued, preserved traces from the period of the first community of brothers, a time when the birth of the brothers' own sons revived the memory of parricide. The brothers' sense of guilt now generated a fear of retaliation, a fear overcome only through a repetition of the crime, carried out against their sons, the perceived vehicles of the father's vengeance. Through the generations, the crime against newborns became transmuted first into the ritual sacrifice of children, later to the sacrifice of an animal upon the birth of a child. Finally, there came into being the prohibition against the eating and killing of animals at the time a child was born. The transition demonstrated the gradual triumph of tender feelings toward the father, and emotional identification with him, such that the brothers eventually transformed the fear of retaliation into concern for the welfare of the next generation. Thus did the subterranean emotional life of the individual and the historical drama of community receive shared expression in the performance of religious ritual.

For Reik, initiation rites revealed most clearly the dramatic quality of ritual as the imitation of an action, such reenactment giving singular insight into the recovery of community. In tribal religions, rites of puberty admitted youths into the society of elders through dramas of death and resurrection, in which initiates participated either as audience to the mystery plays or as ceremonial actors within ritual ordeals meant to signify their own deaths, often through the symbolic act of being devoured. Such initiation rites commonly included the ceremony of circumcision and, in some instances, had participants witness their elders as the symbolic victims of death or murder. Rituals of initiation intended to exert permanent influence on the sons of the community: "It is obvious," Reik stated, "that the drama is enacted in their presence in order to stamp an impressive scene on their imagination in after life."[25] Indeed, such rituals were strongly marked by "their dramatic and plastic form," in close likeness to the work of dreams.[26]

The vivid nature of the punishing scenes to which the sons were witness, or into which they were drawn, served in the first place to ensure that the initiates inwardly renounced those impulses threatening to their elders and to the community. Through the ritual act of circumcision—a symbolic castration—the elders exacted punishment for the incestuous impulses of the sons, the message of the punishment reinforced by the exclusion of women from the initiation mysteries. Further, ceremonial ordeals and, most importantly, the symbolic devouring of the sons, represented punishment for the initiates' murderous, patricidal instincts: through their ritual death, the sons atoned for their murderous wishes, thereby completing their own inward transformation and preparing themselves for their return to society. Finally, such ordeals reflected the persistent, unconscious fear of retaliation, owing to which the elders carefully preserved those rituals which guarded against the vengeance of the sons, and against the disintegration of the emotionally tenuous peace between the generations. Through rites of initiation, the elders reenacted the very crime against which they sought to defend themselves and the community, the imitation of that action which had been recreated as well in the tradition of the totem feast.

In the rites of puberty, genuine reconciliation between fathers and sons, and the complete recovery of community awaited "the second act of the great drama of the initiation ceremonies": the performance of resurrection.[27] Revived from death, the sons shared a new identity with the elders as full members of the community; the ceremonial act of resurrection, Reik explained, "represents this identification in plastic form."[28] Indeed, the theme of identification recast the meaning of the ritual of initiation: the hostile identity between father and son, expressed emotionally in the fear of retaliation, became replaced by bonds of tenderness. Thus, the rites of expiation which created new bonds of brotherhood among the tribal initiates simultaneously made possible the new identity with the father. In recalling the violent death of the father, but affirming the emergence of a compassionate identification between generations, the resurrection of the initiate gave expression to the emotional and historical pathos between father and son.

The rites of puberty developed from the history of community regained, in the course of which the creation of the family resurrected the primal horde, and thus gave new life to the rebellious and murderous impulses of the original crime. Unable to escape those impulses, or the fear of retaliation which inevitably accompanied them, the brothers "were compelled to re-erect the same prohibitions which they had once torn down—a process constantly recurring in the history of mankind."[29] In defending themselves in this way against the revival of the crime and the act of vengeance, they confirmed new bonds of solidarity with each other and, just as importantly, established means for instilling empathy between the generations. As in the totem meal, the imitation of the deed in the rite of initiation allowed emotional atonement and reaffirmed the recovery of community, completing, we would note, the cycle of Aeschylean drama: the Furies of family honor and blood vengeance becoming the Eumenides of social communion and generational peace.

In concluding his study, Reik turned to a consideration of the origins of tragic drama in the rites of Dionysos, comparing the ordeals of initiation to the ancient Dionysian ceremonial which memorialized the sufferings of the god and from which later emerged the ordeals of the tragic hero.[30] The rites of puberty, with the ritual death and resurrection of the initiates, pointed to a twofold origin of the suffering of the hero: his physical agony expressed the son's guilt and his need to atone for the primal crime—an atonement, however, which also, as Freud had argued, recreated the murder of the patriarch, the original sufferer. According to Reik, the reasons for the emotional impact of the earliest Greek drama, in which the audience witnessed the agonies and death of Dionysos, had in fact been indicated by Aristotle, for whom tragedy was, in Reik's words, "the imitation of an occurrence which stimulates fear and pity and, at the same time, brings about a catharsis of these affects."[31] The action of the drama produced in the audience unconscious, emotional identification with the figure who suffered, stirring in the spectator the suppressed desires, inward guilt, and fear of retaliation which now had taken tangible form in front of them. At the same time, by allowing the audience to visualize their emotions and motives, the action created a new perspective: "the spectators see what they unconsciously wished and feared, live again through what once impelled and moved them, and still does; and they allow their moral consciousness to speak, where before only unconscious impulses were urging them."[32] Thus, the performances of tragic drama in the ancient amphitheaters departed from ritual enactments by seeking the expansion of individual moral consciousness.

The nature of moral consciousness Reik explored in the Yom Kippur observance of Kol Nidre, the prayer whose mournful beauty, heard on the eve of the Day of Atonement, gave painfully compelling expression to the need for forgiveness. In seeking absolution and offering repentance for false vows in the year to come, Kol Nidre, in religious and poetic language, provided a single voice to humanity's moral aspiration and its knowledge of its own weakness, the distance between which could be bridged only in the act of atonement to God. Roots of this moral, poetic sensibility Reik sought in ancient ritual observance, specifically the ceremony of the *B'rith*, by which one individual bound his word to another. The *B'rith*, or covenant, included first, the taking of an oath; second, the utterance of a self-curse; and finally, an act of ritual sacrifice confirming the agreement and usually followed by a meal. That ancient ceremony, Reik argued, acknowledged the primal crime: in the self-imprecation, the sons avowed their responsibility for the deed, but ensured against its repetition through the swearing of the oath. In this way, the bond of the covenant recalled the identification forged between father and son in the new, fraternal community, from which bond the *B'rith* derived its own psychological and historical force. The rite of the *B'rith* represented remembrance and atonement, the moral and emotional essence of Kol Nidre.

With the progress of repression across generations, the ritual memorial to the crime—the *B'rith*—became subject to suppression, with the result that the unconscious tendencies toward repetition of the crime, and the need for expiation, became attached to the violation of oaths. The prayer of Kol Nidre, in calling to mind the disavowal of oaths, confessed the violent wish of the patricides who, with agonized conscience, pleaded for pardon from God, who alone could grant forgiveness. In the deeply flowing sadness and sublime striving of Kol Nidre, the observance of Yom Kippur most forcefully emphasized that atonement had become a matter not merely of ritual reenactment, but of moral consciousness.

Kol Nidre, Reik stressed, conveyed its message not only through its poetry, but through the melodies which over generations had been composed for it. The performance of music, and the impression left by it upon the community, became the subject of his final essay on religious ritual, an interpretation of the sounding of the shofar, which announced on the Jewish Days of Awe—Rosh Hashanah and Yom Kippur—God's judgment and the community's desire for repentance. As if to stress the dramatic quality of ritual, Reik approached music, despite its nonvisual nature, as the imitation of an action, the emotional and historical resonances of which remained tangible. The blowing of the shofar—the ram's horn—harkened back to the totemistic period of religion when priests and worshipers, recreating the sound of the totem animal, achieved the "imitation of the paternal voice,"[33] and thus preserved a reminiscence of the original patriarch of the human family. That sound, through which members of the community identified themselves with the father, recalled as well the primal crime; in Reik's words, "it derives its serious significance from the fact that, in the unconscious mental life of the listeners, it represents the anxiety and last death-struggle of the father-god."[34] Thus, the sounding of the shofar, reenacting the final moment of the brothers' rebellion, came to signify both the acknowledgment of guilt and the voice of judgment, an audible reminder of human responsibility and divine presence.

Bringing his discussion of the shofar and the music of ritual to a close, Reik turned once more to a consideration of Dionysian rites and the origins of Greek tragedy. The mimetic power of music also expressed itself in dance, the physical movements of which recreated those of the deity: "music, dance and mimicry always developed from imitation of the god whose first prototype was the father of the primitive horde, and who was changed later into the totem animal."[35] Dionysian ceremony embodied this complete ritual mimesis, in which the threnody and dance performed by the chorus reproduced the dying voice and physical suffering of the divine goat—later, the god—Dionysos. With the development of Greek tragic drama, the performance of music, dance, and poetry gradually gained a status independent of the ritual actions of the original Dionysian chorus. Like the ritual of Dionysos, however, classical Greek drama derived its unconscious emotional and historical meaning from the tragic suffering of the patriarch. "One might perhaps speak in this sense," Reik concluded, "of the birth of music from the soul of tragedy."[36]

Thus did Freudian cultural science depart from Nietzsche, for whom the spirit of music, by defying images, conveyed the objectless longing in all desire, a spirit which, once transformed by sublime imagination into the visual and tangible, became the embodiment of tragic suffering. By reformulating the Nietzschean declaration on the origins of tragedy, Reik emphasized not only that aspect of drama which originated in mimetic action. Through mimesis, generations also retained in fragments the memory of the origins of human community, fragments which preserved their psychological immediacy and authenticity in the persistence of Oedipal impulses in the individual unconscious.[37] The dramatic continuity of human history found confirmation in the recovery of community, the original moments of which Reik described as follows: "The longing for the father and the triumph over the powerful adversary, lived over and over again in phantasy, must have made it possible for the sons to call up again and again the memory of the father's form, his movements and the tone of his voice. It forced the clan with compulsive strength to identify itself again and again by imitation of his voice and movements with the primal father whose return is represented for individuals by their own father."[38] The regaining of community was accompanied by the performance of the first drama—an imitation of the primal deed not only for cathartic, but also mnemonic purposes. Genuine recovery called forth tragic remembrance.

IV

One week after the declaration of the armistice ending the hostilities of the First World War, the Vienna Psychoanalytic Society, having gathered informally once a month during the war, formally reconvened its meetings. As the international association had continued the publication of the *International Journal of Psycho-Analysis* in wartime, so the Viennese had sustained *Imago* throughout the conflict. The Freudian circle in Vienna clearly hoped to resume its full activities as quickly as possible.

The group that met on 19 November 1919, no longer included the four original members of the Psychological Wednesday Society. Max Kahane had drifted from the circle several years before the schism with Alfred Adler in 1911; Wilhelm Stekel had resigned in the year following Adler's departure. Rudolf Reitler, however, had remained a practicing analyst until his death in 1917. The loss of another early member of the society came in 1919. In that year, Victor Tausk, who had received his medical doctorate from the University of Vienna in 1914, and had treated soldiers in psychiatric clinics during the war, took his own life.[39]

The Vienna Society in the immediate postwar years did, however, rebuild itself around a nucleus of pre-1914 members. Following the example of the Berlin circle, Eduard Hitschmann in 1922 founded the Ambulatorium, the first psychoanalytic clinic and training institute in Vienna. Isador Sadger and Maxim Steiner continued as practicing analysts, with Alfred von Winterstein and Theodor Reik themselves becoming practitioners after the war: the Viennese authorities' initial refusal to grant Reik a license to practice therapy gave rise to the debate within the psychoanalytic world over the professional status of lay analysts.[40] One member who had left the society before the war rejoined the circle: in 1923, Fritz Wittels published a biography of Freud; two years later, despite his displeasure with the book, Freud supported Wittels's application for readmission into the Vienna Society, over the objections of other members of the group. The two editors of *Imago* departed the Vienna psychoanalytic circle after the war, one for a new city, the other for a different field of psychology. In 1920, Hanns Sachs became a training analyst at the newly created Psychoanalytic Institute in Berlin. After the rise of Nazism, he emigrated to the United States, where he revived the project of the Viennese movement by founding the journal *American Imago*. With the publication of *The Trauma of Birth*, Otto Rank's work with Freud, Sachs, and the Vienna Society came to an end. Rank subsumed the theory of libido and the Oedipal complex within the birth trauma, now conceived as the driving force within the psyche; completed in 1923, and published the following year, the book brought to a close his long association with Freud.[41]

The Vienna Psychoanalytic Society renewed its activity under circumstances of extreme hardship and uncertainty in postwar Austria, one of the several successor states, it can justifiably be said, to the fallen imperial government of the Habsburgs. To Paul Federn, one of the first Freudians and one of the leaders of the Vienna Society after the war—he assumed its vice-presidency in 1924 and continued in that position until the Nazis dissolved the society in 1938—the social psychological theories and researches of *Totem and Taboo* had acquired unforeseen, contemporary urgency, most immediately in their application to the efforts of the Austrian Social Democrats to bring the First Republic into being from the ruins of the monarchy. In a presentation to the Vienna Society, published in 1919 under the title *On the Psychology of Revolution: The Fatherless Society*, Federn discussed in the light of psychoanalytic understanding the crisis confronting Austria, and the possibilities for creating a "community of brothers [*Brudergemeinschaft*]"[42] from the demise of patriarchal authority.

As Federn explained, the institutions of the old order—monarchical and bourgeois—had drawn to themselves the individual's unconscious longing for the authority and image of the father. With defeat in war and the demise of the Habsburgs, reverence toward the state dissipated, and a fatherless society came into being, reproducing the earliest period of humanity: the original revolt against the father, and the attempt to construct a new society among the rebellious sons. The Austrian revolution, however, did not originate only in the collapse of traditional authority; out of economic and political protest, workers had created their own institutions—the worker and soldier councils—giving republicanism in Austria a new foundation among the laboring masses, a foundation which would disintegrate, Federn feared, as a result of the "suicidal methods"[43] of the general strike. Risen from "the hunger of the cities" and a "revolutionary thirst for freedom"—not, as he pointed out, from an "absence of conscience among individuals" or "Bolshevik influence"—the strike movement released the "destructive tendencies" of the sons' rebellion.[44] By contrast, the worker councils revealed "their psychic structure as brotherhood."[45]

One can see in Federn's psychoanalytic interpretation an attempt to address the Austro-Marxists' dilemma of building into the idea of postwar republican unity a permanent revolutionary aspiration.[46] Thus, for Federn, the council movement would provide—under Social Democratic parliamentary leadership—a political base for the new state, while simultaneously accomplishing a social psychological transformation: "It would be an enormous liberation, if the current revolution, which is a repetition of the primal revolt against the father, were to succeed. The soul of humanity could perhaps become a more beautiful one, the patricidal feature removed from its countenance."[47] Yet, as Federn knew, many Austrians—legitimist, clerical, and middle-class—would seek a revival of the "feudal-bourgeois state"; still others, in pursuit of a father-authority, would willingly grant power to some new actor on the political stage: "With great regularity, therefore, after the downfall of kings, republics have stepped aside in favor of rule by a leader of the nation [*Volksführer*]."[48] Federn demonstrated confidence in the Social Democrats' ability to strengthen support for the new state and to forestall a right-wing resurgence, perceiving in the republican movement the hope of a peaceful resolution to the primal drama; yet, he saw, self-admittedly, no certainties in the moment of recovery.

V

Freud's return to social psychology in the postwar era revealed the continued impact on his thought of the wartime past. In the conclusion of his essay on "The Disillusionment of the War," he had lamented the phenomenon of nationalism, under the influence of which the individual sacrificed to the group his own sense of identity and independence: "It is, to be sure, a mystery why the collective individuals should in fact despise, hate and detest one another—every nation against every other—and even in times of peace. I cannot tell why that is so. It is just as though when it becomes a question of a number of people, not to say millions, all individual moral acquisitions are obliterated, and only the most primitive, the oldest, the crudest mental attitudes are left."[49] When taking up the question of recovery in *Group Psychology and the Analysis of the Ego*, he defined the problem of collective behavior in similar terms, stating that "the individual, outside the primitive group [the supposedly unorganized group, or crowd], possessed his own continuity, his self-consciousness, his traditions and customs, his own particular functions and position, and he kept apart from his rivals. Owing to his entry into an 'unorganized' group he had lost this distinctiveness for a time."[50] Thus, in the first years of the peace, Freud observed wartime attitudes persisting in group psychology, an ominous reflection of social uncertainty and incomplete recovery.

Freud focused on the unorganized group or crowd as the rudimentary unit of collective activity, the examination of which now became necessary and possible due to the process of social dissolution brought on by the war. The spontaneity and transience of crowd formation distinguished such a group from well-established, traditional institutions; yet even those institutions such as the Church and the army—the last standing pillars of former Habsburg rule—shared features with the crowd. Both Church and army revealed common emotional ties on which they depended for their continued survival: specifically, those unconscious, libidinal bonds which created among their members ties of dependence toward the leader of the institution and, simultaneously, toward each other. Such ties on the part of the individual, both to the leader and to the collectivity, ties which gave characteristics of the Church and the army a psychological resemblance to crowd phenomena, demonstrated both the individual's loss of inward independence and the emotional grip which the leader held on his followers, the social psychological issues of most concern to Freud.

A group—whether spontaneously generated or traditionally based—remained united through its members' identification with each other, an identification which derived from a shared psychological attitude toward the group's leader. In the mental life of a member of the group, the leader filled the role of the individual's ego ideal, that psychical agency which served as private conscience and critical observer of the self. Identification between individuals and idealization of the leader gave to the collectivity a libidinal unity, and for that feeling of unity individuals sacrificed a portion of their independent identities. Such emotional identification between individuals, combined with their mutual reverence toward a leader, replicated within even the most spontaneous and impermanent of groups the original condition of collective existence: the primal horde. Group behavior after the war revealed the human being again to be "a horde animal."[51]

The contemporary "revival of the primal horde" demonstrated how individual and group psychology had coexisted within that first human collectivity: "The members of the group were subject to ties just as we see them to-day, but the father of the primal horde was free."[52] The psychology of the primal father became prototypical of patriarchal freedom: "His intellectual acts were strong and independent even in isolation, and his will needed no reinforcement from others. Consistency leads us to assume that his ego had few libidinal ties; he loved no one but himself, or other people only in so far as they served his needs. To objects his ego gave away no more than was barely necessary."[53] Like the revenant of the horde, this patriarchal figure, too, enjoyed a modern, ideological revival: "He, at the very beginning of the history of mankind, was the 'superman' whom Nietzsche only expected from the future."[54] The "uncanny and coercive characteristics of group formations" could be explained psychologically by the fact that individuals perceived that image in the figure of the leader, and responded to it with "an extreme passion for authority."[55]

In the final section of his study of group psychology, Freud described the variety and complexity of a stable civil society: "Each individual is a component part of numerous groups, he is bound by ties of identification in many directions, and he has built up his ego ideal upon the most various models."[56] Although the individual remained part of diverse "group minds," Freud continued, "he can also raise himself above them to the extent of having a scrap of independence and originality."[57] A common danger, however, confronted both the individual and the group psyche in the form of mania, the condition in which "the ego and the ego ideal have fused together, so that the person, in a mood of triumph and self-satisfaction, disturbed by no self-criticism, can enjoy the abolition of his inhibitions, his feelings of consideration for others, and his self-reproaches."[58] One can see here, in what the individual experienced as an expression of mania, a likeness to wartime delirium. In the emotional life of the individual, the opposite of mania—the mood of melancholia—resulted from conflict between the ego and ego ideal, "a conflict in which the ideal, in an excess of sensitiveness, relentlessly exhibits its condemnation of the ego in delusions of inferiority and in self-depreciation."[59] In such melancholy there resided perhaps a social dimension, an emotional ill-treatment imposed by the collective ego ideal upon any individual ego which sought participation beyond the confines of the group in wider circles of humanity—in Freud's words, "an ill-treatment which it encounters when there has been identification with a rejected object."[60]

We have been considering how *Group Psychology and the Analysis of the Ego* expressed Freud's postwar frame of mind. In the society in which he now found himself, he witnessed the contemporary rebirth of the horde as a concrete manifestation of a world which had lost the form and unity of drama. With the disintegration of that dramatic pattern, with the reemergence of the horde in collective behavior, the impassioned group or crowd—the chorus of the drama—no longer sought a common language with which to comprehend and convey the suffering of the individual, but in its striving after complete harmony with a leader succumbed to irrational purpose. The contemporary group relinquished the role of the dramatic chorus as, in Francis Fergusson's words, "an organ of a highly self-conscious community."[61] For Freud, the impulses of the horde—passions resurrected by the war and then carried into the peace—had become the greatest danger to both social and personal recovery.

That danger could also be described as the loss of the sublime. The contrast between the figure of Michelangelo's Moses at the moment of torturous, inward recovery, and that of a self-conceived

Nietzschean superman drawing on and manipulating the impulses of the crowd measured that loss. Did not Max Weber also at the end of the war comment on that absence in his prose soliloquy on "Politics as a Vocation"? He wrote in 1918: "To be sure, mere passion, however genuinely felt, is not enough. It does not make a politician, unless passion as devotion to a 'cause' also makes responsibility to this cause the guiding star of action. And for this, a sense of proportion is needed. This is the decisive psychological quality of the politician: his ability to let realities work upon him with inner concentration and calmness. Hence his *distance* to things and men."[62] Devotion and distance, passion and calm: thus did Freud's vision of Moses, Weber's of a political leader moved by the "ethic of responsibility," assert the civic meaning of the sublime, a meaning undermined by the group psychology of the war and its aftermath.

There perhaps remained in such times the seeker after wider identifications, uninfluenced by the limits of the group mind, a figure of isolation, of private grief and agonized longing. Was such an individual in truth witnessing the defeat of pathos, the irrelevance of the sublime? Did there not exist a deeper pattern, a broader sense of community, a more acute awareness of the self? The search for understanding yet persisted, a demand upon consciousness, an inward source of disquiet.

CONSCIOUSNESS
AS FATE

I

In 1923, Freud sent to Romain Rolland, the French writer and pacifist organizer during the First World War, a copy of *Group Psychology and the Analysis of the Ego.* The gift of the book, and the letter which accompanied it, conveyed Freud's friendship and high esteem for Rolland, but served equally as an invitation to intellectual debate, which the two authors pursued, infrequently but nonetheless faithfully, throughout the following decade. In his letter, Freud conveyed his sincere regard for Rolland as the representative of "the most precious of beautiful illusions, that of love extended to all mankind."[1] Reflecting, however, upon the postwar mentality and its dangers, he continued: "I, of course, belong to a race which in the Middle Ages was held responsible for all epidemics and which today is blamed for the disintegration of the Austrian Empire and the German defeat. Such experiences have a sobering effect and are not conducive to make one believe in illusions."[2] Yet, he confessed that he could not himself entirely escape from Rolland's hope, for

> if this one hope cannot be at least partly realized, if in the course of evolution we don't learn to divert our instincts from destroying our own kind, if we continue to hate one another for minor differences and kill each other for petty gain, if we go on exploiting the great progress made

in the control of natural resources for our mutual destruction, what kind
of future lies in store for us? It is surely hard enough to ensure the perpe-
tuation of our species in the conflict between our instinctual nature and
the demands made upon us by civilization.[3]

During the ensuing years, the never broken discussion with Rolland remained near the center of Freud's meditation on the postwar world. In 1929, Freud wrote *Civilization and Its Discontents;* he
would begin the book by renewing in its pages his conversation
with Rolland. Thus did the French pacifist and mystic become in
Freud's later work one of the figures through whom he maintained
the Viennese dialogue of the prewar years.

In the letter from 1923, there can be seen, clearly visible, the
outline of the argument of *Civilization and Its Discontents.* To Rolland, therefore, Freud not only presented his published examination of postwar group psychology, but offered with it a continued
reflection on the problems of reconstruction—the loss of community, the abandonment of self-independence—which he had raised in
that study. In reexamining those problems in *Civilization and Its
Discontents,* Freud enunciated the demand placed upon consciousness during the time in which he now lived: the demand to rearti-
culate the idea of a universal, human drama, and to recover from
that drama the moment of recognition. In so doing the book completed the early Viennese psychoanalysts' pursuit of cultural science in a time of continual crisis.

II

Freud began the argument of *Civilization and Its Discontents* with a
consideration of the sense of self, of the ego's consciousness of itself in relation to the external world, introducing the question by
reviving his debate with Rolland.[4] One of the discontented, Rolland yet found within humanity a shared sense of near mystical
union with the world, "a sensation of 'eternity', a feeling of something limitless, unbounded—as it were, 'oceanic'."[5] Although a
critic of established religions, Rolland believed that religious senti-
ment reflected that rudimentary, inner sense. In the oceanic feeling, however, Freud himself saw the mental survival of that ego-
feeling original to early childhood which could not define, or only
poorly, the boundaries between the self and the outside world, "a
much more inclusive—indeed, an all-embracing—feeling which

corresponded to a more intimate bond between the ego and the world about it."[6] To that ego-feeling corresponded the ideas belonging to the oceanic sense, "those of limitlessness and of a bond with the universe."[7] Thus, in addressing Rolland's ideas at the outset, Freud chose to consider that mystical aspiration toward union as it appeared in one who during the war had been acutely conscious of his own inward isolation. Through the figure of Rolland, sketched quickly and in broad strokes, he provided an image, faint but discernable, of the solitary individual, overcome by a sense of misery and disenchantment, in search of a universal unity.

The sketch of that individual embodied an image of longing and inward pain, a suffering which called into question the success of human community. One could seek to reduce the feeling of longing and deprivation, a feeling rooted deeply in the sensation of instinctual want, through the denial or limitation of desire, and the attainment of emotional quietude. Instinctual need, however, might also be directed toward a new aim—undergo sublimation— from which an individual "gains the most if one can sufficiently heighten the yield of pleasure from the sources of psychical and intellectual work."[8] Religion invited participation in a collective escape: "Its technique consists in depressing the value of life and distorting the picture of the real world in a delusional manner—which presupposes an intimidation of the intelligence."[9] Still, the devout believer could not avoid encountering pain, at which time "all that is left to him as a last possible consolation and source of pleasure in his suffering is an unconditional submission."[10] Thus did religious belief provide not the only, but the most widely accepted sanction for quietude, for the sacrifice of self-consciousness.

The sufferer, however, might end by rejecting the human community altogether, withdrawing every attachment to it. At this point in the argument, one can detect that Freud considered the oceanic feeling itself to be an attempt at compensating for the perhaps irresistible inclination toward withdrawal and thus, one among the many emotional signs of despair with civilization. The existence of that social despair—especially the indication of such despair in one like Rolland—and its foundation in the experience of the First World War, now brought the book's analysis to the evolution of community, and its effect upon the individual. The life of human community began, Freud wrote, with the attempt to

adjust "social relationships": "If the attempt were not made, the relationships would be subject to the arbitrary will of the individual:
that is to say, the physically stronger man would decide them in the
sense of his own interests and instinctual impulses."[11] By widening
that attempt at socialization, the "further course of cultural development seems to tend towards making the law no longer an expression of the will of a small community—a caste or a stratum of the
population or a racial group—which, in its turn, behaves like a violent individual towards other, and perhaps more numerous, collec-
tions of people."[12] The existence of community thus depended
upon each member's expectation that the renunciation of instinct
was equal and mutual, and that such renunciation, and the law
which followed from it, would not be applied arbitrarily—"broken
in favour of an individual."[13] Genuine community rested upon the
expectation of justice. If it granted remedies to injustice, the community would keep faith with that expectation on the part of its
members, or, at the very least, not plant yet another source of estrangement between them. For in the instinctual need of the individual—that need which existed prior to consciousness of community—there already existed a continual source of opposition to
civilization, as if commitment to the human community itself had
always to be experienced in part as a feeling of inward desolation.

In history, human community had emerged from the destruction of the primal horde, that original human grouping over which
the father had ruled with unrestrained will. With the formation of
the society of brothers, civilization came into being, grounding itself in the need for labor in common, and in that love which the
brothers were now free to apply to the creation of their own families. That bond of love became extended more widely as communal
feeling or affection: "The love which founded the family continues
to operate in civilization both in its original form, in which it does
not renounce direct sexual satisfaction, and in its modified form as
aim-inhibited affection. In each, it continues to carry on its function of binding together considerable numbers of people, and it
does so in a more intensive fashion than can be effected through
the interest of work in common."[14] The progress of repression,
however, accompanied the effort of civilization "to bring people
together into large unities."[15] In the development of civilization,
that original suppression of incestuous impulses and Oedipal hos-

tility which had been required to preserve a sense of solidarity within the new community of brothers, and to eliminate the chief, sexual source of rivalry, ended with the contemporary, increasingly narrow restrictions upon sexual life, constraints onerous to the individual, beyond what was necessary to the community, and impractical of fulfillment. Yet, society strove toward displacing ever larger libidinous quantities toward its own aims. The advance of sexual repression evidenced, in the clearest way, the intensifying, inward conflict generated by civilization, which sought almost desperately to strengthen communal, affectionate ties at the increasingly greater expense of the instinctual, sensual aims of the individual.

The diversion of libido toward the purposes of community indicated an urgency within the dynamic of civilization. The rechanneling of libidinal energy toward community had become necessary to counteract the equally strong human instinct of aggression: "In consequence of this primary mutual hostility of human beings, civilized society is perpetually threatened with disintegration. The interest of work in common would not hold it together; instinctual passions are stronger than reasonable interests."[16] The primal horde fell to an act of violence, the repetition of which the community of brothers had sought strenuously to prevent through collective measures of renunciation and atonement. Further, no contemporary could doubt the ineradicable nature and consequences of human aggression, inescapably demonstrated in "the horrors of the recent World War."[17]

The fact of aggression reflected a more profound conflict within the evolution of civilization, a conflict rooted more deeply than the opposition between the ego and the world, between the individual and community—one rooted in a constant, instinctual duality. The method of moving toward ever deeper dualities led Freud to maintain that "besides the instinct to preserve living substance and to join it into ever larger units, there must exist another, contrary instinct seeking to dissolve those units and to bring them back to their primaeval inorganic state. That is to say, as well as Eros there was an instinct of death."[18] Libido represented the striving of Eros toward its aim; aggression manifested the disintegrative, destructive force within instinctual life. In the light of that dualism, Freud observed that "civilization is a process in the service of Eros, whose purpose is to combine single human individuals, and after that families, then races, peoples and nations, into one great unity, the unity of mankind."[19] History, from this perspective, demonstrated "the struggle between Eros and Death, between the instinct of life and the instinct of destruction, as it works itself out in the human species."[20] Within the individual, that struggle produced a perpetual sensation of uneasy longing and painful apprehension.

A desolate expectation and watchfulness: one perceives the emotional qualities belonging to the sense of guilt, the chief means through which civilization sought to control instinctual aggression. Turned inward, Freud wrote, human aggressivity becomes "taken over by a portion of the ego, which sets itself over against the rest of the ego as super-ego, and which now, in the form of 'conscience', is ready to put into action against the ego the same harsh aggressiveness that the ego would have liked to satisfy upon other, extraneous individuals. The tension between the harsh super-ego and the ego that is subjected to it, is called by us the sense of guilt; it expresses itself as a need for punishment."[21] Experienced as an anxious expectation of punishment, the sense of guilt derived originally from fear of an external figure of authority, whose love—or more specifically, the withdrawal of whose love—was a matter of the greatest moment to the ego. Internalization of the authority in the super-ego preserved that figure and, as an inescapable consequence, generated an inward fear of conscience. Whereas instinctual renunciation could satisfy the demands of the external authority, such renunciation could not completely free the ego from its own censor, as the instinctual wish, according to the laws of preservation in mental life, remained present within the unconscious, and thus known to conscience.

Those who sacrificed most willingly and selflessly in the name of community and humanity, however, seemed most uneasy toward their consciences. In psychoanalytic understanding: "Every renunciation of instinct now becomes a dynamic source of conscience and every fresh renunciation increases the latter's severity and intolerance."[22] That observation led still further into the relationship between aggression and the sense of guilt: conscience not only reflected the punitive attitude and actions of the internalized figure of authority, but also took possession of the ego's aggressivity toward that figure and redirected it toward the self. With every renunciation the ego unconsciously sensed a new stirring of vengeful anger, which on each occasion the super-ego diverted inward.

The psychological origins of the sense of guilt recalled the historical drama of community: "We cannot," Freud stated, "get away from the assumption that man's sense of guilt springs from the Oedipus complex and was acquired at the killing of the father by the brothers banded together."[23] How did a sense of guilt make itself felt in those who had belonged to the primal horde, whose will had been the will of the father, and whose self-consciousness emerged only with the creation of human community? The brothers' conscience, though cast in violence, preserved also the traces of Eros:

> After their hatred had been satisfied by their act of aggression, their love came to the fore in their remorse for the deed. It set up the super-ego by identification with the father; it gave that agency the father's power, as though as a punishment for the deed of aggression they had carried out against him, and it created the restrictions which were intended to prevent a repetition of the deed. And since the inclination to aggressiveness against the father was repeated in the following generations, the sense of guilt, too, persisted, and it was reinforced once more by every piece of aggressiveness that was suppressed and carried over to the super-ego.[24]

Expansion of human community unavoidably deepened the sense of guilt, the painful, inward sensation of a humanity ceaselessly striving toward unity, plagued by its own aggression, solitary in its efforts.

III

In characterizing civilization, Freud defined it as "a special process which mankind undergoes."[25] The argument of *Civilization and Its Discontents*—the dialogue with Rolland—reaffirmed the dramatic nature of that process, an evolutionary process rooted both historically and psychologically in the dualism of Eros and death. In Freud's prose, civilization itself became the subject of a tragedy, as of course it had been in the ancient world in the work of the poet Aeschylus. In the tragic cycle of the *Oresteia*, humanity, under the protective aegis of Wisdom, could not overcome the demons antagonistic to civilization—Furies of vengeance and family loyalty— by expelling them, but only by burying and transforming them.

Thus were those spirits, older than human society, diverted from their aims, but necessarily preserved as objects of collective propitiation and inward atonement. And thus in final fulfillment of the divine oracle, Sophocles' Oedipus, unable to escape his suffering, but now conscious of his fate, traveled to the sacred grove of the Furies at Colonus, there in his last hours to confer his own blessing on the community.

For Freud, the drama of civilization had become an increasingly inward one, from which finally emerged the possibility of conscious recognition, a possibility which had seemed lost to the war and the uncertainties of its aftermath. The sense of guilt that accompanied the progress of civilization, Freud wrote, "remains to a large extent unconscious, or appears as a sort of *malaise*, a dissatisfaction, for which people seek other motivations."[26] The possibility existed, however, for the individual to replace portions of that unconscious feeling of guilt with a conscious understanding of responsibility. To base choices and actions on that understanding could allow for the modification or readjustment of the relations of the individual to community in ways more beneficial to both. Further, the striving for individual consciousness could, as in the ancient tragedies, force the community to confront its own crisis. Authentic recognition, however, would not free the individual from that inward suffering which resulted from the struggle between Eros and death in the development of culture. Such awareness remained tragic, replacing an unconscious sense of despair, a nameless, inward desolation, with the anguish of consciousness, the last, uncompromising manifestation of fate. As in the lives of the Sophoclean heroes—as in the final moments of the life of Oedipus the king at Colonus—consciousness became the most defiant assertion of humanity.

The sacred grove at Colonus: the stillness of images; the reenactment of the ritual; a voiceless drama. Recognition, however, demands the language and measured speech of the amphitheater, the words with which to express a lucid commitment. Through such means, a portion of recognition may lead to the discovery of a calling.

NOTES

CHAPTER 1

1. Max Weber, *The Protestant Ethic and the Spirit of Capitalism* (1904-1905), trans. Talcott Parsons (New York: Charles Scribner's Sons, 1958), 79.

2. Aristotle, *Metaphysics*, trans. W. D. Ross, bk. 1, ch. 2, 982b, in *The Basic Works of Aristotle*, ed. Richard McKeon (New York: Random House, 1941).

3. Sigmund Freud, *The Question of Lay Analysis* (1926), in *The Standard Edition of the Complete Psychological Works of Sigmund Freud*, translated from the German under the general editorship of James Strachey, in collaboration with Anna Freud, assisted by Alix Strachey and Alan Tyson (London: Hogarth Press and the Institute of Psycho-Analysis, 1953-1974), 20: 246.

4. The official membership in 1906-1907, when minutes, attendance, and yearly enrollment were first recorded, numbered seventeen; it grew to thirty-seven in 1910-1911, the year of the schism between Freud and Alfred Adler, reached thirty-two in 1912-1913, and fell to twenty-two by the beginning of the First World War. The attendance at meetings was far lower, averaging ten in 1906-1907, nineteen in 1910-1911, and finally fourteen from 1912 to 1914. These figures were compiled from the attendance and enrollment lists in Herman Nunberg and Ernst Federn, eds., *Minutes of the Vienna Psychoanalytic Society*, 4 vols., trans. M. Nunberg with the assistance of H. Collins (New York: International Universities Press, 1962-1975), hereafter referred to as *Minutes;* they exclude individuals who were guests of the society or visiting members of psychoanalytic societies from other cities. For an analysis of the backgrounds of the medical practitioners who joined the society, see Edward Shorter, "The Two Medical Worlds of Sigmund Freud," in *Freud and the History of Psychoanalysis*, ed. Toby Gelfand and John Kerr (Hillsdale, N. J.: Analytic Press, 1992), 59-78.

5. Sigmund Freud, *Three Essays on the Theory of Sexuality* (1905), in *The Standard Edition*, 7: 135.

6. Sigmund Freud, *The Interpretation of Dreams* (1900), in *The Standard Edition*, 4: 260-61.

7. See Sigmund Freud, *Analysis of a Phobia in a Five-Year-Old Boy* (1909), in *The Standard Edition*, 10: 5-149.

8. Freud, *The Interpretation of Dreams*, 262.

9. Ibid., 262-63.

10. Ibid., 263.

11. See Sigmund Freud, *Delusions and Dreams in Jensen's "Gradiva"* (1907 [1906]), in *The Standard Edition*, 9: 7-95.

12. In his biography of Freud, Peter Gay, however, referred to *Imago* as a journal for the cultural sciences. See Gay, *Freud: A Life for Our Time* (New York: W. W. Norton, 1988), 311.

13. Wundt's *Völkerpsychologie* appeared from 1900 to 1920. In 1912, he published *Elemente der Völkerpsychologie* (*Elements of Folk Psychology: Outlines of a Psychological History of the Development of Mankind*, trans. Edward Leroy Schaub [London: George Allen and Unwin, 1916]), summarizing his argument and material. According to Wundt, the discipline of collective psychology assisted in "the interpretation of the more complicated processes of individual consciousness," furthering the effort "to investigate the complex functions of thought" with "a history of the development of human thought" (*Elements of Folk Psychology*, 3). On Wundt and the cultural sciences in Germany, see Fritz Ringer, *The Decline of the German Mandarins: The German Academic Community* (Cambridge, Mass.: Harvard University Press, 1969; Hanover, N. H.: Wesleyan University Press, University Press of New England, 1990), 312-15, and Woodruff D. Smith, *Politics and the Sciences of Culture in Germany, 1840-1920* (New York: Oxford University Press, 1991), 120-28.

14. E. H. Gombrich, "The Ambivalence of the Classical Tradition: The Cultural Psychology of Aby Warburg (1866-1929)," in *Tributes: Interpreters of Our Cultural Tradition* (Ithaca, N.Y.: Cornell University Press, 1984), 119. Of course, prominent among those seeking to construct a science of culture based upon patterns and structures of consciousness was Wilhelm Dilthey. For Dilthey's conception of the aims and methods of *Geisteswissenschaft*, see Ringer, *Decline of the German Mandarins*, 316-23, and Michael Ermarth, *Wilhelm Dilthey: The Critique of Historical Reason* (Chicago: University of Chicago Press, 1978), 94-108. In the historical profession itself, Karl Lamprecht sought to explain cultural stages in human history, and the transitional periods between them, according to the psychology of the association and organization of sense impressions as pursued, for example, by his Leipzig colleague, Wundt. Lamprecht argued that the mentality of a given historical period made itself known most clearly through its artistic productions. For Lamprecht's theory, and the controversy among historians which it aroused at the turn of the century, see Ringer, *Decline of the German Mandarins*, 302-4, and E. H. Gombrich, *Aby Warburg: An Intellectual Biography*, 2nd ed. (Chicago: University of Chicago Press, 1986), 30-35.

15. On these aspects of Warburg's approach, see Gombrich, *Aby Warburg*, 177-85, and Carlo Ginzburg, "From Aby Warburg to E. H. Gombrich: A Problem of Method," in *Clues, Myths, and the Historical Method*, trans. John and Anne Tedeschi (Baltimore: Johns Hopkins University Press, 1989), 18-22.

16. *The Poetics of Aristotle*, ed. and trans. S. H. Butcher, 4th ed. (London: Macmillan, 1907), ch. 6, 1449b. Freud owned Theodor Gomperz's 1897 translation, for which Gomperz chose the phrase, "imitative representation" [*nachahmende Darstellung*] to translate the Aristotelian notion of mimesis in poetry and tragedy. (*Aristoteles' Poetik*,

trans. and intro. Theodor Gomperz [Leipzig: von Veit, 1897], 11.) Included with the translation was Alfred von Berger's essay, "Truth and Error in Aristotle's Catharsis Theory," in which Berger wrote: "The cathartic treatment of hysteria, which the physicians Dr. Josef Breuer and Dr. Sigmund Freud have described, is well-suited to make the cathartic effect of tragedy intelligible" (Alfred von Berger, "Wahrheit und Irrtum in der Katharsis-Theorie des Aristoteles," in *Aristoteles' Poetik*, 81). On the copy of Gomperz's translation and Berger's essay in Freud's possession, see Robin N. Mitchell-Boyask, "Freud's Reading of Classical Literature and Classical Philology," in *Reading Freud's Reading*, ed. Sander L. Gilman et al. (New York: New York University Press, 1994), 27-29. Translations are my own unless indicated otherwise.

17. Fergusson explained his approach in his analysis of Sophocles' *Oedipus the King*. See Francis Fergusson, *The Idea of a Theater: A Study of Ten Plays: The Art of Drama in Changing Perspective* (Princeton: Princeton University Press, 1949), 13-41.

18. Hans W. Loewald, "Psychoanalysis as an Art and the Fantasy Character of the Psychoanalytic Situation," *Journal of the American Psychoanalytic Association* 23, no. 2 (1975): 279. Reprinted in Hans W. Loewald, *Papers on Psychoanalysis*. New Haven: Yale University Press, 1980.

19. Ibid., 285. More recently, Alvin Frank has written that "the central role of the transference in producing psychic change indelibly stamps clinical psychoanalysis as a biographical process. The analyst is first its facilitator and then, with the process set in motion, this re-enactment's *dramatis personae*" ("Psychic Change and the Analyst as Biographer: Transference and Reconstruction," *International Journal of Psycho-Analysis* 72, no. 1 (1991): 26).

20. Serge Moscovici, *The Age of the Crowd: A Historical Treatise on Mass Psychology*, trans. J. C. Whitehouse (Cambridge: Cambridge University Press, 1985), 256-82, 296-312.

21. Jane Ellen Harrison, *Ancient Art and Ritual* (New York: Henry Holt, 1913), 44.

22. Ibid., 47.

23. Ibid.

24. Gombrich, *Aby Warburg*, 17.

25. *The Poetics of Aristotle*, ch. 9, 1451b. In the Gomperz translation, this passage reads: "jene befasst sich mehr mit dem Allgemeinen, diese mit dem Einzelnen" (*Aristoteles' Poetik*, 20).

CHAPTER 2

1. *Minutes*, vol. 1, 1 April 1908, 359.

2. *Minutes*, vol. 2, 28 October 1908, 31-32.

3. See Hermann Broch, *Hugo von Hofmannsthal and His Time: The European Imagination, 1860-1920*, trans. Michael P. Steinberg (Chicago: University of Chicago Press, 1984), 53-65.

4. Carl E. Schorske, "Politics and the Psyche: Schnitzler and Hofmannsthal," in *Fin-de-Siècle Vienna: Politics and Culture* (New York: Alfred A. Knopf, 1980), 7.

5. Ibid., 8.

6. The *Matrikel* and *Rigorosenprotokolle*, Universitätsarchiv, Universität Wien—the psychoanalysts' registration and graduation forms at the University of Vienna—recorded the professions of fourteen fathers: three businessmen, two civil servants, two journalists, a bank executive, a railroad executive, a lawyer, a physician, a railroad

inspector, a produce merchant, and an accountant. The fathers of Isador Sadger and David Bach died before their sons entered the university. The profession of the elder Sadger is unknown.

7. Hanns Sachs, *Freud, Master and Friend* (Cambridge, Mass.: Harvard University Press, 1944), 158.

8. Ernst Federn et al., "Thirty-Five Years with Freud: In Honor of the Hundredth Anniversary of Paul Federn, M.D.," *Journal of the History of the Behavioral Sciences* 8 (January 1972): 12-13.

9. See Shorter, "The Two Medical Worlds of Sigmund Freud," 71, and Philip L. Becker, "Eduard Hitschmann, 1871-1957: Psychoanalysis of Great Men," in *Psychoanalytic Pioneers*, ed. Franz Alexander, Samuel Eisenstein, and Martin Grotjahn (New York: Basic Books, 1966), 160-68.

10. For the exact business profession of Fritz Wittels's father, see *Freud and the Child Woman: The Memoirs of Fritz Wittels*, ed. Edward Timms (New Haven: Yale University Press, 1995), 12, and for the occupations of David Bach's parents, Henriette Kotlan-Werner, *Kunst und Volk: David Joseph Bach, 1874-1947*, Materialien zur Arbeiterbewegung (Vienna: Europaverlag, 1977), 10. Alfred Adler recorded his father's profession on his university registration form.

11. The Österreichische Nationalbibliothek holds the *Central-Organ des Vereins für Verwertung geistiger Arbeit* 1, no. 1 (9 March 1868) through 1, no. 8 (27 July 1868).

12. See Marcellin Reitler, *Die Personaleinrichtungen der Eisenbahn vom Standpunkte des Denkers und Menschenfreundes: Studien und Vorschläge* (Vienna: Waldheim, 1879), 3-4, and pt. 4. Reitler also composed operettas under the pseudonym "Emil Arter." They can be found in the Österreichische Nationalbibliothek and in the Firestone Library, Princeton University.

13. Paul Roazen, *Brother Animal: The Story of Tausk and Freud* (New York: Alfred A. Knopf, 1969), 8-9.

14. See *Matrikel, Phil.*, summer 1909. In Rank's early youth, his father had worked as a jeweler. See Dennis Klein, *Jewish Origins of the Psychoanalytic Movement* (New York: Praeger, 1981), 108, and E. James Lieberman, *Acts of Will: The Life and Work of Otto Rank* (New York: Free Press, 1985), 1.

15. Theodor Reik, *Fragment of a Great Confession: A Psychoanalytic Autobiography* (New York: Farrar, Strauss, 1949), 230.

16. *The Autobiography of Wilhelm Stekel* (New York: Liveright, 1950), 36-48.

17. Roazen, *Brother Animal*, 10.

18. Ernst Mayer, "400 Jahre Akademisches Gymnasium," in *Festschrift: 400 Jahre Akademisches Gymnasium* (Vienna: Bondi und Sohn, 1953), 14.

19. Five members—Max Kahane, Isador Sadger, Maxim Steiner, David Bach, and Theodor Reik—lived and attended school in Leopoldstadt, the home of the majority of Eastern European Jewish families who settled in Vienna after 1850. Kahane, Sadger, and Steiner attended the *Sperlgymnasium*, Freud's secondary school. Alfred Adler, born in Fünfhaus, a lower-middle-class and working-class district on the outskirts of Vienna, attended *Gymnasium* in the suburb of Hernals. Fritz Wittels and Hanns Sachs received their education at the *Maximiliansgymnasium*, located in the university district. The only titled member of the Vienna Psychoanalytic Society rejected the prestigious education of the *Theresianum*. According to the curriculum vitae in his graduation forms, Alfred von Winterstein left the school after one year in order to attend the somewhat less exclusive *Franz Josefgymnasium* (*Rigorosenprotokolle, Phil.*, no. 3191).

20. *Autobiography of Wilhelm Stekel*, 43-57, 99-100.

21. Max Graf, *Legend of a Musical City* (New York: Philosophical Library, 1945), 106.

22. Max Graf, *Composer and Critic: Two Hundred Years of Music Criticism* (New York: W. W. Norton, 1946), 15, 23-24.

23. Sachs, *Freud, Master and Friend*, 3.

24. Ibid., 39.

25. *Rigorosenprotokolle, Jur.*

26. Roazen, *Brother Animal*, 13-18.

27. There is no record of Winterstein having taken the examinations for a doctorate in law. For an account of his university exams, see his curriculum vitae *(Rigorosenprotokolle, Phil.*, no. 3191). Winterstein's poem, "Der Stundenzeiger," appeared in *Die Fackel* 11, no. 285-86 (27 July 1909): 17-19. In 1909, he returned to the University of Vienna to obtain a degree in philosophy (*Matrikel, Phil.*, summer 1909-summer 1911). In *Die Fackel* 13, no. 338 (6 December 1911), an advertisement appeared for a collection of his poetry, *Gedichte*, published by Hugo Heller.

28. In their registration forms, Reitler and Winterstein recorded their religion as Catholic. According to Ernst Federn, Reitler's family had converted from Judaism (conversation with the author).

29. Sachs, *Freud, Master and Friend*, 22.

30. Federn et al., "Thirty-Five Years with Freud," 13.

31. One of Alfred Adler's biographers states that Adler officially converted to Protestantism (Phyllis Bottome, *Alfred Adler: A Biography* [New York: G. P. Putnam's Sons, 1939], 4). Adler's university registration forms, however, show that at least throughout his education he recorded his religion as Jewish. Although her father was Jewish, Victor Tausk's wife adhered to Christianity. Tausk chose to be baptized a Protestant before their wedding. He never ceased, however, to identify himself as Jewish, and few were aware of his conversion. (Sigmund Freud, *The Psychopathology of Everyday Life* [1901], 1919 ed., in *The Standard Edition*, 6: 92-93; Roazen, *Brother Animal*, 11.) Although born Jewish, Otto Rank described himself on the university registration form in 1908 as "non-confessional" (*Konfessionslos*). In the same year, he formally converted to Catholicism so as to justify to the government changing his name from Rosenfeld to Rank, thereby dissociating himself from his father. In 1922, he returned to Judaism. (See Klein, *Jewish Origins of the Psychoanalytic Movement*, 110, n. 28.) Max Graf recalled, "When my son was born, I wondered whether I should not remove him from the prevailing antisemitic hatred, which at the time was preached in Vienna by a very popular man, Doctor Lueger. I was not certain whether it would not be better to have my son brought up in the Christian faith. Freud advised me not to do this" (Max Graf, "Reminiscences of Professor Sigmund Freud," *Psychoanalytic Quarterly* 11, no. 4 [1942]: 473).

32. Max Graf, *Wagner-Probleme und andere Studien* (Vienna: Wiener Verlag, [1900]), 148.

33. Ibid., 150.

34. Graf, *Legend of a Musical City*, 79.

35. Ibid., 174. See also 181.

36. Sachs, *Freud, Master and Friend*, 25-27.

37. Ibid., 27-28.

38. Ibid., 28.

39. Fritz Wittels, *Der Taufjude* (Vienna: M. Breitenstein, 1904), 12.

40. Ibid., 30.

41. Ibid.
42. Ibid., 19.
43. Ibid., 38.
44. Ibid., 35. (Johann Wolfgang von Goethe, *Faust: Part I*, trans. Bayard Taylor, revised and edited by Stuart Atkins [New York: Macmillan, Collier Books, 1962], lines 1339-40.)
45. Otto Weininger, *Sex and Character* (London: William Heinemann, [1906]), 54.
46. Ibid., 130-31.
47. Ibid., 83.
48. Ibid., see 135. The translation is my own. The 1906 translation referred to *Wille zum Wert* as a craving or desire for value.
49. Ibid., 162.
50. Ibid., 161.
51. Ibid., 346.
52. Otto Rank, *Tagebücher II*, 24 February 1904, Box 1a, Otto Rank Papers, Rare Book and Manuscript Library, Columbia University.
53. For information on Rank's father, family life, schooling, and employment, see Klein, *Jewish Origins of the Psychoanalytic Movement*, 116-29, and appendix B.
54. Rank, *Tagebücher II*, 3 May 1904.
55. Rank, *Tagebücher II*, 4 April 1904.
56. Rank, *Tagebücher II*, 22 February 1904.
57. See Klein, *Jewish Origins of the Psychoanalytic Movement*, 121.
58. Wilhelm Stekel, "Der Fall Otto Weininger," *Die Wage*, no. 45 (5 November 1904): 1031.
59. Eduard Hitschmann, "Schopenhauer. Von P. J. Möbius," *Wiener klinische Rundschau* 19, no. 18 (7 May 1905): 317.
60. Ibid.
61. Ibid., 318.
62. *Minutes*, vol. 2, 12 January 1910, 383.
63. Schorske, "Explosion in the Garden: Kokoschka and Schoenberg," in *Fin-de-Siècle Vienna*, 363.
64. Walter Benjamin, "Karl Kraus" (1931), in *Reflections: Essays, Aphorisms, Autobiographical Writings*, ed. Peter Demetz, trans. Edmund Jephcott (New York: Harcourt Brace Jovanovich, 1978), 271.
65. Karl Kraus, *Die demolirte Literatur*, in vol. 2 of *Frühe Schriften, 1892-1900*, ed. Johannes J. Braakenburg (Munich: Kosel Verlag, 1979), 278-79.
66. Ibid., 281. In his essay, "The Overcoming of Naturalism," Hermann Bahr had written: "When nervousness becomes completely liberated and man, especially the artist, becomes entirely subordinate to the nerves, without regard for the rational and sensuous, then the lost joy will return to art. The imprisonment in the external and the bondage of reality cause great pain. . . . Naturalism was a lamentation for the artist, since he had to serve it. But now he removes the tablets from the real and inscribes his own laws on them." (Hermann Bahr, "The Overcoming of Naturalism" [1891], in *The Vienna Coffeehouse Wits 1890-1938*, ed. and trans. Harold B. Segel [West Lafayette, Ind.: Purdue University Press, 1993], 51.)
67. Hanns Sachs, trans., *Soldaten-Lieder und andere Gedichte, von Rudyard Kipling* (Leipzig: Julius Zeitler, 1910), 1.
68. Ibid., 2.

69. Ibid., 1. It is interesting to note that in 1917 the Italian Marxist philosopher and antifascist organizer Antonio Gramsci also published his own translation of Kipling: the poem "If," which Gramsci described as "a breviary for anticlericals [*breviario per laici*], an example of a morality unpolluted by Christianity which can be accepted by all men." (Cited in James Joll, *Antonio Gramsci* [Harmondsworth: Penguin Books, 1978], 44.)

70. Theodor Reik, *Richard Beer-Hofmann* (Leipzig: Sphinx, 1911), 9.

71. Ibid., 9.

72. Ibid., 3.

73. Ibid., 18-19.

74. Ibid., 39.

75. Sachs, *Freud, Master and Friend,* 39-40.

76. Karl Kraus, "Die Kinderfreunde," *Die Fackel* 7, no. 187 (5 November 1905): 19.

77. Karl Kraus, "Der Prozess Riehl," *Die Fackel* 8, no. 211 (13 November 1906): 19.

78. Ibid., 9

79. Ibid., 10.

80. Ibid., 11.

81. Ibid., 25.

82. *Minutes*, vol. 2, 12 January 1910, 388.

83. Fritz Wittels, *Die sexuelle Not* (Vienna: C. W. Stern, 1909), [ix].

84. Ibid., [xiii].

85. *Freud and the Child Woman,* 71. Wittels wrote the drafts of his memoirs in the early 1940s, never publishing them himself.

86. Ibid., 50.

87. Ibid., 48.

88. Edward Timms, *Karl Kraus, Apocalyptic Satirist: Culture and Catastrophe in Habsburg Vienna* (New Haven: Yale University Press, 1986), 99-100.

89. Karl Kraus, *Die Fackel* 10, no. 266 (30 November 1908): 20.

90. *Minutes*, vol. 2, 16 December 1908, 89. In all quotations from the published minutes, bracketed additions appear in the minutes themselves and have not been added by the author.

91. *Minutes*, vol. 2, 12 January 1910, 391.

92. Sigmund Freud to Karl Kraus, 11 November 1906, *Briefe von Freud an Karl Kraus*, in the Wiener Stadt- und Landesbibliothek (IN 109.725). This letter is reprinted in Michael Worbs, *Nervenkunst: Literatur und Psychoanalyse im Wien der Jahrhundertwende* (Frankfurt am Main: Europäische Verlagsanstalt, 1983), 158. Typescripts of other letters from Freud to Kraus are included in *Handschriftliches aus dem Archiv der Fackel herausgegeben von Karl Kraus* (Vienna: Antiquariat und Autographenhandlung Heinrich Hinterberger, [1950]), in the Wiener Stadt- und Landesbibliothek (IN 258.675).

93. For an exploration of the correspondence between Freud and Kraus, and a comparison of their views on sexual morality, see Timms, *Karl Kraus, Apocalyptic Satirist*, 64-67, 94-103.

94. Sigmund Freud to Carl Jung, 13 February 1910, *The Freud/Jung Letters: The Correspondence between Sigmund Freud and C. G. Jung*, ed. William McGuire, trans. Ralph Manheim and R. F. C. Hull (Princeton: Princeton University Press, 1974), 295.

95. Graf, "Reminiscences of Professor Sigmund Freud," 470.

96. William McGrath pointed out the influence of Wagnerianism on David Bach's desire to create a bridge between high culture and the working class. See McGrath, *Dionysian Art and Populist Politics in Austria* (New Haven: Yale University Press, 1974), 217-18.

97. Graf, *Wagner-Probleme und andere Studien,* [7].

98. Ibid., 21-22.

99. Ibid., [7-8].

100. Ibid., [5]. While a student at the University of Vienna, Graf had supported the rebellion of *Jung Wien.* He now rejected it: "The old criticism was rigid, dogmatic, narrow-minded; the new flexible, without convictions, indulgent. . . . It made no value judgments, that was its chief weapon." See ibid., [10].

101. Ibid., [6].

102. Ibid., 78.

103. Ibid., 80.

104. Ibid., 83-84.

CHAPTER 3

1. *Autobiography of Wilhelm Stekel,* 104.

2. Max Kahane, *Grundriss der inneren Medicin für studierende und praktische Ärzte* (Leipzig: Franz Deuticke, 1901), 580.

3. Wilhelm Stekel, "Traumleben und Traumdeutung," *Neues Wiener Tagblatt,* 29 January 1902, 1.

4. For the location of Freud's lectures, see Alfred von Winterstein, "Meine Erin-nerungen an Freud," manuscript in the possession of Dr. Ernst Federn, 1; see also Josef and Renée Gicklhorn, *Sigmund Freuds akademische Laufbahn im Lichte der Dokumente* (Vienna: Urban und Schwarzenberg, 1960), 165.

5. See Rudolf Reitler, *Mitteilungen der Thermal-Kuranstalt für partielle Trocken-Heissluft-Behandlung* 1, no. 1 (March 1903): 1. The Österreichische Nationalbibliothek has five numbers of the *Mitteilungen* from March 1903 through July 1904.

6. See "Besuch bei Dr. Alfred Adler," *Neues Wiener Tagblatt,* 1 July 1928, 5-6, cited in Carl Furtmüller, "Alfred Adler: A Biographical Essay," in Alfred Adler, *Superiority and Social Interest: A Collection of Later Writings,* ed. Heinz L. and Rowena R. Ansbacher, 2nd ed. (Evanston, Ill.: Northwestern University Press, 1970), 336 n. 8. On the creation of the Wednesday group, see also Ernest Jones, *The Life and Work of Sigmund Freud,* vol. 2 (New York: Basic Books, 1955), 7-8.

7. Winterstein, "Meine Erinnerungen an Freud," 1. I am grateful to Dr. Ernst Federn for allowing me to quote from this document.

8. Winterstein took his last course in law in the summer semester of 1908. During his first semester in the school of philosophy—the summer of 1909—together with logic and ethics, Winterstein enrolled for "Anatomical and Physiological Introduction to the Study of Nervous Illnesses." He formally registered for Freud's course, "Lectures on the Theory of Neurosis and Psychoanalysis" [*Vorträge uber Neurosenlehre und Psychoanalyse*] in the winter semester, 1909-1910. See *Matrikel, Phil.,* summer 1909-summer 1911.

9. Winterstein, "Meine Erinnerungen an Freud," 2.

10. Ibid.

11. Sachs, *Freud, Master and Friend,* 42.

12. Ibid., 41.

13. Ibid., 42.

14. Ibid., 43.

15. Ibid.

16. Ibid., 44.

17. Ibid. For the years of Sachs's attendance at Freud's lectures, see Elke Mühl-leitner, *Biographisches Lexikon der Psychoanalyse: Die Mitglieder der Psychologischen Mittwoch-Gesellschaft und der Wiener Psychoanalytischen Vereinigung 1902-1938* Tübingen: Edition Diskord, 1992), 279.

18. Fritz Wittels, *Sigmund Freud: His Personality, His Teaching, and His School*, translated by Eden and Cedar Paul (New York: Dodd, Mead, 1924), 129-30.

19. Ibid., 130. (Wilhelm Hauff, *Mittheilungen aus den Memoiren des Satan*, vol. 6 of *Sämmtliche Werke* [Stuttgart: Friedrich Brodhag'sche Buchhandlung, 1837], 19.) For the date of Wittels's attendance at Freud's lectures, see *Freud and the Child Woman*, 33. In Theodor Reik's words, psychoanalysis offered "something derived not from psychology textbooks but from the premonitions and visions of Goethe, Shakespeare, Dostoyevsky, Schopenhauer, and Nietzsche" (Theodor Reik, *From Thirty Years with Freud* [New York: Farrar and Rinehart, 1940], 26).

20. David Bach, "Oesterreichischer Universitätsjammer," *Arbeiter Zeitung*, 6 December 1903, 2-3; 8 December 1903, 2-3; and 18 December 1903, 2-3.

21. *Rigorosenprotokolle, Phil.*, no. 1074.

22. For Bach's career, see Henriette Kotlan-Werner, *Kunst und Volk*, 16; Max Graf, "Totenkränze," *Weltpresse*, 7 May 1948, 6; and Alfred Magaziner, "David Bach schuf Konzerte für die Arbeiter," *Rentner und Pensionist* (June 1977): 17.

23. Bach, "Oesterreichischer Universitätsjammer," 6 December 1903, 3.

24. Ibid.

25. Ibid.

26. Ibid.

27. Ibid.

28. Ibid.

29. Ibid., 8 December 1903, 2.

30. Max Graf, *Richard Wagner im "Fliegenden Holländer": Ein Beitrag zur Psychologie künstlerischen Schaffens* (Leipzig: Franz Deuticke, 1911), "Vorwort," and Isador Sadger, *Heinrich von Kleist: Eine pathographisch-psychologische Studie* (Wiesbaden: J. F. Bergmann, 1909), 58.

31. *Minutes*, vol. 1, February 5, 1908, 299.

32. Ibid., 301-2.

33. Alfred Adler, "Der Arzt als Erzieher" (1904), in *Heilen und Bilden: Ärtzlich-pädagogische Arbeiten des Vereins für Individualpsychologie*, ed. Alfred Adler and Carl Furtmüller (Munich: Ernst Reinhardt, 1914), 1-10.

34. Ibid., 3.

35. Ibid., 5.

36. Alfred Adler, "Das sexuelle Problem in der Erziehung," in Heinrich and Lily Braun, eds., *Die Neue Gesellschaft: Sozialkritische Wochenschrift* 1, no. 50 (1905): 361. I am grateful to Dr. Heinz L. Ansbacher for having provided me with a copy of this article.

37. Ibid.

38. Ibid.

39. Sadger was the brother of Wittels's stepmother, Rubin Wittels's second wife, Malke Sadger. See *Freud and The Child Woman*, 163 n. 5.

40. Wittels, *Die sexuelle Not*, 15. The essay first appeared in *Die Fackel* 8, no. 219-20 (22 February 1907): 1-22. According to Wittels, Freud, after having read the essay, personally asked Wittels to join the Vienna Society. (*Freud and the Child Woman*, 48.)

41. Wittels, *Die sexuelle Not*, 16.

42. The essay first appeared in *Die Fackel* 9, no. 238 (16 December 1907): 1-24; it was republished in *Die sexuelle Not*.

43. Wittels, *Die sexuelle Not*, 88.

44. Wittels's essay on female assassins, discussed by the society on 10 April 1907, was published almost a year later in *Die Fackel* 9, no. 246-47 (12 March 1908): 26-38, and reprinted in *Die sexuelle Not*. On 15 May 1907, Wittels delivered to the society his paper on female physicians, which had appeared in *Die Fackel* 9, no. 225 (3 May 1907): 10-24; he republished it in *Die sexuelle Not*.

45. *Minutes*, vol. 1, 10 April 1907, 165.

46. Wittels, *Die sexuelle Not*, 183.

47. *Minutes*, vol. 1, 10 April 1907, 162.

48. Ibid.

49. Ibid., 163.

50. *Minutes*, vol. 1, 15 May 1907, 196.

51. *Minutes*, vol. 1, 11 March 1908, 351.

52. *Minutes*, vol. 1, 15 May 1907, 197.

53. Ibid., 199.

54. *Minutes*, vol. 2, 16 December 1908, 86.

55. Ibid.

56. Ibid., 89.

57. David Bach, "Beim Schreiben," *Arbeiter Zeitung*, 4 October 1904, 1.

58. Ibid., 2.

59. Ibid., 3.

60. Klein, *Jewish Origins of the Psychoanalytic Movement*, 121.

61. See Rank, *Tagebücher IV*, Box 1a, Otto Rank Papers, Columbia University.

62. In his article, "Drei Psycho-Analysen von Zahleneinfällen und obsedirenden Zahlen," Adler referred to an individual who had communicated with him on a self-analysis. Age, birth date, and family circumstances indicate that the individual was Otto Rank. (*Psychiatrisch-Neurologische Wochenschrift*, 7 October 1905, 265-66.)

63. Jones, *Life and Work of Sigmund Freud*, vol. 2, 8.

64. See Klein, *Jewish Origins of the Psychoanalytic Movement*, 128.

65. Freud recalled, "One day a young man who had passed through a technical training college introduced himself with a manuscript which showed very unusual comprehension. We persuaded him to go through the *Gymnasium* [Secondary School] and the University and to devote himself to the non-medical side of psychoanalysis" (*On the History of the Psycho-Analytic Movement* [1914], in *The Standard Edition*, 14: 25).

66. Otto Rank, *Der Künstler: Ansätze zu einer Sexual-Psychologie* (Vienna: Hugo Heller, 1907), 16.

67. Ibid., 15. In translating these and the following passages, I have consulted *The Artist* (1925), 4th ed., trans. Eva Salomon with the assistance of E. James Lieberman, in *Journal of the Otto Rank Association* 15, no. 1 (summer 1980): 5-63.

68. Ibid., 16-17.

69. Ibid., 16.

70. Ibid., 24.

71. Ibid., 26.

72. Ibid., 33.

73. Ibid., 35.

74. Ibid., 55.

75. Ibid.

76. Ibid.

77. Ibid., 56.

78. Ibid.

79. Ibid.

80. Sigmund Freud, *The Interpretation of Dreams*, 264.

81. *Minutes*, vol. 2, 10 March 1909, 174. For discussion of Rank's book, *The Incest Theme in Literature and Legend*, see Chapters 4 and 6 below.

82. Aeschylus, *Agamemnon*, trans. Richmond Lattimore, lines 174-78, in *The Complete Greek Tragedies*, ed. David Grene and Richmond Lattimore (Chicago: University of Chicago Press, 1953). In 1964, the new editorial board of *American Imago*, headed by Harry Slochower, introduced the passage from Aeschylus as the journal's motto: Πάθει μάθος, Through suffering, wisdom. The board also stated its decision to translate *"Geisteswissenshaften"* as the "Humanities" in its pages. ("Program of American Imago," *American Imago* 21, no. 1-2 [spring-summer 1964]: 5.) A psychoanalyst, Harry Slochower began his career as a professor of German and comparative literature at Brooklyn College. In 1952, the college launched a McCarthyite purge of its professors and dismissed him from the faculty. Slochower remained as editor of *American Imago* until his death in 1991. See Ellen Schrecker, *No Ivory Tower: McCarthyism and the Universities* (New York: Oxford University Press, 1986), 167-71, 285, 306, and Sophie Wilkins, "Harry Slochower: *Der springende Punkt*," in Maynard Solomon, ed., *Myth, Creativity, Psychoanalysis: Essays in Honor of Harry Slochower* (Detroit: Wayne State University Press, 1978), 16-22.

CHAPTER 4

1. Max Graf, "Richard Wagner und das dramatische Schaffen," *Österreichische Rundschau* 9 (November-December 1906): 115.

2. Ibid.

3. Ibid. (Wilhelm Dilthey, *Das Erlebnis und die Dichtung: Lessing, Goethe, Novalis, Hölderlin* (Leipzig: B. G. Teubner, 1906], 145.) In the passage which he cited, however, Graf deviated from Dilthey's original statement by emphasizing in typeface the phrase *"seinem allgemeinen Gesetzen gemäss."* In this way, perhaps, Graf chose to distinguish in Dilthey's work the universal psychologist from the historicist philosopher.

4. Graf, "Richard Wagner und das dramatische Schaffen," 115.

5. Ibid., 121.

6. Max Graf, "Probleme des dramatischen Schaffens," *Österreichische Rundschau* 10 (January-March 1907): 337.

7. *Rigorosenprotokolle, Med.*, 1872-1894, 328.

8. For the years of Sadger's attendance at Freud's lectures, see Mühlleitner, *Biographisches Lexikon der Psychoanalyse*, 282.

9. Isador Sadger, "Wie wirken Hydro- und Elektrotherapie bei Nervenkrankheiten?" in *Fortschritte der Hydrotherapie*, ed. A. Strasser and B. Buxbaum (Vienna: Urban und Schwarzenberg), 220.

10. Klein, *Jewish Origins of the Psychoanalytic Movement*, 140.

11. Isador Sadger, "Ferdinand Raimund: Eine pathologische Studie," *Die Wage* 1. Halbjahr, no. 23 (1898): 387-89; no. 24 (1898): 402-4; no. 25 (1898): 421-23; and "War Goethe eine pathologische Erscheinung?," *Deutsche Revue über das gesamte nationale Leben der Gegenwart* 24, no. 2 (April-June 1899): 72-96. For information on Sadger's background, publications, and career, see Mühlleitner, *Biographisches Lexikon der Psychoanalyse*, 282-83.

12. Sadger, "Ferdinand Raimund," 388.

13. Ibid., 404.

14. Ibid., 422.

15. Ibid.

16. Ibid.

17. Freud to Jung, 5 March 1908, *The Freud/Jung Letters*, 130.

18. Isador Sadger, *Konrad Ferdinand Meyer: Eine pathographisch-psychologische Studie* (Wiesbaden: J. F. Bergmann, 1909), 15.

19. Ibid., 6.

20. *Minutes*, vol. 1, 4 December 1907, 255.

21. Ibid., 256.

22. Ibid., 255.

23. Ibid.

24. Ibid., 257.

25. Ibid.

26. Ibid.

27. *Minutes*, vol. 1, 11 December 1907, 259.

28. Ibid., 260-61.

29. Ibid., 261.

30. Ibid., 262.

31. Ibid., 262-63.

32. Ibid., 264.

33. Ibid.

34. Ibid., 268-69.

35. Ibid., 265.

36. Ibid., 267. According to Wittels, the psychology of creativity diverted the movement from its true aim: "Wittels is opposed to this method of writing biographies of poets. For the temptation would be too great to use the unwritten dictionary of unconscious meanings, which one has in one's mind. It is more fruitful to apply Freudian teachings to life itself, to make people understand the sexual need. At the present time, the psychologies of poets are of no advantage either for Freud's teachings or for the public in general" (ibid.).

37. Ibid., 265.

38. Heller, who founded his publishing firm in 1905, began to organize lectures and readings at his bookstore in 1907. Presenters included Hugo von Hofmannsthal, Heinrich Mann, Thomas Mann, and Rainer Maria Rilke. See Worbs, *Nervenkunst*, 143-46.

39. Sigmund Freud, "Creative Writers and Day-Dreaming" (1908 [1907]), in *The Standard Edition*, 9: 153.

40. Ibid.

41. *Minutes*, vol. 1, 11 December 1907, 265-66.

42. Ibid., 266.

43. Ibid.

44. In the preface, Graf stated that he first presented his study of "The Flying Dutchman" to the Vienna Psychoanalytic Society, certainly prior to October 1906, as there is no record of it in the published minutes.

45. Max Graf, *Richard Wagner im "Fliegenden Holländer,"* 9.

46. Ibid., 20.

47. Ibid., 22.

48. Ibid., 45.

49. Graf, "Richard Wagner und das dramatische Schaffen," 113.

50. Max Graf, *Die innere Werkstatt des Musikers* (Stuttgart: Ferdinand Enke, 1910), 187.

51. Ibid., 228.

52. Ibid., 249-50.

53. Rank, *Der Künstler,* 46.

54. David Bach, " 'Elektra' von Richard Strauss," *Arbeiter Zeitung,* 26 March 1909, 1.

55. Ibid.

56. Ibid.

57. Ibid.

58. Ibid.

59. Ibid., 1-2.

60. Ibid., 2.

61. In this regard, compare Richard Wollheim's conclusion: "For all his attachment to the central European tradition of romanticism, a work of art remained for Freud what historically it had always been: a piece of work" (Richard Wollheim, "Freud and the Understanding of Art," in *On Art and the Mind: Essays and Lectures* [London: Allen Lane, 1973], 218).

62. Rank, *Der Künstler,* 56.

63. Weininger, *Sex and Character,* 345.

64. *Minutes,* vol. 1, 17 October 1906, 15.

65. Ibid., 16-17.

66. *Minutes,* vol. 1, 24 October 1906, 23.

67. Ibid., 28.

68. *Minutes,* vol. 2, 31 March 1909, 186.

69. Ibid., 187.

70. Ibid., 186.

71. Ibid., 187.

72. Ibid.

73. Ibid.

74. Ibid.

75. Ibid., 188.

76. Ibid.

77. Ibid., 188-89.

78. Ibid., 189. Michael Worbs noted Freud's statement at the meeting—"It is also one of the poet's tasks to facilitate our empathy with his hero, not to draw him as such a repulsive individual that we cannot take any interest in his fate" (ibid., 190)—commenting that "Brecht would have characterized this conception of the dramatist's task as an Aristotelian one" (Worbs, *Nervenkunst,* 267).

79. *Minutes,* vol. 2, 31 March 1909, 193.

80. Ibid., 194.

81. Ibid.

82. Ibid.

83. Bach, " 'Elektra' von Richard Strauss," 2.

84. *Minutes*, vol. 1, 24 October 1906, 23.

85. Wilhelm Stekel, *Dichtung und Neurose: Bausteine zur Psychologie des Künstlers und des Kunstwerkes* (Wiesbaden: J. F. Bergmann, 1909), 5.

86. *Minutes*, vol. 2, 14 October 1908, 7.

87. Karl Kraus, *Die Fackel* 9, no. 229 (2 July 1907): 4.

88. Karl Kraus, *Die Fackel* 9, no. 237 (2 December 1907): 9-10.

89. Karl Kraus, *Die Fackel* 10, no. 256 (5 June 1908): 19.

90. Ibid., 20.

91. Ibid., 20-21. (*King Lear* I.ii.125-28.)

92. Kraus, *Die Fackel* 10, no. 256 (5 June 1908): 21.

93. Ibid., 22.

94. Karl Kraus, *Die Fackel* 11, no. 300 (9 April 1910): 27.

95. Karl Kraus, *Die Fackel* 10, no. 256 (5 June 1908): 23. (Johann Wolfgang von Goethe, "The Sorcerer's Apprentice," in *Selected Verse*, ed. David Luke [Harmondsworth: Penguin Books, 1964], 173-77.) For a discussion of Kraus's critique of Freudian interpretations of creativity and his final disenchantment with psychoanalysis, see Timms, *Karl Kraus, Apocalyptic Satirist*, 103-14.

96. *Minutes*, vol. 2, 14 October 1908, 9.

97. *Minutes*, vol. 2, 5 May 1909, 224-25.

98. Ibid., 224.

CHAPTER 5

1. *Minutes*, vol. 1, 11 December 1907, 261.

2. Ibid., 265.

3. Freud to Jung, 11 November 1909, *The Freud/Jung Letters*, 260.

4. Much has been written on the subject of Freud's identification with Leonardo, beginning with Ernest Jones's biography of Freud. For an overview of the literature, see Joseph D. Lichtenberg, "Freud's Leonardo: Psychobiography and Autobiography of Genius," *Journal of the American Psychoanalytic Association* 26, no. 4 (1978): 863-80.

5. Sigmund Freud, "On Psychotherapy" (1905 [1904]), in *The Standard Edition*, 7: 260-61.

6. Erwin Panofsky, "Artist, Scientist, Genius: Notes on the 'Renaissance-Dämmerung,' " in Wallace K. Ferguson, et al., *The Renaissance: Six Essays* (New York: Harper and Row, Harper Torchbooks, 1962), 128.

7. Carlo Ginzburg has explained how this tendency crossed class lines. See Ginzburg, *The Cheese and the Worms: The Cosmos of a Sixteenth-Century Miller*, trans. John and Anne Tedeschi (Baltimore: Johns Hopkins University Press, 1980), 121-26.

8. E. H. Gombrich, preface to *Leonardo da Vinci: Hayward Gallery, London*, ed. Martin Kemp and Jane Roberts (London: South Bank Centre and Yale University Press, 1989), 1. Elsewhere Gombrich noted that once Leonardo had broken with traditional patterns of design, in his work "any increase in that imaginative freedom we call 'art' demanded an equal intensification of those studies we call 'scientific'. . . . To give substance to a figure that had emerged from the artist's *imaginativa* and been adjusted *levando e ponendo*, nothing less would suffice than a knowledge of those laws of growth

and proportion by which Nature herself would create it" (E. H. Gombrich, "Leonardo's Method for Working out Compositions," in *Norm and Form*, 4th ed. [London: Phaidon Press, 1985], 62-63).

9. On concepts of the liberal and fine arts in the Renaissance, see Paul Oskar Kristeller, "The Modern System of the Arts," in *Renaissance Thought and the Arts: Collected Essays*, expanded ed. (Princeton: Princeton University Press, 1990), 178-89.

10. Gombrich, preface to *Leonardo da Vinci: Hayward Gallery, London*, 1-2.

11. For a history and description of the *Trattato della Pittura*, see Kenneth Clark, *Leonardo da Vinci*, rev. and intro. Martin Kemp (London: Penguin Books, 1993), 125-38.

12. On the relation of Leonardo's *paragone* to the conceptualization of the liberal and fine arts, see Kristeller, "The Modern System of the Arts," 183-84.

13. Martin Kemp, ed., *Leonardo on Painting: An Anthology of Writings by Leonardo da Vinci with a Selection of Documents Relating to his Career as an Artist*, trans. Martin Kemp and Margaret Walker (New Haven: Yale University Press, 1989), 10.

14. Panofsky, "Artist, Scientist, Genius," 130-31. Paolo Rossi emphasized that Leonardo did not, however, advocate a complete fusion of mechanical and liberal pursuits: "In reality, Leonardo's polemic, like that of many other artists of the fifteenth century, did not intend to overcome the age-old opposition between the mechanical and liberal arts. Rather, it tended to justify the insertion of painting and sculpture within the list of the so-called liberal arts" (Paolo Rossi, "Mechanical Arts and Philosophy in the Sixteenth Century," in *Philosophy, Technology, and the Arts in the Early Modern Era*, trans. Salvator Attanasio [New York: Harper and Row, Torchbook Library, 1970], 29).

15. Kemp, ed., *Leonardo on Painting*, 10.

16. Ibid.

17. Ibid., 19.

18. Ibid., 193.

19. Ibid., 202.

20. Ibid., 193.

21. Irma A. Richter, ed., *The Notebooks of Leonardo da Vinci* (Oxford: Oxford University Press, 1952; Oxford: Oxford University Press, World's Classics, 1990), 7.

22. See E. H. Gombrich, "Leonardo on the Science of Painting: Towards a Commentary on the 'Trattato della Pittura,' " in *New Light on Old Masters* (Chicago: University of Chicago Press, 1986), 32-60.

23. See Kemp, ed., *Leonardo on Painting*, 15, 16, and Martin Kemp, " 'Disciple of Experience,' " in *Leonardo da Vinci: Hayward Gallery, London*, 13.

24. Kemp, ed., *Leonardo on Painting*, 18.

25. Ibid., 23.

26. Ibid., 37.

27. Ibid., 26.

28. Ibid., 46. The passage is completed, "while poetry ends in words, with which it vigorously praises itself."

29. Panofsky, "Artist, Scientist, Genius," 147.

30. Ibid., 140. Rossi also stressed Leonardo's "decisive contribution to the invention of a precise method for the representation and description of reality," such a method equaling in the descriptive sciences "the invention of the telescope or of the microscope in the seventeenth century" (Rossi, "Mechanical Arts and Philosophy in the Sixteenth Century," 28-29).

31. Richter, ed., *The Notebooks of Leonardo da Vinci*, 7.

32. Martin Kemp, "Leonardo Then and Now," in *Leonardo da Vinci: Hayward Gallery, London*, 11.

33. See Panofsky, "Artist, Scientist, Genius," 166-82. Similarly, Rossi emphasized that "before the figure of the artist was identified with that of the 'genius,' in the Florentine studios of the fifteenth century, like that of Verrochio, Ghirlandaio, and Brunelleschi, for perhaps the first time a fusion had been effected between technical and scientific activities, and manual labor and theory. . . . Here, alongside the arts of stone-cutting and pouring bronze, as well as painting and sculpture, apprentices were taught the rudiments of anatomy, optics, calculus, perspective, and geometry, as well as the projected construction of vaults and the digging of canals" (Rossi, "Mechanical Arts and Philosophy in the Sixteenth Century," 22-23).

34. Sigmund Freud to Martha Bernays, 19 October 1885, *The Letters of Sigmund Freud*, ed. Ernest L. Freud, trans. Tania and James Stern (New York: Basic Books, 1960), 173.

35. Sigmund Freud to Ernest Jones, 15 April 1910, *The Complete Correspondence of Sigmund Freud and Ernest Jones 1908-1939*, ed. R. Andrew Paskauskas (Cambridge, Mass.: Harvard University Press, Belknap Press, 1993), 51.

36. Sigmund Freud to Eduard Silberstein, 13 August 1874, *The Letters of Sigmund Freud and Eduard Silberstein 1871-1881*, ed. Walter Boehlich, trans. Arnold J. Pomerans (Cambridge, Mass.: Harvard University Press, Belknap Press, 1990), 48.

37. Sigmund Freud, "Contribution to a Questionnaire on Reading" (1907), in *The Standard Edition*, 9: 246. Freud kept as part of his library Merejkowski's *Leonardo Da Vinci: Ein Biographischer Roman aus der Wende des 15. Jahrhunderts*, translated by Carl von Guetschow and published in 1903. (See Jutta Birmele, "Strategies of Persuasion: The Case of *Leonardo Da Vinci*," in *Reading Freud's Reading*, 146 n. 25.) The novel's original date of publication in Russian was 1902. (See "Indexes and Bibliographies," in *The Standard Edition*, 24: 125.) An English translation by Herbert Trench was published in the same year, and entitled, *The Romance of Leonardo da Vinci*. For the date of the original English-language publication, see the 1912 edition (New York: G. P. Putnam's Sons).

38. Sigmund Freud, *Leonardo da Vinci and a Memory of His Childhood* (1910), in *The Standard Edition*, 11: 131.

39. Ibid., 76.

40. Ibid.

41. Ibid.

42. Ibid., 77.

43. Ibid.

44. Ibid., 69.

45. Sigmund Freud, *Delusions and Dreams in Jensen's "Gradiva,"* 9.

46. Freud, *Leonardo da Vinci and a Memory of His Childhood*, 82. The much commented upon mistranslation of "vulture" for "kite" would have satisfied Leonardo as further proof of the superiority of visual impressions over words. (See especially Meyer Schapiro, "Leonardo and Freud: An Art-Historical Study," *Journal of the History of Ideas* 17, no. 2 [April 1956]: 147-78.) Our concern, however, is with Freud's interpretation of the memory as given in his source, and how that interpretation elucidates his views on art and science.

47. Ibid., 90.

48. Ibid., 92.

49. Ibid., 98.

50. Ibid., 110-11.

51. Ibid., 117.

52. Ibid., 117-18. Here Freud followed the traditional designation of the seated figure of St. John the Baptist as Bacchus.

53. Ibid., 123.

54. Ibid., 124-25.

55. Ibid., 134.

56. Ibid., 136.

57. Ibid., 63.

58. In discussing psychoanalysis as both science and art, Harry Slochower, in his inaugural issue as editor of *American Imago*, wrote that "psychoanalysis is a system which aims at establishing universal laws of human motivation." (Harry Slochower, "Applied Psychoanalysis As a Science and As An Art," *American Imago* 21, nos. 1-2 [spring-summer, 1964]: 167.) He continued, however, that "the universality which psychoanalysis aims at is by way and through the individual, in his concreteness and sensuousness." (ibid.) Slochower concluded, "Psychoanalysis, like art, replaces an abstract-conceptual dialectic by a material-contentual dialectic which aims to uncover the dynamics of emotion without pretending to offer final formulas." (ibid., 172-73.)

59. See Yosef Hayim Yerushalmi, "Freud on the 'Historical Novel': From the Manuscript Draft (1934) of *Moses and Monotheism*," *International Journal of Psycho-Analysis* 70, no. 3 (1989): 375-95.

60. Freud, *Leonardo da Vinci and a Memory of His Childhood*, 136-37.

61. Ibid., 137.

62. Ibid.

63. Ibid.

Chapter 6

1. Freud to Jung, 14 November 1911, *The Freud/Jung Letters*, 463.

2. It is worth noting that at this time Freud made an adjustment in therapeutic focus similar to the shift which he introduced in the study of culture. In "Remembering, Repeating and Working-Through," he stressed the importance to psychoanalytic technique of those cases in which "the patient does not *remember* anything of what he has forgotten and repressed, but *acts* it out. He reproduces it not as a memory but as an action; he *repeats* it, without, of course, knowing that he is repeating it." (Sigmund Freud, "Remembering, Repeating and Working-Through" [1914], in *The Standard Edition* 12: 150.)

3. See *Minutes*, vol. 3, 12 October 1910, 8, and *Statuten der Wiener Psychoanalytischen Vereinigung* (Vienna: Moriz Frisch, 1910).

4. Jones, *Life and Work of Sigmund Freud*, vol. 2, 146.

5. See *Minutes*, vol. 3, 12 October 1910, 9; and 19 October 1910, 17.

6. Of these members, twenty-one participated in at least half of the society's meetings that year. In the first year for which we have a record, 1906-1907, the membership numbered nineteen, of which nine individuals attended at least half of the discussions. These figures were determined from the membership and attendance lists published in *Minutes*.

7. *Minutes*, vol. 2, 23 February 1910, 423-28. A revised version of Adler's essay was published in Alfred Adler, *Co-operation Between the Sexes: Writings on Women, Love*

and Marriage, Sexuality and Its Disorders, ed. and trans. Heinz L. and Rowena R. Ansbacher (Garden City, N. Y.: Doubleday Anchor Books, 1978), 32-34.

8. *Minutes*, vol. 2, 23 February 1910, 432.

9. Ibid., 433.

10. *Minutes*, vol. 3, 16 November 1910, 59.

11. Ibid.

12. Ibid.

13. Alfred Adler, "Die psychische Behandlung der Trigeminusneuralgie," *Zentralblatt* 1 (1910): 22.

14. Ibid., 16.

15. Ibid., 17.

16. Ibid.

17. Ibid.

18. Alfred Adler, "Über männliche Einstellung bei weiblichen Neurotikern," *Zentralblatt* 1 (1910): 177.

19. Ibid.

20. Ibid.

21. Alfred Adler, "Beitrag zur Lehre vom Widerstand," *Zentralblatt* 1 (1910): 218.

22. *Minutes*, vol. 3, 4 January 1911, 102-3.

23. Ibid., 104.

24. Ibid., 103-4.

25. *Minutes*, vol. 3, 1 February 1911, 142.

26. Ibid.

27. Ibid.

28. Ibid., 143.

29. Ibid.

30. Ibid., 141.

31. Ibid., 142.

32. Ibid., 145.

33. Ibid., 146.

34. Ibid., 147.

35. Ibid.

36. Ibid., 149.

37. Ibid., 147.

38. *Minutes*, vol. 3, 22 February 1911, 171-72.

39. Rudolf Reitler, "Kritische Bemerkungen zu Dr. Adler's Lehre vom 'männlichen Protest,'" *Zentralblatt* 1 (1910): 581.

40. Ibid., 582.

41. Ibid.

42. *Minutes*, vol. 3, 22 February 1911, 168.

43. Ibid., 175.

44. *Minutes*, vol. 3, 8 February 1911, 156.

45. *Minutes*, vol. 3, 22 February 1911, 175-76.

46. *Minutes*, vol. 3, 1 February 1911, 150.

47. *Minutes*, vol. 3, 22 February 1911, 173.

48. Ibid., 172.

49. Ibid., 173.

50. *Minutes*, vol. 3, 1 March 1911, 179.

51. Jones, *Life and Work of Sigmund Freud*, vol. 2, 133.

52. Freud to Jung, 15 June 1911, *The Freud/Jung Letters*, 428.

53. *Minutes*, vol. 3, 11 October 1911, 283.

54. *Minutes*, vol. 3, 5 October 1910, 2. In his memoirs, Wittels gave his own account of those events surrounding the unnecessary and ill-fated libel suit against him by Kraus on behalf of Irma Karczewska for Wittels's thinly veiled fictional characterization of her in his novel *Ezechiel der Zugereiste* (Berlin: Egon Fleischel, 1910). More a coda than a cause for his breach with Kraus, the suit determined the timing of his taking leave of the circles of both Kraus and Freud. See *Freud and the Child Women*, 85-103.

55. *Minutes*, vol. 3, 11 October 1911, 281.

56. *Minutes*, vol. 2, 7 February 1909, 159.

57. Graf's name was crossed from the attendance book for the year 1913-1914. See *Minutes*, vol. 4, "Appendix," 309.

58. *Minutes*, vol. 1, 5 February 1908, 301. Freud apparently compelled Graf to come to a decision. Graf recalled that "I was unable and unwilling to submit to Freud's 'do' or 'don't'—with which he once confronted me—and nothing was left for me but to withdraw from his circle" (Graf, "Reminiscences of Professor Sigmund Freud," 475).

59. Sachs recalled his first meeting with Freud: "My translation of Kipling's *Barrack-Room Ballads* had been published (it was the farewell, or rather the tombstone, for my purely literary interests) and I went one afternoon, not without some heartbeating, to present a copy to Freud" (Sachs, *Freud, Master and Friend*, 50).

60. Freud to Jung, 27 June 1911, *The Freud/Jung Letters*, 432.

61. See *Matrikel, Phil.*, winter 1907-summer 1911, Universitätsarchiv, Universität Wien.

62. Theodor Reik, *From Thirty Years with Freud*, 25.

63. Ibid.

64. See Reik, *Fragment of a Great Confession*, 301. Reik's dissertation for the Philosophy Faculty at the university was a psychoanalytic study of Gustave Flaubert's *The Temptation of St. Anthony*, the first dissertation to utilize psychoanalysis. On 10 July 1911, Reik submitted the thesis, which was passed on 7 October 1911. (Universitätsarchiv, Universität Wien, *Rigorosenprotokolle, Phil.*, no. 3283.) He published it under the title *Flaubert und seine "Versuchung des Heiligen Antonius": Ein Beitrag zur Künstlerpsychologie* (Minden, Westfalen: J. C. C. Bruns, 1912). Otto Rank submitted his dissertation, a psychoanalytic study of the Lohengrin legend, on 3 June 1912, and received approval from his readers on 13 June. (Universitätsarchiv, Universität Wien, *Rigorosenprotokolle, Phil.*, no. 3465.) Rank had already published *Die Lohengrinsage: Ein Beitrag zu ihrer Motivgestaltung und Deutung* (Leipzig: Franz Deuticke, 1911) in the *Papers on Applied Psychology*.

65. See Freud to Jung, 1 January 1908, *The Freud/Jung Letters*, 105 n. 1; Freud to Jung, 14 February 1908, *The Freud/Jung Letters*, 117.

66. On attempts to secure a publisher for *Imago*, see Sigmund Freud to Sándor Ferenczi, 5 October 1911, *The Correspondence of Sigmund Freud and Sándor Ferenczi: Volume 1, 1908-1914*, ed. Eva Brabant, Ernst Falzeder, and Patrizia Giampieri-Deutsch, under the supervision of André Haynal, trans. Peter T. Hoffer (Cambridge, Mass.: Harvard University Press, Belknap Press, 1993), 302; Freud to Ferenczi, 21 October 1911, *The Correspondence of Sigmund Freud and Sándor Ferenczi: Volume 1*, 306; Freud to Jung, 20 October 1911, *The Freud/Jung Letters*, 451; Freud to Jung, 2 November 1911,

The Freud/Jung Letters, 453; Sachs, *Freud, Master and Friend*, 64-65; and Jones, *Life and Work of Sigmund Freud*, vol. 2, 89.

67. Freud to Jung, 12 November 1911, *The Freud/Jung Letters*, 458.

68. Freud to Jung, 14 November 1911, *The Freud/Jung Letters*, 463.

69. Freud to Jung, 16 November 1911, *The Freud/Jung Letters*, 464.

70. See Freud to Jung, 27 June 1911, *The Freud/Jung Letters*, 432; and Freud to Jones, 9 August 1911, *The Complete Correspondence of Sigmund Freud and Ernest Jones*, 113.

71. For the date of its appearance, see Sigmund Freud to James Jackson Putnam, 28 March 1912, *James Jackson Putnam and Psychoanalysis: Letters between Putnam and Sigmund Freud, Ernest Jones, William James, Sandor [sic] Ferenczi, and Morton Prince, 1877-1917*, ed. Nathan G. Hale, Jr., trans. Judith Bernays Heller (Cambridge, Mass.: Harvard University Press, 1971), 137.

72. Freud to Jung, 10 January 1912, *The Freud/Jung Letters*, 480.

73. Ibid.

74. Freud to Jones, 28 April 1912, *The Complete Correspondence of Sigmund Freud and Ernest Jones*, 138.

75. Carl G. Jung, "Wandlungen und Symbole der Libido. Beiträge zur Entwicklungsgeschichte des Denkens. I," *Jahrbuch für psychoanalytische und psychopathologische Forschungen* 3, no. 1 (1911): 120-227. This was published with pt. 2 as *Psychology of the Unconscious: A Study of the Transformations and Symbolisms of the Libido: A Contribution to the History of the Evolution of Thought*, trans. Beatrice M. Hinkle, supplementary vol. B of *The Collected Works of C. G. Jung*, Bollingen Series 20 (Princeton: Princeton University Press, 1991). For a discussion of the term imago, see Jean Laplanche and J.-B. Pontalis, *The Language of Psycho-Analysis*, trans. Donald Nicholson-Smith (New York: W. W. Norton, 1973), 211.

76. Jung, *Psychology of the Unconscious*, 48.

77. Ibid.

78. Ibid., n. 6.

79. Sachs, *Freud, Master and Friend*, 65.

80. Hanns Sachs, "Carl Spitteler," *Imago* 2, no. 1 (1913): 74.

81. Ibid., 73-74.

82. Sigmund Freud, "The Dynamics of Transference" (1912), in *The Standard Edition*, 12: 100.

83. Ibid., 102.

84. Sigmund Freud, "On the Universal Tendency to Debasement in the Sphere of Love" (1912), in *The Standard Edition*, 11: 181.

85. Otto Rank and Hanns Sachs, "Entwicklung und Ansprüche der Psychoanalyse," *Imago* 1, no. 1 (1912): 16. Rank and Sachs also coauthored a programmatic outline on the application of psychoanalysis to the cultural sciences, *Die Bedeutung der Psychoanalyse für die Geisteswissenschaften* (Wiesbaden: J. F. Bergmann, 1913). (*The Significance of Psychoanalysis for the Mental Sciences*, trans. Charles R. Payne [New York: Nervous and Mental Disease Publishing Co., 1916].)

86. On the Sociological Society, see Josef Langer, "Allgemeine gesellschaftliche Hintergründe für die Entwicklung der Soziologie in Österreich," in *Geschichte der österreichischen Soziologie*, ed. Josef Langer (Vienna: Verlag für Gesellschaftskritik, 1988), 14. I am grateful to Johannes Reichmayr for providing me with this reference.

87. Hanns Sachs, "Die Bedeutung der Psychoanalyse für Probleme der Soziologie," *Zentralblatt* 2 (1911-1912): 469.

88. Hanns Sachs, "Über Naturgefühl," *Imago* 1, no. 2 (1912): 128.
89. Ibid., 129.
90. Ibid.
91. Ibid.
92. Ibid., 130.
93. Ibid.
94. Ibid., 130-31.
95. Ibid., 131.
96. Ibid.
97. Alfred von Winterstein, "Psychoanalytische Anmerkungen zur Geschichte der Philosophie," *Imago* 2, no. 2 (1913): 209.
98. Ibid.
99. Ibid., 208.
100. Ibid., 198
101. Ibid., 206
102. Ibid., n. 1. Ernst Kris later commented that for the application of narrative form in art, "the shortcut of visual imagination must be replaced by words which can evoke the vision in others" (Ernst Kris, *Psychoanalytic Explorations in Art* [Madison, Conn.: International Universities Press, 1952], 38).
103. Winterstein, 198.
104. Ibid.
105. See ibid., 176, 223.
106. Ibid., 221. For a discussion of Winterstein's essay, see also Patrizia Giampieri-Deutsch, "Alfred von Winterstein und die Rolle der Philosophie in den Diskussion der Mittwoch-Gesellschaft," in *Aus dem Kreis um Sigmund Freud: Zu den Protokollen der Wiener Psychoanalytischen Vereinigung,* ed. Ernst Federn and Gerhard Wittenberger (Frankfurt am Main: Fischer Taschenbuch, 1992), 77-88.
107. Theodor Reik, *Arthur Schnitzler als Psycholog* (Minden, Westfalen: J. C. C. Bruns, 1913), 187.
108. Commenting on the use of the concept of imago, Reik wrote: "We often said: this or that character is a father-imago. That does not mean that the character is the copy [*Abbild*] of the actual father, rather that it represents the projection of a specific idea [*Vorstellung*] of the father, of an emotional attitude [*Gefühlseinstellung*] toward the father" (ibid., 192-93).
109. Ibid., 196.
110. Ibid., 195.
111. See ibid., 197-98.
112. Otto Rank, *The Incest Theme in Literature and Legend: Fundamentals of a Psychology of Literary Creation,* trans. Gregory C. Richter (Baltimore: Johns Hopkins University Press, 1992), 572.
113. Freud to Jung, 12 February 1911, *The Freud/Jung Letters,* 391.
114. Freud to Jung, 20 August 1911, *The Freud/Jung Letters,* 438.
115. See Jung, *Psychology of the Unconscious,* 86.
116. Freud to Jung, 1 September 1911, *The Freud/Jung Letters,* 441.
117. Ibid.
118. Sigmund Freud, "Die Inzestscheu," *Imago* 1, no. 1 (1912): 17.
119. Ibid., 18.
120. C. G. Jung, "Wandlungen und Symbole der Libido. II," *Jahrbuch* 4, no. 1 (1912): 162-464. (*Psychology of the Unconscious,* pt. 2, 115-414.)

121. Sigmund Freud, *Totem and Taboo: Some Points of Agreement between the Mental Lives of Savages and Neurotics* (1913 [1912-13]), in *The Standard Edition*, 13: xiii.

122. Ibid.

123. As Francis Huxley wrote, Frazer "was a materialist in the Darwinian style in that he translated structure into habit and thus into function—though the habits he was interested in were all ritual." Huxley continued, "These rituals, though many and disparate, had yet something in common with each other; indeed, it seemed that there was a large ritual form in which they were once embodied, here known as totemism, there as sacred kingship, while the form of these forms was the universal pattern, the life and death of the incarnate deity" (Francis Huxley, "Psychoanalysis and Anthropology," in *Freud and the Humanities*, ed. Peregrine Horden [London: Duckworth, 1985], 131). On the importance for Freud of Frazer's differentiation of religious and social aspects of totemism, his study of the horror of incest in totemic communities, his account of taboo prohibitions, and his analysis of magic, see Edwin R. Wallace, *Freud and Anthropology: A History and Reappraisal* (New York: International Universities Press, 1983), 65-68, 72-77, 85-86.

124. Sigmund Freud, "Über einige Übereinstimmungen im Seelenleben der Wilden und der Neurotiker. I. Die Inzestscheu," *Imago* 1, no. 1 (1912): 17-33; "II. Das Tabu und die Ambivalenz der Gefühlsregungen," *Imago* 1, no. 3, (1912): 213-27 and 1, no. 4 (1912): 301-33; "III. Animismus, Magie und Allmacht der Gedanken," *Imago* 2, no. 1 (1913): 1-21; and "IV. Die infantile Wiederkehr des Totemismus," *Imago* 2, no. 4 (1913): 357-408.

125. Freud, *Totem and Taboo*, 2.

126. Ibid., 3.

127. Ibid., 4.

128. Ibid.

129. Ibid., 17.

130. Ibid., 21.

131. Ibid., 22.

132. Ibid.

133. Ibid., 21.

134. Ibid., 34.

135. Ibid., 35.

136. Ibid., 72.

137. Ibid., 73.

138. Ibid., 91-92.

139. Ibid., 92.

140. At the meeting of the Vienna Psychoanalytic Society devoted to Sachs's presentation on the feeling for nature, Freud applied his interpretation of animism to the contemporary concerns of the culture critics among his followers: "Art, which previously had the loftiest and most meaningful directions, has become directionless ('art for art's sake'). The same thing holds true for aesthetics, which is also a secondary psychic achievement, becoming possible only after the decline of something else—namely, the animistic world-outlook. Thus, there seems to be nothing in our midst that one could explain without reaching back into the whole of prehistory" (*Minutes*, vol. 3, 13 December 1911, 353).

141. Freud, *Totem and Taboo*, 108.

142. Ibid.

143. Ibid., 126.

144. Ibid., 132.

145. Ibid., 139. Freud relied on William Robertson Smith, *The Religion of the Semites: The Fundamental Institutions*, 2nd ed. (1894; reprint, New York: Schocken Books, 1972). Discussing the practice of animal sacrifice, the Scottish biblical scholar and anthropologist wrote, "When an unclean animal is sacrificed it is also a sacred animal. If the deity to which it is devoted is named, it is the deity which ordinarily protects the sanctity of the victim, and, in some cases, the worshippers either in words or by symbolic disguise claim kinship with the victim and the god. Further, the sacrifice is generally limited to certain solemn occasions, usually annual, and so has the character of a public celebration. In several cases the worshippers partake of the sacred flesh, which at other times it would be impious to touch. All this is exactly what we find among totem peoples. Here also the sacred animal is forbidden food, it is akin to the men who acknowledge its sanctity, and if there is a god it is akin to the god. And, finally, the totem is sometimes sacrificed at an annual feast, with special and solemn ritual" (Smith, *The Religion of the Semites*, 294-95).

146. Freud, *Totem and Taboo*, 142.

147. Ibid., 143.

148. In December 1912, Freud expressed his view of religion as the internalization of the father's actions to a meeting of the Vienna Psychoanalytic Society: "Law is what the father does; religion, what the son has" (*Minutes*, vol. 4, 11 December 1912, 136).

149. Freud, *Totem and Taboo*, 144.

150. Ibid., 146.

151. Ibid., 150.

152. Ibid., 149.

153. Ibid., 150.

154. Ibid., 151-52.

155. In a paper presented to the 1912 International Congress of Art History in Rome, Aby Warburg traced in the astrological images of the frescoes of the Palazzo Schifonoja a similar process of the return of the repressed. Warburg interpreted the figure of the man holding a rope, who was associated in one of the frescoes with the zodiacal symbol of the ram, as the penultimate stage in the reemergence of the image of Perseus from classical antiquity. According to Warburg, the Greek Perseus had appeared in the Middle Ages as an astrological symbol first in the guise of an Indian Decan with a double axe, later distorted a second time as a Decan with a rope, until reemerging as the figure in the Palazzo Schifonoja. Ultimately, a student of Raphael returned Perseus to his original form for the ceiling of the Farnesina in Rome. (See Gombrich, *Aby Warburg*, 192-95.)

156. Freud, *Totem and Taboo*, 156.

157. Ibid.

158. Ibid., 161.

159. According to Patrick Mahony, in the concluding essay of *Totem and Taboo*, Freud's writing style itself relied in part on a "mimetic structure," in that "his text becomes a temporal artifact of narrative suspense in its own right: the objective chronological difficulties spill over into the diverse mappings of origins from mythology and secondary historical sources and into Freud's own theory and narrative elaboration of it. The imbrication of shifting time levels truly imitates the enmeshing of thought and deed which preoccupies Freud at the end of his text" (Patrick Mahony, *Freud as a Writer*, expanded ed. [New Haven: Yale University Press, 1987], 25).

160. In December 1912, Freud told the Vienna Psychoanalytic Society that "one can discuss the relationships of the libido to the psychology of religion and to the evolution of civilization without having, as Jung thinks, to modify the concept" (*Minutes*, vol. 4, 11 December 1912, 136).

161. As commentators have pointed out, Freud assumed that the memory of the primal crime also survived as part of the individual's "archaic heritage," preserved and transmitted within the unconscious. The contributions of *Totem and Taboo* to cultural science, however, do not rise or fall with that assumption—certainly not for the Viennese—as the discussion in the following chapter will demonstrate.

CHAPTER 7

1. Sigmund Freud, "Thoughts for the Times on War and Death: (I) The Disillusionment of the War (II) Our Attitude towards Death" (1915), in *The Standard Edition*, 14: 275-300.

2. In connection with the painter Christoph Haitzmann's demonological case history, Freud turned to Haitzmann's illustrations of the Devil—visions contemporaneous with the painter's illness—to help interpret Haitzmann's neurosis. See Sigmund Freud, "A Seventeenth-Century Demonological Neurosis" (1923 [1922]), in *The Standard Edition*, 19: 72-105.

3. The essays were first published together as *Probleme der Religionspsychologie: I. Teil: Das Ritual* (Leipzig: Internationaler Psychoanalytischer Verlag, 1919).

4. Sigmund Freud to Sándor Ferenczi, 17 October 1912, *The Correspondence of Sigmund Freud and Sándor Ferenczi: Volume 1*, 411.

5. Sigmund Freud to Karl Abraham, 6 January 1914, in Jones, *Life and Work of Sigmund Freud*, vol. 2, 366.

6. Sigmund Freud, "The Moses of Michelangelo" (1914), in *The Standard Edition*, 13: 213.

7. Marthe Robert, *From Oedipus to Moses: Freud's Jewish Identity*, trans. Ralph Manheim (Garden City, N. Y.: Doubleday Anchor Books, 1976), 142.

8. See Yosef Hayim Yerushalmi, *Freud's Moses: Judaism Terminable and Interminable* (New Haven: Yale University Press, 1991), 70-74.

9. E. H. Gombrich, "Freud's Aesthetics," *Encounter* 26, no. 1 (January 1966): 33.

10. Wollheim, "Freud and the Understanding of Art," 208.

11. For an examination of Freud, Morelli, and late nineteenth-century investigative methods, see Carlo Ginzburg, "Clues: Roots of an Evidential Paradigm" in *Clues, Myths, and the Historical Method*, 96-125.

12. Richard Wollheim noted that through this interpretation Freud resolved the question as to whether the sculpture represented a "study of character" or a "study of action." (Wollheim, "Freud and the Understanding of Art," 208.) "By seeing it as a study in suppressed action, that is self-mastery, we can also see it as a study in character and at the same time avoid any inconsistency with the compositional indications" (ibid., 209).

13. Freud, "The Moses of Michelangelo," 229. Jack Spector characterized Freud's analysis as a "dramatic interpretation, with its series of imagined stages, and with its potential for his own identification" (Jack J. Spector, *The Aesthetics of Freud: A Study in Psychoanalysis and Art* [New York: McGraw-Hill, 1974], 131). As Spector wrote, "Freud combined the cinematographic with the psychological in considering the statue's form as the epitome of preliminary postures and emotional attitudes" (ibid., 132).

14. Freud, "The Moses of Michelangelo," 233.

15. Ibid., 220.

16. Ibid., 229.

17. Ibid., 233.

18. Ibid., 228.

19. For the interpretation of the pathos of the Jewish prophets as in part rooted in a conflict between their concern for God and his Law, and their loyalty to their people, see Abraham J. Heschel, *The Prophets*, (New York: Harper and Row, 1962), 24, 38, 121-22, 315, 423.

20. Sigmund Freud, "Thoughts for the Time on War and Death: (I) The Disillusionment of War," 276-77.

21. Ibid., 279.

22. Theodor Reik, *Ritual: Psycho-Analytic Studies: The Psychological Problems of Religion: I* (1946; reprint, Westport, Conn.: Greenwood Press, 1975), 1. In the prefatory remarks to his *Arthur Schnitzler als Psycholog* dated August 1913, Reik also referred to this conversation in which Freud pointed out to him analogies between the procedure of psychoanalysis and that of Morelli (Reik, *Arthur Schnitzler als Psycholog*, iv). Certainly, Reik must have been aware of the identity of the author of "The Moses of Michelangelo" when the essay first appeared in *Imago*.

23. Reik, *Ritual*, 16. Emphasis in the 1946 American edition of *Ritual*. In the 1919 German edition, the phrase read, "*Charakter der Aktion*," without emphasis. (Reik, *Das Ritual*, xvi.)

24. Reik, *Ritual*, 60.

25. Ibid., 108.

26. Ibid., 140.

27. Ibid., 118.

28. Ibid., 125-26.

29. Ibid., 155.

30. Reik referred the reader to Jane Ellen Harrison, who, in *Ancient Art and Ritual*, had traced one of the roots of Greek tragedy to the performance of initiation rites (ibid., 161 n. 3). Harrison wrote that " 'initiation' is of tremendous importance, and we should expect, what in fact we find, that all this emotion that centres about it issues in *dromena*, 'rites done'" (Harrison, *Ancient Art and Ritual*, 106). Upon examining such rituals, it became possible to "understand now who and what was the god who arose out of the rite, the *dromenon* of tribal initiation, the rite of the new, the second birth. He was Dionysos" (ibid., 113).

31. Reik, *Ritual*, 164. The definition reads, "die Nachahmung eines Geschehens . . . , die Furcht und Mitleid erregt und zugleich eine Katharsis dieser Affekte bewirkt" in the 1919 German edition (Reik, *Das Ritual*, 129).

32. Reik, *Ritual*, 164-65. Reik likened this process to the course of psychoanalytic therapy, without further elaborating on the analogy. His description of drama, however, seemed to provide an account of the process and nature of transference as Hans W. Loewald would describe it years later in "Psychoanalysis as an Art and the Fantasy Character of the Psychoanalytic Situation." See chapter 1 above.

33. Reik, *Ritual*, 258.

34. Ibid., 259.

35. Ibid., 298.

36. Ibid., 304.

37. It should be emphasized that the issue here is not only one of the content of ritual, but of its form. Ritual mimesis was representation in the form of an action, and thus its formal qualities also pointed to its origins in historical acts. Ernst Kris commented on how the advance of repression influenced this formal element: "The historical development of dramatic art during a comparatively late, the so-called classical, phase of Greek civilization was, according to well-documented assumptions, preceded by various stages in which no rigorous separation between audience and stage existed. All were potential actors, participating in festival or ritual, celebrating or reliving what myth had taught them as the essence of tradition. . . . The development from magic ritual to dramatic art in Greek civilization has many analogies in other culture areas. The common element of these developments is the tendency to the reduction of action and its more or less complete replacement by other experiences" (Kris, *Psychoanalytic Explorations in Art*, 40).

38. Reik, *Ritual*, 298-99.

39. For Tausk's graduation from the medical school, see *Rigorosenprotokolle, Med.*, 1903-1930, 843. For his psychological writings, see *Sexuality, War, and Schizophrenia: Collected Psychoanalytic Papers*, ed. Paul Roazen, trans. Eric Mosbacher et al. (New Brunswick, N. J.: Transaction Publishers, 1991).

40. See "Discussion on Lay Analysis," *International Journal of Psycho-Analysis* 8 (1927): 174-283, and "Concluding Remarks on the Question of Lay Analysis," *International Journal of Psycho-Analysis* 8 (1927): 392-401.

41. For a recent account of Rank's break with Freud, see Peter L. Rudnytsky, *The Psychoanalytic Vocation: Rank, Winnicott, and the Legacy of Freud* (New Haven: Yale University Press, 1991), 31-45. The book interprets the continued relevance of Rank's immediate post-Freudian writings in the light of developments in psychoanalytic object relations theory.

42. Paul Federn, *Zur Psychologie der Revolution: die vaterlose Gesellschaft* (Leipzig: Brüder Suschitzky, 1919), 22.

43. Ibid., 6.

44. Ibid., 5

45. Ibid., 17. According to Federn, Bolshevism, like the councils and strike movement, represented "the primal tendency of mankind toward a new order" (ibid., 24). While he saw in the council organization a defense against the "dictatorship of the proletariat," Federn believed that the idea of common ownership "genuinely represented the progress from the fatherlessness of society to the brother principle" (ibid). Dictatorship in Russia arose not from Bolshevism alone, but also as a response to the war and to the sabotage organized by the former Entente powers and their newly allied bourgeois states.

46. On the Austro-Marxists' political choice between republic and revolution in the immediate aftermath of the war, see Anson Rabinbach, *The Crisis of Austrian Socialism: From Red Vienna to Civil War 1927-1934* (Chicago: University of Chicago Press, 1983), 18-31, and Tom Bottomore, introduction to *Austro-Marxism*, ed. and trans. Tom Bottomore and Patrick Goode (Oxford: Clarendon Press, 1978), 37-44.

47. Federn, *Zur Psychologie der Revolution: die vaterlose Gesellschaft*, 22.

48. Ibid., 28.

49. Freud, "Thoughts for the Time on War and Death: (I) The Disillusionment of War," 288.

50. Sigmund Freud, *Group Psychology and the Analysis of the Ego* (1921), in *The Standard Edition*, 18: 86-87. For a review of the book within the context of turn-of-the-

century crowd psychology, see Jaap van Ginneken, "The Killing of the Father: The Background of Freud's Group Psychology," *Political Psychology* 5, no. 3 (September 1984): 391-414.

51. Freud, *Group Psychology and the Analysis of the Ego*, 121.

52. Ibid., 123.

53. Ibid.

54. Ibid.

55. Ibid., 127. In *The Age of the Crowd*, Serge Moscovici applied the concept of mimesis to interpret the role of identification in Freud's group psychology. Identification encompassed both "the act of imitating, of reproducing a model" and "a feeling of attachment" (Moscovici, *The Age of the Crowd*, 257). Moscovici, however, proposed the existence of two "autonomous and irreducible" desires: the erotic, which tended toward "inamoration," and the mimetic, which tended toward identification, or attachment to a model (ibid., 270). "With regard to the individual," he wrote, "the erotic tendency is paramount over the mimetic one, whereas in the case of the mass, the opposite is the case" (ibid., 271). The "resurrection of *imago*" referred to the process which maintained "the continuity of identifications in the course of history" (ibid., 301-2). That process occurred chiefly as the transmission of "idealised" images of persons and events (ibid., 311).

56. Freud, *Group Psychology and the Analysis of the Ego*, 129.

57. Ibid.

58. Ibid., 132.

59. Ibid.

60. Ibid., 133.

61. Fergusson, *The Idea of a Theater*, 29.

62. Max Weber, "Politics as a Vocation" (1919 [1918]), in *From Max Weber: Essays in Sociology*, ed. H. H. Gerth and C. Wright Mills (New York: Oxford University Press, 1946, 1975), 115.

CHAPTER 8

1. Sigmund Freud to Romain Rolland, 4 March 1923, *The Letters of Sigmund Freud*, 341.

2. Ibid.

3. Ibid., 341-42. On the correspondence between Freud and Rolland, see David James Fisher, "Sigmund Freud and Romain Rolland: The Terrestrial Animal and His Great Oceanic Friend," *American Imago* 33, no. 1 (spring 1976): 1-59, and David S. Werman, "Sigmund Freud and Romain Rolland," *International Review of Psycho-Analysis* 4, no. 2 (1977): 225-42.

4. In July 1929, Freud wrote to Rolland for his agreement to open the book in this way; Rolland assented. (Freud to Rolland, 14 July 1929, *The Letters of Sigmund Freud*, 388.)

5. Sigmund Freud, *Civilization and Its Discontents* (1930 [1929]), in *The Standard Edition*, 21: 64.

6. Ibid., 68.

7. Ibid.

8. Ibid., 79.

9. Ibid., 84.

10. Ibid., 85.

11. Ibid., 95.
12. Ibid.
13. Ibid.
14. Ibid., 102.
15. Ibid., 103.
16. Ibid., 112.
17. Ibid.
18. Ibid., 118-19.
19. Ibid., 122.
20. Ibid.
21. Ibid., 123. As Paul Ricoeur wrote, culture's "supreme ruse is to make death work against death" (Ricoeur, *Freud and Philosophy: An Essay in Interpretation*, trans. Denis Savage [New Haven: Yale University Press, 1970], 309).
22. Freud, *Civilization and Its Discontents*, 128.
23. Ibid., 131.
24. Ibid., 132.
25. Ibid., 122. See also 96.
26. Ibid., 135-36.

BIBLIOGRAPHY

I. ARCHIVES

Otto Rank Papers, Rare Book and Manuscript Library, Columbia University
Sigmund Freud Gesellschaft, Vienna
Universitätsarchiv, Universität Wien
Wiener Stadt- und Landesbibliothek

II. SIGMUND FREUD: LETTERS CITED

Briefe von Freud an Karl Kraus. 25 September 1906 and 18 November 1906. IN 109.723 and IN 109.725. Wiener Stadt- und Landesbibliothek.

The Complete Correspondence of Sigmund Freud and Ernest Jones 1908-1939. Edited by R. Andrew Paskauskas. Cambridge, Mass.: Harvard University Press, Belknap Press, 1993.

The Correspondence of Sigmund Freud and Sándor Ferenczi: Volume 1, 1908-1914. Edited by Eva Brabant, Ernst Falzeder, and Patrizia Giampieri-Deutsch, under the supervision of André Haynal. Translated by Peter T. Hoffer. Cambridge, Mass.: Harvard University Press, Belknap Press, 1993.

The Freud/Jung Letters: The Correspondence between Sigmund Freud and C. G. Jung. Edited by William McGuire. Translated by Ralph Manheim and R. F. C. Hull. Princeton: Princeton University Press, 1974.

Handschriftliches aus dem Archiv der Fackel herausgegeben von Karl Kraus. Sigmund Freud, 2 October 1904, 2 October 1906, 7 October 1906, 31 October 1906. Vienna: Antiquariat und Autographenhandlung Heinrich Hinterberger, [1950]. IN 258.675. Wiener Stadt- und Landesbibliothek

James Jackson Putnam and Psychoanalysis: Letters between Putnam and Sigmund Freud, Ernest Jones, William James, Sandor [sic] Ferenczi, and Morton Prince, 1877-1917.

Edited by Nathan G. Hale, Jr. Translated by Judith Bernays Heller. Cambridge, Mass.: Harvard University Press, 1971.

The Letters of Sigmund Freud. Edited by Ernst L. Freud. Translated by Tania and James Stern. New York: Basic Books, 1960.

The Letters of Sigmund Freud to Eduard Silberstein 1871-1881. Edited by Walter Boehlich. Translated by Arnold J. Pomerans. Cambridge, Mass.: Harvard University Press, Belknap Press, 1990.

III. SIGMUND FREUD: WORKS CITED

The Standard Edition of the Complete Psychological Works of Sigmund Freud. 24 vols. Edited by James Strachey in collaboration with Anna Freud, assisted by Alix Strachey and Alan Tyson. London: Hogarth Press and the Institute of Psycho-Analysis, 1953-1974.

Studies on Hysteria (1893-1895). With Josef Breuer. Vol. 2.

The Interpretation of Dreams (1900). Vol. 4.

The Psychopathology of Everyday Life (1901). Vol. 6.

"On Psychotherapy" (1905 [1904]). Vol. 7.

Three Essays on the Theory of Sexuality (1905). Vol. 7.

Jokes and their Relation to the Unconscious (1905). Vol. 8.

Delusions and Dreams in Jensen's "Gradiva" (1907 [1906]). Vol. 9.

"Creative Writers and Day-Dreaming" (1908 [1907]). Vol. 9.

"Contribution to a Questionnaire on Reading" (1907). Vol. 9.

Analysis of a Phobia in a Five-Year-Old Boy (1909). Vol. 10.

Leonardo da Vinci and a Memory of His Childhood (1910). Vol. 11.

"On the Universal Tendency to Debasement in the Sphere of Love" (1912). Vol. 11.

"The Dynamics of Transference" (1912). Vol. 12.

"Remembering, Repeating and Working-Through" (1914). Vol. 12.

Totem and Taboo: Some Points of Agreement between the Mental Lives of Savages and Neurotics (1913 [1912-13]). Vol. 13.

"The Moses of Michelangelo" (1914). Vol. 13.

On the History of the Psycho-Analytic Movement (1914). Vol. 14.

"Thoughts for the Time on War and Death (I) The Disillusionment of the War (II) Our Attitude towards Death" (1915). Vol. 14.

Group Psychology and the Analysis of the Ego (1921). Vol. 18.

"A Seventeenth-Century Demonological Neurosis" (1923 [1922]). Vol. 19.

The Question of Lay Analysis (1926). Vol. 20.

Civilization and Its Discontents (1930 [1929]). Vol. 21.

Moses and Monotheism: Three Essays (1939 [1934-38]). Vol. 23.

IV. VIENNA PSYCHOANALYTIC SOCIETY: MINUTES

Andreas-Salomé, Lou. *The Freud Journal of Lou Andreas-Salomé.* Translated by Stanley A. Levy. New York: Basic Books, 1964.

Lobner, Hans, ed. "Die behandlungstechnischen Diskussionen der Wiener Psychoanalytischen Vereinigung (1923-1924)." *Jahrbuch der Psychoanalyse* 10: 169-204. Published in English as "Discussions on Therapeutic Technique in the Vienna Psychoanalytic Society (1923-1924)." Translated by Hans Lobner. *Sigmund Freud House Bulletin* 2 (1978): 15-33.

Nunberg, Herman and Federn, Ernst, eds. *Minutes of the Vienna Psychoanalytic Society*. 4 vols. Translated by M. Nunberg with the assistance of H. Collins. New York: International Universities Press, 1962-1975. Published in German as *Protokolle der Wiener Psychoanalytischen Vereinigung*. 4 vols. Frankfurt am Main: S. Fischer, 1976-1981.

"Zur Genese des Fetischismus." In *Aus dem Kreis um Sigmund Freud Zu den Protokollen der Wiener Psychoanalytischen Vereinigung*, edited by Ernst Federn and Gerhard Wittenberger. Frankfurt am Main: Fischer Taschenbuch, 1992. Published in English as "Freud and Fetishism: Previously Unpublished Minutes of the Vienna Psychoanalytic Society." Translated by Louis Rose. *Psychoanalytic Quarterly* 57, no. 2 (April 1988): 147-66.

V. VIENNA PSYCHOANALYTIC SOCIETY: WORKS CITED

Adler, Alfred. "Der Arzt als Erzieher" (1904). In *Heilen und Bilden: Ärztlich-pädagogische Arbeiten des Vereins für Individualpsychologie*, edited by Alfred Adler and Carl Furtmüller. Munich: Ernst Reinhardt, 1914.

————. "Das sexuelle Problem in der Erziehung." *Die Neue Gesellschaft: Sozialkritische Wochenschrift* 1, no. 50 (1905): 360-62.

————. "Drei Psycho-Analysen von Zahleneinfällen und obsedirenden Zahlen." *Psychiatrisch-Neurologische Wochenschrift* 7, no. 28 (7 October 1905): 263-67.

————. "Der psychische Hermaphroditismus im Leben und Neurose." *Fortschritte der Medizin* 28 (1910): 486-93. Revised version published as "Masculine Protest and a Critique of Freud." In *Co-operation Between the Sexes: Writings on Women, Love and Marriage, Sexuality and Its Disorders*, edited and translated by Heinz L. and Rowena R. Ansbacher. Garden City, N. Y.: Doubleday Anchor Books, 1978.

————. "Die psychische Behandlung der Trigeminusneuralgie." *Zentralblatt* 1 (1910): 10-29. Revised version published as "The Psychic Treatment of Trigeminal Neuralgia." In *The Practice and Theory of Individual Psychology*, translated by P. Radin. Totowa, N. J.: Littlefield, Adams, 1973.

————. "Über männliche Einstellung bei weiblichen Neurotikern." *Zentralblatt* 1 (1910): 174-78. Revised version published as "The Masculine Attitude in Female Neurotics." In *The Practice and Theory of Individual Psychology*, translated by P. Radin. Totowa, N. J.: Littlefield, Adams, 1973.

————. "Beitrag zur Lehre vom Widerstand." *Zentralblatt* 1 (1910): 214-19. Revised version published as "The Concept of Resistance during Treatment." In *The Practice and Theory of Individual Psychology*, translated by P. Radin. Totowa, N. J.: Littlefield, Adams, 1973.

Bach, David, "Oesterreichischer Universitätsjammer." *Arbeiter Zeitung*, 6 December 1903, 2-3; 8 December 1903, 2-3; 18 December 1903, 2-3.

————. "Beim Schreiben." *Arbeiter Zeitung*, 7 October 1904, 1-3.

————. " 'Elektra' von Richard Strauss." *Arbeiter Zeitung*, 26 March 1909, 1-2.

Federn, Paul. *Zur Psychologie der Revolution: Die vaterlose Gesellschaft*. Leipzig: Brüder Suschitzky, 1919.

Graf, Max. *Wagner-Probleme und andere Studien*. Vienna: Wiener Verlag, [1900].

————. "Richard Wagner und das dramatische Schaffen." *Österreichische Rundschau* 9 (November-December 1906): 111-21.

————. "Probleme des dramatischen Schaffens." *Österreichische Rundschau* 10 (January-March 1907): 326-37.

————. *Die innere Werkstatt des Musikers.* Stuttgart: Ferdinand Enke, 1910.

————. *Richard Wagner im "Fliegenden Holländer": Ein Beitrag zur Psychologie künstlerischen Schaffens.* Leipzig: Franz Deuticke, 1911.

————. "Reminiscences of Prof. Sigmund Freud." *Psychoanalytic Quarterly* 11, no. 4 (1942): 465-76.

————. *Legend of a Musical City.* New York: Philosophical Library, 1945.

————. *Composer and Critic: Two Hundred Years of Music Criticism.* New York: W. W. Norton, 1946.

————. "Totenkränze." *Weltpresse*, 7 May 1948, 6.

Hitschmann, Eduard. "Schopenhauer. Von P. J. Möbius." *Wiener klinische Rundschau* 19, no. 18 (7 May 1905): 317-18.

Kahane, Max. *Grundriss der inneren Medicin für studierende und praktische Ärzte.* Leipzig: Franz Deuticke, 1901.

Rank, Otto. *Der Künstler: Ansätze zu einer Sexual-Psychologie.* Vienna: Hugo Heller, 1907.

————. *Die Lohengrinsage: Ein Beitrag zu ihrer Motivgestaltung und Deutung.* Leipzig: Franz Deuticke, 1911.

————. *Das Inzest-Motiv in Dichtung und Sage: Grundzüge einer Psychologie des dichterischen Schaffens.* Leipzig: Franz Deuticke, 1912. Published in English as *The Incest Theme in Literature and Legend: Fundamentals of a Psychology of Literary Creation*, translated by Gregory C. Richter. Baltimore: Johns Hopkins University Press, 1992.

————. *The Artist* (1925). 4th ed. Translated by Eva Solomon with the assistance of E. James Lieberman. In *Journal of the Otto Rank Association* 15, no. 1 (summer 1980): 5-63.

Rank, Otto, and Hanns Sachs. "Entwicklung und Ansprüche der Psychoanalyse." *Imago* 1, no. 1 (1912): 1-16.

————. *Die Bedeutung der Psychoanalyse für die Geisteswissenschaften.* Wiesbaden: J. F. Bergmann, 1913. Published in English as *The Significance of Psychoanalysis for the Mental Sciences*, translated by Charles R. Payne. New York: Nervous and Mental Disease Publishing Co., 1916.

Reik, Theodor. *Richard Beer-Hofmann.* Leipzig: Sphinx, 1911.

————. *Flaubert und seine "Versuchung des heiligen Antonius": Ein Beitrag zur Künstlerpsychologie.* Minden, Westfalen: J. C. C. Bruns, 1912.

————. *Arthur Schnitzler als Psycholog.* Minden, Westfalen: J. C. C. Bruns, 1913.

————. *Probleme der Religionspsychologie: I. Teil: Das Ritual.* Leipzig: Internationaler Psychoanalytischer Verlag, 1919.

————. *Ritual: Psycho-Analytic Studies: The Psychological Problems of Religion: I.* Translated by Douglas Bryan. 1946. Reprint, Westport, Conn.: Greenwood Press, 1975.

————. *From Thirty Years with Freud.* New York: Farrar and Rinehart, 1940.

————. *Fragment of a Great Confession: A Psychoanalytic Autobiography.* New York: Farrar, Strauss, 1949.

Reitler, Rudolf, ed. *Mitteilungen der Thermal-Kuranstalt für partielle Trocken-Heissluft-Behandlung* 1, no. 1 (March 1903).

————. "Kritische Bermerkungen zu Dr. Adler's Lehre vom 'männlichen Protest.'" *Zentralblatt* 1 (1910): 580-86.

Sachs, Hanns, trans. *Soldaten-Lieder und andere Gedichte, von Rudyard Kipling.* Leipzig: Julius Zeitler, 1910.

———. "Die Bedeutung der Psychoanalyse für Probleme der Soziologie." *Zentralblatt* 2 (1911-1912): 464-69.

———. "Über Naturgefühl." *Imago* 1, no. 2 (1912): 119-31.

———. "Carl Spitteler." *Imago* 2, no. 1 (1913): 73-77.

———. *Freud, Master and Friend.* Cambridge, Mass.: Harvard University Press, 1944.

Sadger, Isador. "Wie Wirken Hydro- und Elektrotherapie bei Nervenkrankheiten?" *Fortschritte der Hydrotherapie*, edited by A. Strasser and B. Buxbaum. Vienna: Urban und Schwarzenberg, 1897.

———. "Ferdinand Raimund: Eine pathologische Studie." *Die Wage*, 1. Halbjahr, no. 23 (1898): 387-89; no. 24 (1898): 402-4; no. 25 (1898): 421-23.

———. "War Goethe eine pathologische Erscheinung?" *Deutsche Revue über das gesamte nationale Leben der Gegenwart* 24, no. 2 (April-June 1899): 72-96.

———. *Konrad Ferdinand Meyer: Eine pathographisch-psychologische Studie.* Wiesbaden: J. F. Bergmann, 1908.

———. *Heinrich von Kleist: Eine pathographisch-psychologische Studie.* Wiesbaden: J. F. Bergmann, 1909.

———. *Aus dem Liebesleben Nicolaus Lenaus.* Leipzig: Franz Deuticke, 1909.

Statuten der Wiener Psychoanalytischen Vereinigung. Vienna: Moriz Frisch, 1910.

Stekel, Wilhelm. "Traumleben und Traumdeutung." *Neues Wiener Tagblatt*, 29 January 1902, 1-3; 30 January 1902, 1-3.

———. "Der Fall Otto Weininger." *Die Wage* 7, no. 44, 29 October 1904, 1004-9; no. 45, 5 November 1904, 1031-34.

———. *Dichtung und Neurose: Bausteine zur Psychologie des Künstlers und des Kunstwerkes.* Wiesbaden: J. F. Bergmann, 1909.

———. *The Autobiography of Wilhelm Stekel.* New York: Liveright, 1950.

Tausk, Victor. *Sexuality, War, and Schizophrenia: Collected Psychoanalytic Papers*, edited by Paul Roazen. Translated by Eric Mosbacher et al. New Brunswick, N. J.: Transaction Publishers, 1991.

Winterstein, Alfred von. "Der Stundenzeiger." *Die Fackel* 11, nos. 285-286 (27 July 1909): 17-19.

———. "Psychoanalytische Anmerkungen zur Geschichte der Philosophie." *Imago* 2, no. 2 (1913): 175-237.

———. "Meine Erinnerungen an Freud." Manuscript in the possession of Dr. Ernst Federn.

Wittels, Fritz. *Der Taufjude.* Vienna: M. Breitenstein, 1904.

———. *Die sexuelle Not.* Vienna: C. W. Stern, 1909.

———. *Ezechiel der Zugereiste.* Berlin: Egon Fleischel, 1910.

———. *Sigmund Freud: His Personality, His Teaching, and His School.* Translated by Eden and Cedar Paul. New York: Dodd, Mead, 1924.

———. *Freud and the Child Woman: The Memoirs of Fritz Wittels.* Edited by Edward Timms. New Haven: Yale University Press, 1995.

VI. FREUD, VIENNESE PSYCHOANALYSIS, AND CULTURAL SCIENCE: WORKS CITED

Aeschylus. *Agamemnon.* Translated by Richmond Lattimore. In *The Complete Greek Tragedies*, edited by David Grene and Richmond Lattimore. Chicago: University of Chicago Press, 1953.

Aristotle. *Aristoteles' Poetik*. Edited and translated by Theodor Gomperz. Leipzig: von Veit, 1897.

———. *The Poetics of Aristotle*. Edited and translated by S. H. Butcher. 4th ed. London: Macmillan, 1907.

———. *Metaphysics*. Translated by W. D. Ross. In *The Basic Works of Aristotle*, edited by Richard McKeon. New York: Random House, 1941.

Bahr, Hermann. "The Overcoming of Naturalism" (1891). In *The Vienna Coffeehouse Wits 1890-1938*, edited and translated by Harold B. Segel. West Lafayette, Ind.: Purdue University Press, 1993.

Becker, Philip. "Eduard Hitschmann, 1871-1957." In *Psychoanalytic Pioneers*, edited by Franz Alexander, Samuel Eisenstein, and Martin Grotjahn. New York: Basic Books, 1966.

Benjamin, Walter. "Karl Kraus" (1931). In *Reflections: Essays, Aphorisms, Autobiographical Writings*, edited by Peter Demetz, translated by Edmund Jephcott. New York: Harcourt Brace Jovanovich, 1978.

Berger, Alfred von. "Wahrheit und Irrtum in der Katharsis-Theorie des Aristoteles." In *Aristoteles' Poetik*, edited and translated by Theodor Gomperz. Leipzig: von Veit, 1897.

Birmele, Jutta. "Strategies of Persuasion: The Case of *Leonardo Da Vinci*." In *Reading Freud's Reading*, edited by Sander L. Gilman et al. New York: New York University Press, 1994.

Bottome, Phyllis. *Alfred Adler: A Biography*. New York: G. P. Putnam's Sons, 1939.

Bottomore, Tom. Introduction to *Austro-Marxism*, edited and translated by Tom Bottomore and Patrick Goode. Oxford: Clarendon Press, 1978.

Broch, Hermann. *Hugo von Hofmannsthal and His Time: The European Imagination, 1860-1920*. Translated by Michael P. Steinberg. Chicago: University of Chicago Press, 1984.

Clark, Kenneth. *Leonardo da Vinci*. Revised and introduced by Martin Kemp. Harmondsworth: Penguin Books, 1993.

"Concluding Remarks on the Question of Lay Analysis." *International Journal of Psycho-Analysis* 8 (1927): 392-401.

Dilthey, Wilhelm. *Das Erlebnis und die Dichtung: Lessing, Goethe, Novalis, Hölderlin*. Leipzig: B. G. Teubner, 1906.

"Discussion on Lay Analysis." *International Journal of Psycho-Analysis* 8 (1927): 174-283.

Ermarth, Michael. *Wilhelm Dilthey: The Critique of Historical Reason*. Chicago: University of Chicago Press, 1978.

Federn, Ernst, with Annie Urbach, Heinrich Meng, and Edoardo Weiss. "Thirty-Five Years with Freud: In Honor of the Hundredth Anniversary of Paul Federn, M. D." *Journal of the History of the Behavioral Sciences* 8 (January 1972): 7-55.

Fergusson, Francis. *The Idea of a Theater: A Study of Ten Plays: The Art of Drama in Changing Perspective*. Princeton: Princeton University Press, 1949.

Fisher, David James. "Sigmund Freud and Romain Rolland: The Terrestrial Animal and His Great Oceanic Friend." *American Imago* 33, no. 1 (spring 1976): 1-59.

Frank, Alvin. "Psychic Change and the Analyst as Biographer: Transference and Reconstruction." *International Journal of Psycho-Analysis* 72, no. 1 (1991): 22-26.

Furtmüller, Carl (1946). "Alfred Adler: A Biographical Essay." In *Superiority and Social Interest: A Collection of Later Writings*, edited by Heinz L. and Rowena R. Ansbacher. 2nd ed. Evanston, Ill.: Northwestern University Press, 1970.

Gay, Peter. *Freud: A Life for Our Time*. New York: W. W. Norton, 1988.

Giampieri-Deutsch, Patrizia. "Alfred von Winterstein und die Rolle der Philosophie in den Diskussion der Mittwoch-Gesellschaft." In *Aus dem Kreis um Sigmund Freud: Zu den Protokollen der Wiener Psychoanalytischen Vereinigung*, edited by Ernst Federn and Gerhard Wittenberger. Frankfurt am Main: Fischer Taschenbuch, 1992.

Gicklhorn, Josef, and Renée Gicklhorn. *Sigmund Freuds akademische Laufbahn im Lichte der Dokumente*. Vienna: Urban und Schwarzenberg, 1960.

Ginneken, Jaap van. "The Killing of the Father: The Background of Freud's Group Psychology." *Political Psychology* 5, no. 3 (September 1984): 391-414.

Ginzburg, Carlo. *The Cheese and the Worms: The Cosmos of a Sixteenth-Century Miller*. Translated by John and Anne Tedeschi. Baltimore: Johns Hopkins University Press, 1980.

————. *Clues, Myths, and the Historical Method*. Translated by John and Anne Tedeschi. Baltimore: Johns Hopkins University Press, 1989.

Goethe, Johann Wolfgang von. *Faust: Part I*. Translated by Bayard Taylor, revised and edited by Stuart Atkins. New York: Macmillan, Collier Books, 1962.

————. *Selected Verse*. Edited by David Luke. Harmondsworth: Penguin Books, 1964.

Gombrich, E. H. "Freud's Aesthetics." *Encounter* 26, no. 1 (January 1966): 30-40.

————. "The Ambivalence of the Classical Tradition: The Cultural Psychology of Aby Warburg (1866-1929)." In *Tributes: Interpreters of Our Cultural Tradition*. Ithaca, N. Y.: Cornell University Press, 1984.

————. "Leonardo's Method for Working out Compositions." In *Norm and Form*. 4th ed. London: Phaidon Press, 1985.

————. *Aby Warburg: An Intellectual Biography*. 2nd ed. Chicago: University of Chicago Press, 1986.

————. "Leonardo on the Science of Painting: Towards a Commentary on the 'Trattato della Pittura.'" In *New Light on Old Masters*. Chicago: University of Chicago Press, 1986.

Harrison, Jane Ellen. *Ancient Art and Ritual*. New York: Henry Holt, 1913.

Hauff, Wilhelm. *Mittheilungen aus den Memoiren des Satan*. Vol. 6 of *Sämmtliche Werke*. Stuttgart: Friedrich Brodhag'sche Buchhandlung, 1837.

Heschel, Abraham J. *The Prophets*. New York: Harper and Row, 1962.

Huxley, Francis. "Psychoanalysis and Anthropology." In *Freud and the Humanities*, edited by Peregrine Horden. London: Duckworth, 1985.

Joll, James. *Antonio Gramsci*. Harmondsworth: Penguin Books, 1978.

Jones, Ernest. *The Life and Work of Sigmund Freud*. 3 vols. New York: Basic Books, 1953-1957.

Jung, Carl G. "Wandlungen und Symbole der Libido. Beiträge zur Entwicklungsgeschichte des Denkens." *Jahrbuch für psychoanalytische und psychopathologie Forschungen* 3, no. 1 (1911): 120-227; 4, no. 1 (1912): 162-464. Published in English as *Psychology of the Unconscious: A Study of the Transformations and Symbolisms of the Libido: A Contribution to the History of the Evolution of Thought*. Translated by Beatrice M. Hinkle. Supplementary vol. B of *The Collected Works of C. G. Jung*. Bollingen Series 20. Princeton: Princeton University Press, 1991.

Kemp, Martin, ed. *Leonardo on Painting: An Anthology of Writings by Leonardo da Vinci with a Selection of Documents Relating to his Career as an Artist*. Translated by Martin Kemp and Margaret Walker. New Haven: Yale University Press, 1989.

Kemp, Martin, and Jane Roberts, eds. *Leonardo da Vinci: Hayward Gallery, London*. London: South Bank Centre and Yale University Press, 1989.

Klein, Dennis B. *Jewish Origins of the Psychoanalytic Movement.* New York: Praeger, 1981.

Kotlan-Werner, Henriette. *Kunst und Volk: David Josef Bach, 1874-1947.* Materialen zur Arbeiterbewegung. Vienna: Europaverlag, 1977.

Kraus, Karl. *Die demolirte Literatur.* In vol. 2 of *Frühe Schriften, 1892-1900,* edited by Johannes J. Braakenburg. Munich: Kosel Verlag, 1979.

————. "Die Kinderfreunde." *Die Fackel* 7, no. 187 (5 November 1905).

————. "Der Prozess Riehl." *Die Fackel* 8, no. 211 (13 November 1906).

————. *Die Fackel* 9, no. 229 (2 July 1907).

————. *Die Fackel* 9, no. 237 (2 December 1907).

————. *Die Fackel* 10, no. 256 (5 June 1908).

————. *Die Fackel* 11, no. 300 (9 April 1910).

————. *Die Fackel* 13, no. 338 (6 December 1911).

Kris, Ernst. *Psychoanalytic Explorations in Art.* Madison, Conn.: International Universities Press, 1952.

Kristeller, Paul Oskar. "The Modern System of the Arts." In *Renaissance Thought and the Arts: Collected Essays.* Expanded edition. Princeton: Princeton University Press, 1990.

Langer, Josef. "Allgemeine gesellschaftliche Hintergründe für die Entwicklung der Soziologie in Österreich." In *Geschichte der österreichischen Soziologie,* edited by Josef Langer. Vienna: Verlag für Gesellschaftskritik, 1988.

Laplanche, Jean, and J.-B. Pontalis. *The Language of Psycho-Analysis.* Translated by Donald Nicholson-Smith. New York: W. W. Norton and Co., 1973.

Lichtenberg, Joseph. "Freud's Leonardo: Psychobiography and Autobiography of Genius." *Journal of the American Psychoanalytic Association* 26, no. 4 (1978): 863-80.

Lieberman, E. James. *Acts of Will: The Life and Work of Otto Rank.* New York: Free Press, 1985.

Loewald, Hans W. "Psychoanalysis as an Art and the Fantasy Character of the Psychoanalytic Situation." *Journal of the American Psychoanalytic Association* 23, no. 2 (1975): 277-99. Reprinted in Hans W. Loewald, *Papers on Psychoanalysis.* New Haven: Yale University Press, 1980.

Magaziner, Alfred. "David Bach schuf Konzerte für die Arbeiter." *Rentner und Pensionist,* June 1977, 17.

Mahony, Patrick. *Freud as a Writer.* Expanded ed. New Haven: Yale University Press, 1987.

Mayer, Ernst. "400 Jahre Akademisches Gymnasium." In *Festschrift: 400 Jahre Akademisches Gymnasium.* Vienna: Bondi und Sohn, 1953.

McGrath, William. *Dionysian Art and Populist Politics in Austria.* New Haven: Yale University Press, 1974.

Merejkowski, Dmitri. *The Romance of Leonardo da Vinci.* Translated by Herbert Trench. New York: G. P. Putnam's Sons, 1912.

Mitchell-Boyask, Robin N. "Freud's Reading of Classical Literature and Classical Philology." In *Reading Freud's Reading,* edited by Sander L. Gilman et al. New York: New York University Press, 1994.

Moscovici, Serge. *The Age of the Crowd: A Historical Treatise on Mass Psychology.* Translated by J. C. Whitehouse. Cambridge: Cambridge University Press, 1985.

Mühlleitner, Elke. *Biographisches Lexikon der Psychoanalyse: Die Mitglieder der Psychologischen Mittwoch-Gesellschaft und der Wiener Psychoanalytischen Vereinigung 1902-1938.* Tübingen: Edition Diskord, 1992.

Panofsky, Erwin. "Artist, Scientist, Genius: Notes on the 'Renaissance-Dämmerung.'" In Wallace K. Ferguson et al., *The Renaissance: Six Essays*. New York: Harper and Row, Harper Torchbooks, 1962.

"Program of *American Imago*." *American Imago* 21, nos. 1-2 (spring-summer 1964): 5.

Rabinbach, Anson. *The Crisis of Austrian Socialism: From Red Vienna to Civil War 1927-1934*. Chicago: University of Chicago Press, 1983.

Reitler, Marcellin, ed. *Central-Organ des Vereins für Verwertung geistiger Arbeit* 1, no. 1 (9 March 1868)—no. 8 (27 July 1868).

———. *Die Personaleinrichtungen der Eisenbahn vom Standpunkte des Denkers und Menschenfreundes: Studien und Vorschläge*. Vienna: Waldheim, 1879.

Richter, Irma A., ed. *The Notebooks of Leonardo da Vinci*. Oxford: Oxford University Press, 1952; Oxford: Oxford University Press, World's Classics, 1990.

Ricoeur, Paul. *Freud and Philosophy: An Essay on Interpretation*. Translated by Denis Savage. New Haven: Yale University Press, 1970.

Ringer, Fritz. *The Decline of the German Mandarins: The German Academic Community, 1890-1933*. Cambridge, Mass.: Harvard University Press, 1969; Hanover, N. H.: Wesleyan University Press, University Press of New England, 1990.

Roazen, Paul. *Brother Animal: The Story of Freud and Tausk*. New York: Alfred A. Knopf, 1969.

Robert, Marthe. *From Oedipus to Moses: Freud's Jewish Identity*. Translated by Ralph Manheim. Garden City, N.Y.: Doubleday Anchor Press, 1976.

Rossi, Paolo. "Mechanical Arts and Philosophy in the Sixteenth Century." In *Philosophy, Technology, and the Arts in the Early Modern Era*, translated by Salvator Attanasio. New York: Harper and Row, Torchbook Library, 1970.

Rudnytsky, Peter L. *The Psychoanalytic Vocation: Rank, Winnicott, and the Legacy of Freud*. New Haven: Yale University Press, 1991.

Schapiro, Meyer. "Leonardo and Freud: An Art-Historical Study." *Journal of the History of Ideas* 17, no. 2 (April 1956): 147-78.

Schorske, Carl E. *Fin-de-Siècle Vienna: Politics and Culture*. New York: Alfred A. Knopf, 1980.

Schrecker, Ellen W. *No Ivory Tower: McCarthyism and the Universities*. New York: Oxford University Press, 1986.

Shorter, Edward. "The Two Medical Worlds of Sigmund Freud." In *Freud and the History of Psychoanalysis*, edited by Toby Gelfand and John Kerr. Hillsdale, N. J.: Analytic Press, 1992.

Slochower, Harry. "Applied Psychoanalysis As a Science and As An Art." *American Imago* 21, nos. 1-2 (spring-summer 1964): 165-74.

Smith, William Robertson. *The Religion of the Semites: The Fundamental Institutions*. 2nd ed. 1894. Reprint. New York: Schocken Books, 1972.

Smith, Woodruff. *Politics and the Sciences of Culture in Germany, 1840-1920*. New York: Oxford University Press, 1991.

Sophocles. *Oedipus at Colonus*. Translated by Robert Fitzgerald. In *The Complete Greek Tragedies*, edited by David Grene and Richmond Lattimore. Chicago: University of Chicago Press, 1954.

Spector, Jack J. *The Aesthetics of Freud: A Study in Psychoanalysis and Art*. New York: McGraw-Hill, 1974.

Timms, Edward. *Karl Kraus, Apocalyptic Satirist: Culture and Catastrophe in Habsburg Vienna*. New Haven: Yale University Press, 1986.

Wallace, Edwin R. *Freud and Anthropology: A History and Reappraisal.* New York: International Universities Press, 1983.

Weber, Max. *The Protestant Ethic and the Spirit of Capitalism* (1904-1905). Translated by Talcott Parsons. New York: Charles Scribner's Sons, 1958.

———. "Politics as a Vocation" (1919 [1918]). In *From Max Weber: Essays in Sociology,* edited by H. H. Gerth and C. Wright Mills. New York: Oxford University Press, 1946, 1975.

Weininger, Otto. *Sex and Character.* London: William Heinemann, [1906].

Werman, David S. "Sigmund Freud and Romain Rolland." *International Review of Psycho-Analysis* 4, no. 2 (1977): 225-42.

Wilkins, Sophie. "Harry Slochower: *Der springende Punkt.*" In *Myth, Creativity, Psychoanalysis: Essays in Honor of Harry Slochower,* edited by Maynard Solomon. Detroit: Wayne State University Press, 1978.

Wollheim, Richard. "Freud and the Understanding of Art." In *On Art and the Mind: Essays and Lectures.* London: Allen Lane, 1973. Republished in *The Cambridge Companion to Freud,* edited by Jerome Neu. Cambridge: Cambridge University Press, 1992.

Worbs, Michael. *Nervenkunst: Literatur und Psychoanalyse im Wien der Jahrhundertwende.* Frankfurt am Main: Europäische Verlagsanstalt, 1983.

Wundt, Wilhelm. *Elements of Folk Psychology: Outlines of a Psychological History of the Development of Mankind.* Translated by Edward Leroy Schaub. London: George Allen and Unwin, 1916.

Yerushalmi, Yosef Hayim. "Freud on the 'Historical Novel': From the Manuscript Draft (1934) of *Moses and Monotheism.*" *International Journal of Psycho-Analysis* 70, no. 3 (1989): 375-95.

———. *Freud's Moses: Judaism Terminable and Interminable.* New Haven: Yale University Press, 1991.

VII. Freud, Viennese Psychoanalysis, and Cultural Science: Selected Works

Adams, Laurie Schneider. *Art and Psychoanalysis.* New York: HarperCollins, Icon Editions, 1993.

Alford, C. Fred. *The Psychoanalytic Theory of Greek Tragedy.* New Haven: Yale University Press, 1992.

Anzieu, Didier. "The Place of Germanic Language and Culture in Freud's Discovery of Psychoanalysis between 1895-1900." *International Journal of Psycho-Analysis* 67, no. 2 (1986): 219-36.

Berlin, Jeffrey B., and Elizabeth J. Levy. "On the Letters of Theodor Reik to Arthur Schnitzler." *Psychoanalytic Review* 65, no. 1 (spring 1978): 109-30. Republished in *Psychoanalysis and Old Vienna: Freud, Reik, Schnitzler, Kraus,* edited by Murray H. Sherman. New York: Human Sciences Press, 1978.

Bernfeld, Suzanne Cassirer. "Freud and Archeology." *American Imago* 8, no. 2 (June 1951): 107-28.

Bettelheim, Bruno. *Freud's Vienna and Other Essays.* New York: Random House, Vintage Books, 1991.

Bocock, Robert. *Freud and Modern Society: An Outline and Analysis of Freud's Sociology.* New York: Holmes and Meier, 1978.

Bowlby, John. "Psychoanalysis as Art and Science." *International Review of Psycho-Analysis 6*, no. 1 (1979): 3-14.

Boyer, John W. "Freud, Marriage and Late Viennese Liberalism: A Commentary from 1905." *Journal of Modern History 50*, no. 1 (March 1978): 72-102.

Brenkman, John. "Family, Community, Polis: The Freudian Structure of Feeling." *New Literary History 23*, no. 4 (autumn 1992): 923-54.

Brome, Vincent. *Freud and His Early Circle*. New York: William Morrow, Apollo Edition, 1969.

Brunner, José. *Freud and the Politics of Psychoanalysis*. Oxford: Blackwell, 1995.

Butler, Eliza M. *The Tyranny of Greece over Germany*. New York: Macmillan, 1935.

Certeau, Michel de. *The Writing of History*. Translated by Tom Conley. New York: Columbia University Press, 1988.

Collins, Bradley I. *Leonardo, Psychoanalysis, and Art History: A Critical Study of Psychobiographical Approaches to Leonardo da Vinci*. Evanston, Ill.: Northwestern University Press, 1997.

Decker, Hannah. *Freud in Germany: Revolution and Reaction in Science, 1893-1907*. New York: International Universities Press, 1977.

Deigh, John. "Freud's Later Theory of Civilization: Changes and Implications." In *The Cambridge Companion to Freud*, edited by Jerome Neu. Cambridge: Cambridge University Press, 1992.

Devereux, George. *Dreams in Greek Tragedy: An Ethno-Psychoanalytical Study*. Oxford: Blackwell, 1976.

Edmunds, Lowell. "The Cults and the Legend of Oedipus." *Harvard Studies in Classical Philology 85* (1981): 221-38.

Eissler, K. R. *Leonardo da Vinci: Psychoanalytic Notes on the Enigma*. New York: International Universities Press, 1961.

———. *Talent and Genius: The Fictitious Case of Tausk Contra Freud*. New York: Grove Press, 1971.

Fromm, Erich. *Sigmund Freud's Mission: An Analysis of His Personality and Influence*. New York: Harper and Row, Harper Colophon Books, 1972.

Gay, Peter. *Freud, Jews and Other Germans: Masters and Victims in Modernist Culture*. New York: Oxford University Press, 1978.

———. *Freud for Historians*. New York: Oxford University Press, 1985.

———. *A Godless Jew: Freud, Atheism, and the Making of Psychoanalysis*. New Haven: Yale University Press, 1987.

Gilman, Sander L. *The Case of Sigmund Freud: Medicine and Identity at the Fin de Siècle*. Baltimore: Johns Hopkins University Press, 1993.

———. "Sigmund Freud and the Sexologists: A Second Reading." In *Reading Freud's Reading*, edited by Sander L. Gilman et al. New York: New York University Press, 1994.

Ginneken, Jaap van. *Crowds, Psychology, and Politics, 1871-1899*. Cambridge: Cambridge University Press, 1992.

Goldstein, Bluma. *Reinscribing Moses: Heine, Kafka, Freud, and Schoenberg in a European Wilderness*. Cambridge, Mass.: Harvard University Press, 1992.

Gresser, Moshe. *Dual Allegiance: Freud as a Modern Jew*. Albany, N. Y.: State University of New York Press, 1994.

Grosskurth, Phyllis. *The Secret Ring: Freud's Inner Circle and the Politics of Psychoanalysis*. Reading, Mass.: Addison-Wesley, 1991.

Hauser, Arnold. "The Psychological Approach: Psychoanalysis and Art." In *The Philosophy of Art History*. Evanston, Ill.: Northwestern University Press, 1985.

Hoffer, Peter T. "The Concept of Phylogenetic Inheritance in Freud and Jung." *Journal of the American Psychoanalytic Association* 40, no. 2 (1992): 517-30.

Homans, Peter. *Jung in Context: Modernity and the Making of a Psychology*. 2nd ed. Chicago: University of Chicago Press, 1995.

Huber, Wolfgang. *Psychoanalyse in Österreich seit 1933*. Vienna: Geyer-Edition, 1977.

Hyman, Stanley Edgar. "Psychoanalysis and the Climate of Tragedy." In *Freud and the 20th Century*, edited by Benjamin Nelson. New York: Meridian Books, 1957.

Kerr, John. *A Most Dangerous Method: The Story of Jung, Freud, and Sabina Spielrein*. New York: Random House, Vintage Books, 1994.

Knox, Bernard M. W. *Oedipus at Thebes: Sophocles' Tragic Hero and His Time*. New York: W. W. Norton, 1957.

———. *The Heroic Temper: Studies in Sophoclean Tragedy*. Berkeley and Los Angeles: University of California Press, 1964, 1983.

Kroeber, A. L. "Totem and Taboo: An Ethnologic Psychoanalysis." *American Anthropologist* 22 (January 1920): 48-55.

———. "Totem and Taboo in Retrospect." *American Journal of Sociology* 45, no. 3 (November 1939): 446-51. Republished in *Psychoanalysis and History*, edited by Bruce Mazlish. Rev. ed. New York: Grosset and Dunlap, Universal Library, 1971.

Kurzweil, Edith. *The Freudians: A Comparative Perspective*. New Haven: Yale University Press, 1989.

Lloyd-Jones, Hugh. "Psychoanalysis and the Study of the Ancient World." In *Freud and the Humanities*, edited by Peregrine Horden. London: Duckworth, 1985.

Mann, Thomas. "Freud's Position in the History of Modern Culture" (1929). Translated by Clara Willard and Smith Ely Jelliffe. In *Freud As We Knew Him*, edited by Hendrik M. Ruitenbeek. Detroit: Wayne State University Press, 1973.

———. "Freud and the Future" (1936). In *Essays of Three Decades*, translated by H. T. Lowe-Porter. New York: Alfred A. Knopf, 1947.

Marcus, Steven. *Freud and the Culture of Psychoanalysis: Studies in the Transition from Victorian Humanism to Modernity*. New York: W. W. Norton, 1984.

Marcuse, Herbert. *Eros and Civilization: A Philosophical Inquiry into Freud*. Boston: Beacon Press, 1955.

Neu, Jerome. "Genetic Explanation in *Totem and Taboo*." In *Freud: A Collection of Critical Essays*, edited by Richard Wollheim. Garden City, N. Y.: Doubleday Anchor Books, 1974.

Oxaal, Ivar. "The Jewish Origins of Psychoanalysis Reconsidered." In *Freud in Exile: Psychoanalysis and its Vicissitudes*, edited by Edward Timms and Naomi Segal. New Haven: Yale University Press, 1988.

Paul, Robert A. "Freud's Anthropology: A Reading of the 'Cultural Books.'" In *The Cambridge Companion to Freud*, edited by Jerome Neu. Cambridge: Cambridge University Press, 1992.

———. *Moses and Civilization: The Meaning Behind Freud's Myth*. New Haven: Yale University Press, 1996.

Pick, Daniel. "Freud's *Group Psychology* and the History of the Crowd." *History Workshop Journal* 40 (autumn 1995): 39-61.

Reichmayr, Johannes. *Spurensuche in der Geschichte der Psychoanalyse*. Frankfurt am Main: Nexus, 1990.

Rieff, Philip. *Freud: The Mind of the Moralist*. New York: Viking Press, 1959.

Roazen, Paul. *Freud and His Followers.* New York: Alfred A. Knopf, 1975.

Robert, Marthe. *The Psychoanalytic Revolution: Sigmund Freud's Life and Achievement.* Translated by Kenneth Morgan. New York: Harcourt, Brace and World, 1966.

Rose, Louis. "The Moral Journey of the First Viennese Psychoanalysts." *Psychoanalytic Quarterly* 61, no. 4 (October 1992): 590-623.

Roth, Michael S. *Psycho-Analysis as History: Negation and Freedom in Freud.* Ithaca, N. Y.: Cornell University Press, 1987.

Rudnytsky, Peter L. *Freud and Oedipus.* New York: Columbia University Press, 1987.

——. "Freud's Pompeian Fantasy." In *Reading Freud's Reading,* edited by Sander L. Gilman et al. New York: New York University Press, 1994.

Schorske, Carl E. "Freud: The Psychoarcheology of Civilizations." In *The Cambridge Companion to Freud,* edited by Jerome Neu. Cambridge: Cambridge University Press, 1992.

Segal, Charles. *Tragedy and Civilization: An Interpretation of Sophocles.* Cambridge, Mass.: Harvard University Press, 1981.

——. "Sophocles' *Oedipus Tyrannus:* Freud, Language, and the Unconscious." In *Freud and Forbidden Knowledge,* edited by Peter L. Rudnytsky and Ellen Handler Spitz. New York: New York University Press, 1994.

Sherman, Murray H. "Reik, Schnitzler, Freud and 'The Murderer.'" *Psychoanalytic Review* 65, no. 1 (spring 1978): 68-94. Republished in *Psychoanalysis and Old Vienna: Freud, Reik, Schnitzler, Kraus,* edited by Murray H. Sherman. New York: Human Sciences Press, 1978.

Simon, Bennett. *Tragic Drama and the Family: Psychoanalytic Studies from Aeschylus to Beckett.* New Haven: Yale University Press, 1988.

——. "Recognition in Greek Tragedy: Psychoanalytic on Aristotelian Perspectives." In *Freud and Forbidden Knowledge,* edited by Peter L. Rudnytsky and Ellen Handler Spitz. New York: New York University Press, 1994.

Spitz, Ellen Handler. *Art and Psyche: A Study in Psychoanalysis and Aesthetics.* New Haven: Yale University Press, 1985.

Spruell, Vann. "Crowd Psychology and Ideology: A Psychoanalytic View of the Reciprocal Effects of Folk Philosophies and Personal Actions." *International Journal of Psycho-Analysis* 69, no. 2 (1988): 171-78.

Stepansky, Paul E. *In Freud's Shadow: Adler in Context.* Hillsdale, N. J.: Analytic Press, 1983.

Szasz, Thomas. *Karl Kraus and the Soul Doctors: A Pioneer Critic and his Criticism of Psychiatry and Psychoanalysis.* Baton Rouge: Louisiana State University Press, 1976.

Taft, Jessie. *Otto Rank: A Biographical Study.* New York: Julian Press, 1958.

Ticho, Ernst. "The Influence of the German-Language Culture on Freud's Thought." *International Journal of Psycho-Analysis* 67, no. 2 (1986): 227-34.

Timms, Edward. "Freud's Library and His Private Reading." In *Freud in Exile: Psychoanalysis and its Vicissitudes,* edited by Edward Timms and Naomi Segal. New Haven: Yale University Press, 1988.

Trilling, Lionel, *Freud and the Crisis of Our Culture.* Boston: Beacon Press, 1955.

Turner, A. Richard. *Inventing Leonardo.* Berkeley and Los Angeles: University of California Press, 1992.

Werman, David S. "On the Nature of the Oceanic Experience." *Journal of the American Psychoanalytic Association* 34, no. 1 (1986): 123-39.

Wollheim, Richard. *Freud.* Glasgow: Fontana/Collins, 1971.

——. *The Mind and Its Depths.* Cambridge, Mass.: Harvard University Press, 1993.

Yovel, Yirmiyahu. "Spinoza and Freud: Self-Knowledge as Emancipation." In *The Adventures of Immanence*. Vol. 2 of *Spinoza and Other Heretics*. Princeton: Princeton University Press, 1989.

INDEX

Abraham, Karl, 149
Adler, Alfred, 15, 52, 180n. 19;
  "Controversial Problems of
  Psychoanalysis: 1. Sexuality and
  Neurosis," 118; criticism of Wittels's
  conception of revolution, 60; on
  effect of psychoanalysis on art, 79;
  emphasis on artist's early work, 73;
  emphasis on social reform through
  education, 58; founding of
  psychological society, 122; on
  Freud's theory of childhood, 57;
  "The Masculine Protest as the
  Central Problem of the Neurosis,"
  119; notion of "irritated psyche,"
  119; notion of masculine protest,
  116, 117-18, 119-20; "On the
  Masculine Attitude in Female
  Neurotics," 117; opposition to
  psychoanalysis, 28, 115-17; "The
  Physician as Educator," 57; "Psychic
  Hermaphroditism in Life and
  Neurosis," 116; "The Psychic
  Treatment of Trigeminal
  Neuralgia," 117; rejection of
  Oedipal theory, 118; rejection of
  theories of repression and libido,
115, 116, 117-20; religious
  background, 181n. 31; "The Sexual
  Problem in Education," 58, 62; on
  transference in the therapeutic
  situation, 119
Adler, Leopold, 29
Adler, Max, 127
Aerztliche Standeszeitung, 57
Aeschylus, 48; and drama, 158; *Oresteia*,
  66, 175-76
Aesthetic form, 77
Aggression, 153, 173; and guilt, 174-75
Akademisches Gymnasium, 30
Ambulatorium, 162
American Imago, 163, 187n. 82
Ananke, 105, 109
Animism, 139-40, 198n. 140
"Animism, Magic and the Omnipotence
  of Thoughts" (Freud), 139-40
Anschluss, 11
Anthropology, British school of, 22, 136
Anticorruptionism, 40, 133, 145
Applied psychoanalysis, 12, 110
Arbeiter Zeitung, 54
Aristotle: definition of tragedy, 21, 159,
  178n. 16; idea of history, 23; *Poetics*,
  21, 23

219